Isabel Hardman is a journalist and broadcaster. She is Assistant Editor of *The Spectator* and presents *Week in Westminster* on BBC Radio 4. In 2015, she was named 'Journalist of the Year' at the Political Studies Association's annual awards. She lives in London.

Why We Get the *Wrong* Politicians

ISABEL HARDMAN

Atlantic Books
London

First published in hardback and trade paperback in Great Britain in 2018 by Atlantic Books, an imprint of Atlantic Books Ltd.

This edition published in 2019

10 9 8 7 6 5

A CIP catalogue record for this book is available from the British Library.

Paperback ISBN: 978 1 78239 975 9
E-book ISBN: 978 1 78239 974 2

Printed and bound by CPI Group (UK) Ltd, Croydon, CR0 4YY

Atlantic Books
An imprint of Atlantic Books Ltd
Ormond House
26–27 Boswell Street
London
WC1N 3JZ

www.atlantic-books.co.uk

CONTENTS

———

AUTHOR'S NOTE

By necessity, a great deal of the research for this book has taken place in off-the-record interviews with politicians and members of their staff or families. Any quotes that are either unattributed or lacking a reference in the endnotes are from interviews with the author.

PREFACE TO THE PAPERBACK EDITION

Not long after the publication of this book, British politics reached such a low point that I wondered whether readers might prefer something called *How We Can Do Without Politicians*.

It wasn't just the way in which the political class has handled Brexit – the sort of 'handling' you might see from a person who trips over while carrying a tray full of mugs – but also the political climate more generally. MPs have faced yet more threats to their safety from the far right, to the extent that some have become afraid to leave the Parliamentary estate. A few commentators suggested that the mobs outside the Palace of Westminster were merely an inevitable expression of the anger felt by both sides about the way politicians were messing up Brexit. But this shows quite how low our political debate has sunk. Even fools don't deserve to be threatened and harassed, yet certain writers believe that politicians are fair game.

Should our politicians be fair game? It's pretty difficult to feel proud of the way the political system is functioning at the moment, and I'm not at all delighted that events since this book was first published have only served to underline many of the conclusions I reach. But as I hope readers will see, I also reach a conclusion about politicians individually that some may find disappointing: they are not selfish, venal, lazy caricatures. What is far worse than the few fools and failures that every parliament seems to contain is the fact that the House of Commons is – both structurally and culturally – not working, and that will remain the case no matter how many snap elections we have over the next few years.

The current political climate isn't going to improve matters. Why on earth would anyone with a vaguely decent perspective on life and a few hobbies want to go anywhere near Parliament? Politicians have long been held in low esteem, but what we have seen emerge over the past few years has been a special type of hatred, in which the daily abuse of MPs has become so normal that I fear we are all being brutalised by it. It is now not just those typing below the line on comments threads, or people who think it a good use of their time to set up anonymous accounts. It is also politicians and other members of the Westminster Bubble, including journalists and staffers. Accusing others of low political motives, of plots and even of being 'traitors' is now par for the course among people who know each other and who formerly looked up to each other too. Politics has become uglier, and the long-term effect of that will be that people who don't want to waste their time around those who behave abhorrently will just stay away altogether.

The response from some quarters to predictions like this is that politicians should be thick-skinned, given how hard the job is. We certainly don't want people who can't deal with difficult ideas, opposition and long hours. But thick-skinned isn't the same as being comfortable in one's skin, and ugly politics rarely attracts those valuable people who have the latter quality. Politicians need to be at ease with themselves so that they can learn and then show the rest of us what it is to disagree well, and how we can live together better as a nation. The splits in our society go far beyond politics and Brexit, but those two matters often show most sharply how many of us are forgetting to disagree well. Our politics is going wrong, and that is harming our wider social fabric.

Perhaps, though, the debacle surrounding Brexit has at least shown us quite how badly our political system needs to change. We cannot carry on with a political class that has grown used to dodging important decisions on social care, infrastructure and, yes, Brexit. Brexit has been the reckoning for those who have grown used to procrastinating in the hope that the next minister or indeed the next government might end up having to take the awkward decision instead. Few policy areas have the legal deadline that leaving the European Union had as soon as Theresa May had triggered Article 50 – and yet she did so without a clear idea of the kind of decision she wanted to make, let alone the kind that Parliament would allow her to make.

In the meantime, important issues including social care have languished on the back burner, and the crises within those sectors have only grown. It's not just that Westminster culture tolerates indecision, but also that those who have made it into Parliament are rarely the ones who know what it is to be on the sharp end of a crisis. Yes, MPs see many more people who are vulnerable and desperate for help than most of the rest of us do, but in order to enter Parliament, you need money, and a lot of it at that. As this book shows, this excludes vast swathes of the population who could be excellent, compassionate parliamentarians but who just cannot afford the job interview. We therefore end up with a political class that cannot instinctively see the impact of bad policies – or of failing to implement any policies – on the most vulnerable.

I had expected that writing a book with this title and containing these conclusions might make me unpopular with MPs. This would be rather inconvenient, given that my day job is to work with them on stories. But while a couple of the MPs I single out have taken to avoiding me in the corridors of power, most parliamentarians have been not only grateful that someone has explained the maddening nature of their job, but also largely in agreement with my assessment of the problems with the current political system. If even the people in the political bubble agree that something needs to change, then surely we have an opportunity to do something?

There has also been more talk of Parliament 'taking back control' of law-making, something I explore further in the updated section on Brexit in Chapter 12. Having failed to take advantage of the mechanisms for scrutiny that are already available to them, MPs then decided that they'd like to start rewriting laws, specifically the ones enabling Britain to leave the European Union. Speaker John Bercow was accused of being part of a plot against the government – and against Brexit – when he changed House of Commons procedure to allow an amendment that would speed up the government's response to a defeat on the Brexit 'meaningful vote'. Brexiteers were furious and Remainers delighted at what they saw as MPs being given more power over the process.

I have avoided offering my own opinions on the politics of Brexit and other big issues in this book, but one thing I am confident of is that Parliament is not en route to becoming more powerful as a result of Britain leaving the European Union. The changes attempted by rebel, largely pro-Remain MPs have been too piecemeal to really improve the scrutiny of legislation, while Brexiteer ministers have behaved in a cavalier fashion largely because they know they will get away with it.

But at least there is now an appetite among MPs to make Parliament more powerful. At least we have a debate about whether the legislature should be able to write real, meaningful laws. At least we have ended up in a situation where the executive realises that delaying decisions isn't without political cost.

For us to get the best possible politicians, we need to capitalise on that hunger while we can. MPs now have a taste for holding up legislation until it works, and maybe even for writing laws themselves, if only they had the resources and training to do so. The political parties are talking a good game on social mobility, knowing that it resonates with swing voters. But until the parties open up Parliament to people who would be good MPs, rather than merely to those who can afford to be MPs, then they are only talking, not changing.

I wonder, then, if those who read this book and are moved by it one way or the other might ask their MP or local political party what they could do about its conclusions. Is your MP really content that Parliament is working the way it should? Do they really think the Commons is approving legislation that is well drafted and that has the consequences the government claimed it would? Wouldn't your MP like more power? Perhaps your local MP is Theresa May, in which case the answer would almost certainly be 'yes', given the (largely self-inflicted) predicament she ended up in as prime minister. But whether you are in a constituency represented by an MP from the governing party or one from an opposition group, you'll most likely find that your local politician isn't happy with the current system.

The current system doesn't need a revolution before it changes. Most of the reforms proposed in this book could be implemented in the mid-term of a parliament, and without much fanfare. Some would cost more money, because they would involve giving parliamentarians the proper resources to ensure that policy really is going to work. But the money saved by avoiding dropping more people into crisis would make these reforms worthwhile. And to get those reforms, we need MPs to feel that it is politically expedient to campaign for them, to take every opportunity to try to get the government of the day to agree.

This matters to those on the left and the right of politics, as well as those of us whose political convictions wobble around like a blancmange. Presumably, when you vote for a party, you do so hoping that at least a handful of its policies end up being implemented. If you're a diehard political activist, you may yearn for your party to build the new Jerusalem by implementing every single one of its policies. Either way, you are being ill-served by the current system, under which governments are able to implement their policies in the scrappiest and most thoughtless way possible. This not only embarrasses the party in power, but also damages people's lives. No one, whether card-carrying loyalist or swing voter, really wants that.

You might not get to the end of this book feeling that Parliament is for you. But my hope for every reader is that you go away feeling that Parliament must and can change. You don't need to stand for election yourself to play your part in ensuring that we get a much better political system than the one we are lumbered with now.

Isabel Hardman, January 2019

___

A MISTRUSTED CLASS

'What have you done? Oh my God. What the fuck have you done?' Anne Milton's best friend wasn't taking the news of her election as an MP very well at all. The new member for Guildford had previously worked as a nurse, but was now heading into Parliament to do a job that would be more bewildering than anything she had encountered on a hospital ward.

Soon, it would be voters who would be asking her – and all her colleagues who had just been elected – what the fuck they had done: with their money, their health service, and all the promises they were led to believe would be fulfilled if enough people backed their party.

Milton was about to enter the Westminster Bubble, a place popular folklore would have us believe seethes with venal, selfish characters who love nothing more than to ruin everyone else's lives, in between having affairs with their secretaries.

The Westminster Bubble first cropped up in the late 1990s as a description of the tight community of politicians, researchers, think tanks and journalists around Parliament. It has gained increasingly negative connotations as an insular community in which insignificant things seem enormous and the things that matter to everyone else are ignored. Bubble members are out of touch with the rest of the world, and their lack of understanding of the people they purport to represent leads them to make serious mistakes on a regular basis.

Voters largely agree with this characterisation. MPs are the least trusted professional group – below estate agents, bankers and journalists – with just 21 per cent of Britons saying they'd trust an MP to tell the truth. The public don't like politics as a line of work generally, but they also tell pollsters that the quality of the politicians is the feature they dislike the most.[1] Voters are angry with politicians, ignoring their instructions, for instance, during the EU referendum of 2016, and then again in the snap election of 2017 in which Theresa May instructed the country to give her a bigger mandate.

What are voters most angry with? Often it's the sex-and-sleaze scandals that make their way into the press. But perhaps even these wouldn't matter so much if the public had confidence that the people they were electing knew what they were doing and weren't going to make ordinary people's lives worse. When the government makes a mistake, it means people lose their home, or their ability to buy food, or their chance to have life-saving surgery. If the government making such mistakes is full of people who appear to be enjoying themselves rather too much, then that stings all the more.

But this book will not be a grand tour of thieving philanderers. In fact, it's worth warning you now that while there are some venal politicians, there are many more who are decent human beings. And while the examples of wrongdoing over the years are spectacular, doesn't every walk of life have its villains? Teachers are rightly respected by society for doing an incredibly difficult job. But in 2016/17, the National Council for Teaching and Leadership banned 42 teachers for sexual misconduct.[2]

Analysis by the General Medical Council of its decisions to suspend or erase doctors from the medical register in 2015 found that 24 of the people into whose hands we put our lives had been 'struck off' for inappropriate relations with colleagues (five) or patients (19), and nine had lost their place on the register due to 'sexual issues'. Those 'issues' ranged from voyeurism to sexual assault, and one offence included a minor under 13 years old.[3]

Listing these decisions by other professional bodies regulating public servants isn't an act of whataboutery, where someone tries to defend their actions by pointing to the actions of someone else. Just because there are teachers and doctors who act inappropriately does not make it acceptable that there are politicians who do so too. The question is whether politicians as a group are more likely proportionately to be evil, venal people or whether just as we accept that there will always be some bent coppers, we have to accept that not all the people we elect will turn out to be good eggs.

Unfortunately for those who'd like a polemic about how very wrong so many of our politicians are, I don't think this is actually the most serious problem afflicting Westminster. I joined the lobby – the group of journalists who work in and cover the day-to-day goings-on of Parliament – in 2011, and while I have met my share of politicians who are either too selfish or too stupid to deserve the honour of representing their constituents, I have largely become more disillusioned by the way the vast majority of decent, well-meaning types are ill-used by Parliament itself.

So the next important question is whether Parliament turns good eggs into bad. Just take this exchange on the BBC's *Question Time* in 2014 involving the left-wing populist comedian Russell Brand.

A member of the audience confronted the comedian, telling him to 'stand for Parliament. If you're gonna campaign, then stand, OK? You have the media profile for it.'

Brand replied: 'My problem would be, mate, I'd stand for Parliament but I'd be scared that I'd become one of them.'[4]

Brand clearly thinks that going into politics would force him to change in some way to become like other politicians. It's clearly not a resemblance he aspires to. He obviously thinks that being like all the other politicians in Westminster would represent some kind of erosion of his good character.

Perhaps he fears he might trudge willingly into a cash-for-access scandal. Or that the Westminster Bubble might turn him into a sex pest, or an anti-Semite. Does Parliament turn MPs into sleazebags, or were some of them always like this? And if the latter is true, then how did they become MPs in the first place?

The expenses scandal gave many people a clear grievance against all politicians. That was unforgivable in itself, but what was worse was that a culture of unacceptable behaviour had sprung up. And that is what this book is about. It is about how we get the wrong political cultures, which lead to us having an unrepresentative, often unprepared and frequently unhappy bunch of politicians who end up passing bad laws causing personal disasters on small or catastrophic scales to people who then flood their constituency surgeries in crisis. Cultures are more dangerous than individuals: they continue with each changing of the guard of bad guys, and are so pernicious that even those employed to scrutinise them can sometimes miss what's going on or fail to recognise how bad their effects are.

Who are these people anyway?

The rogues' gallery of MPs who got things very wrong indeed is horrifying enough. But that's not the full extent of the definition of 'wrong politicians'. Parliament doesn't look like the rest of us. It might be that a fully representative parliament wouldn't necessarily be best for the country, as it is rather handy, after all, for a fair number of your lawmakers to have an understanding of the law from their previous occupation. But this book will show that there just isn't an opportunity for the best to get into the corridors of power anyway.

In the 2017 Parliament, 29 per cent of UK-educated MPs went to private schools. While this is a record low for the years that the Sutton Trust, which campaigns for better social mobility in this country, holds data, it is still disproportionate compared to the general population, which is around 7 per cent privately educated.[5] In addition, one in ten of the privately educated MPs for whom the Sutton Trust holds data went to one school: Eton College, the alma mater of 19 prime ministers. Eton places a high value on the importance of public service, but it is staggering that just one school has produced so many MPs when there are entire towns in this country that have never been represented by someone who was born and schooled locally.

It's not just educational background. Despite women making up more than half the population, only 32 per cent of MPs elected in 2017 were female. It was only in the 2015 Parliament that the number of female MPs who've ever been elected to the House of Commons passed the number of men who were sitting on the green benches at that very moment. The 2017 election saw the percentage of MPs from ethnic minority backgrounds rise from 6.3 per cent to

7.8 per cent, even though roughly 14 per cent of the population is black or minority ethnic. And while 18 per cent of the population has either a long-term health condition or a disability, just under 1 per cent – eight MPs – of those elected in 2017 are disabled. This has an impact on the perceptions of those looking at the ladder from afar, whether as schoolchildren or adults aspiring to be politicians.

We have a parliament weirdly full of career politicians and strangely lacking in experience from sectors such as science and technology, retail and manual work. The 2015 Parliament contained 107 people who had been 'politicians/political organisers' in their previous life, but just 16 former schoolteachers. Even those who had previously worked as either solicitors or barristers were fewer in number (89) than the career politicians. And perhaps the 'business' category in the House of Commons Library research that lists MPs' former occupations includes amongst its 192 members those who have worked in corner shops or Asda – but perhaps not.

A question that is asked less frequently but is perhaps more important than how representative our politicians are is how good they are. Surely we want to attract people to Parliament who are the brightest and the best in order to ensure the smooth running of the country so that the rest of us can get on with our lives? But how can we tell how good someone is at being an MP? As we shall see in this book, the only 'appraisal' an MP ever gets is the next general election, and there is no set job description to assess them against anyway. And though you may have been supremely bright in your previous life as a mechanical engineer, you still might not have the right skill set for Parliament. Perhaps the best way to work out whether MPs are much cop is to see what they produce in Parliament. Yet this book will argue that all too often Parliament approves bad laws and doesn't even notice it's doing it. It's not just

MPs' friends who find themselves asking 'What the fuck have you done?' It's the general public – and often even the MPs themselves.

Are they normal?

'Do I think my colleagues are normal?' asked David Cameron when we sat down for coffee in his constituency. 'Er, mostly. But I think politics attracts people who are more disposed towards getting totally absorbed in it.'

So what lies behind the predisposition to getting sucked into the Westminster Bubble? Perhaps the starkest contrast between politicians and others working in high-pressure jobs became obvious to me when I was attending a series of events for army officers and their families in 2016. A handful of MPs were also present. They were of similar 'rank', but you could tell the difference between politician and soldier instantly. It wasn't just their physical deportment, but something more inherent. The military men and women were not arrogant. But neither were they brittle. They seemed quietly comfortable in their skins. This is not something you encounter very often in Parliament, and it jarred. Politicians might have to appear gregarious and confident, able to persuade people to elect them in the first place. But these two attributes can exist without someone having much contentment about themselves.

Military life is hard. It involves months away from family and years of moving around the country to different bases. But it does involve meritocracy and, in a career sense at least, a sense of stability. Even though soldiers endure and risk immeasurably more than MPs can even imagine, they seem more grounded. Perhaps what makes MPs brittle is the fact that they become more and more dependent on the whims of the voters, and more and more disillusioned about what they can achieve. Or perhaps it is the case that brittle people are more likely to go into politics.

What is striking about politicians is how many of them have had dysfunctional upbringings, even if their social backgrounds were ostensibly comfortable. Many MPs and candidates describe difficult relationships with their parents, and particularly their fathers. One candidate told me: 'My dad left my mother when I was very little and was barely involved, and so I have always had this endless desire to prove to him that I'm actually worth knowing, that I've made something of myself. But because he's not around, I'll never satisfy that desire. So I just keep going.'

Of the 2015 intake MPs who have spoken about their upbringing, 39 grew up without fathers, including 15 Tories and 21 Labour. Michael Gove was adopted at four months old. Eight MPs were raised by a single-parent dad. Of course, single-parent households are far happier and healthier places to grow up than toxic 'nuclear' families in which a marriage has died long ago and the air is thick with tension and resentment. Even parents who enjoy a healthy marriage can be abusive, controlling, or emotionally detached from their children. And so whether or not an MP had a difficult upbringing is far more difficult to assess than merely looking at figures for fatherlessness.

One of the MPs who has spoken very movingly about her difficult upbringing is Caroline Flint, who was first elected Labour MP for Don Valley in 1997. She kept her background quiet for many years, worrying about being judged for it. Her mother was 17 when she gave birth, and Flint never knew her father. She was then adopted by her mother's new husband, Peter Flint, when she was two and a half years old, but only discovered her adoption certificate as a ten-year-old. Initially, the presence of both her mother and her adoptive father's names confused her, and 'I thought I must be some changeling child that had been left or something like that,' she says.

A happy childhood changed a couple of years after this, when her mother and Peter Flint broke up, and he cut off all ties with his adoptive daughter, but stayed in touch with her two half-siblings. 'The end of his relationship with me, that was hard, because I suddenly lost half my family,' says Flint. 'Emotionally that was tough because suddenly it dawned on me that he hadn't really wanted me.' Her mother's troubled relationship with alcohol worsened, and at sixteen Flint also lost the grandparents who had supported her mother. She barely spoke about her home life to schoolmates. 'You did feel embarrassed about it and it's also that whole thing about not wanting to bring people home because you're not quite sure what you're going to come home to.'

She lived away from home twice during her teens. The first time she lodged with a family friend to finish her O levels when her mother, brother and sister went to live with her grandparents in Fleetwood. The second time, the whole family were back in London, but because her mother's alcoholism and its impact on their relationship was so bad, Flint was given a charity grant to live elsewhere while studying for her A levels. She then went to university having concluded that 'if I could just get to university, I could have a better choice over what I could do in life.'

Flint didn't go to her own graduation because she was worried that her mother might turn up drunk, despite not admitting this to anyone else at the time. Her mother had died of cirrhosis when she won her seat in 1997, and though she had been in the Commons for more than a decade by the time we spoke about her history for this book, Flint admitted that her early life experiences still drive her at work. 'I still feel I'm having to prove myself even today,' she says. 'But I have also come to realise that I have a lot to be proud of and I shouldn't be so hard on myself.'

Her Labour colleague Liam Byrne feels the same motivation as a result of his father's battle with alcoholism, which eventually killed him. 'You are constantly driving for perfectionism all the time because what you learn as a child, or what you try and do as a child, is you try and make everything all right, so you develop a kind of subconscious idea that if only you can make everything OK then your parent will stop drinking, and harmony will be restored. And also because there is a degree of shame that is involved, you develop pretty impenetrable armour plating and you have to wear that in public so no one can see into your private problems.

'So that kind of combination of developing armour plating and, you know, driving for perfection in everything, those are two things that are very common in children of alcoholics, and they are two things that you need in public life.' He admits that this made him a 'very tough bastard to work for', but his perfectionism also landed him some of the most difficult jobs in government, such as immigration and deficit reduction.

Politics itself is addictive. Many who leave find it difficult to go cold turkey. One former political adviser told me, in a slightly jittery manner, that he had been forced to take up long-distance running as a means of replicating the regular adrenalin hit that he'd grown used to from his parliamentary work. Another spent weeks in the mental equivalent of Renton's bedroom in *Trainspotting*, trying to shake his dependency on the drug called Westminster. A former Number 10 press secretary said he noticed that 'people actually stand up straighter when I tell them my job title'. Those regular hits of adrenalin and power have a profound effect.

In his book *The Winner Effect*, neuroscientist Ian Robertson describes how the brains of people in power change as they experience more of it. Power – and sex – causes a surge in testosterone, he writes, adding that 'high testosterone levels further increase the appetite for power and sex, in a politico-erotic vicious circle'. Testosterone boosts dopamine levels, and dopamine is a 'key element in motivation – in getting clear in our minds what we want, and setting out to get it. Winning changes how we feel and think by racking up testosterone and the dopamine-sensitive brain systems responsible for an action-oriented approach.' This can be addictive, 'particularly in people with a high need for power'.[6] Robertson is writing about political leaders rather than lowly backbenchers, but every politician has to win, not just the candidate selection and their seat, but also the game of rising up the greasy pole in Parliament, an addiction that can be very difficult indeed to feed, given the unpredictability of the political career ladder.

The addiction extends to those who work in politics but aren't in office. In his account of his time as General Secretary of the Labour Party, *Inside Out*, Peter Watt speaks repeatedly of politics as a drug. It was one that took him further and further away from his family as he became embroiled deeper and deeper in party scandals. That's what addictions do: they take people away from even those they love the most. David Cameron was unusual in that he seemed to be able to seal different parts of his life in Tupperware, switching off, or 'chillaxing', as he called it, from government to spend time with his wife and family in a way that many colleagues in Parliament couldn't understand. They didn't seem to like the idea of someone who wasn't an addict like them, but rather the political equivalent of a social smoker, able to dip in and out when they fancied.

Few politicians would admit to being addicted to power. They do, however, readily admit to being addicted to Westminster. When Tony Blair – who Robertson profiles as someone with a need for power that eclipsed his good judgement – returned to Parliament in 2012 to speak to lobby journalists, he was asked by one curious hack why on earth he had agreed to come back into the lions' den. His face lit up. 'I just wanted to remember what it was like,' he said.[7] Perhaps for the former prime minister, it was like a visit to his old school, remembering the smells and atmosphere that never really go away. Or perhaps he still wanted just one more hit before he went clean.

It is wrong to say that someone who is addicted to politics isn't also driven by the thought of how confusing and often unjust the benefits system is, or by a desire to get a better deal for women fleeing domestic violence. But given the life that MPs live, whatever it is that does drive them must be very strong and compelling. Otherwise they wouldn't bother.

Angry Young Things

For some, the addiction strikes early. Student politics can be as off-putting to people as it can be a feeder for Westminster. But with 86 per cent of the MPs elected in 2017 having at least one university degree,[8] university political societies will have been where many of them cut their teeth before entering Westminster, even if they spent a couple of decades doing something completely different between graduating and being elected. And most researchers who work for MPs have just graduated from university too, which further shrinks the net for people who are drawn into politics and who consider Parliament to be the sort of place where they belong.

During and after university, aspiring politicians can become members of the youth wings of their parties. These are as earnest as you might expect of a group of people who consider politics important when only a small proportion of their peers are actually even voting. But they can also be menacing places.

Strange personality cults can develop around those who are seen to have influence on whether someone becomes an MP, even if they are as far from power as the young people who flock to them.

One cult that went badly wrong was in the youth wing of the Conservative Party. Like most cults, it looked so attractive on the surface. But bubbling beneath that were tensions, plots – and bullying. When a young Tory activist, Elliott Johnson, committed suicide in September 2015, what most had dismissed as young people playing at politics was revealed to be something far darker. It turned out that Johnson, who had struggled with mental health problems for a long while before he died, had ended up in the middle of an internecine war between different factions of the party's youth wing.

Suicides always raise questions. Johnson's parents squarely blamed the Conservative Party and an activist called Mark Clarke, who they claimed had bullied him. Clarke had been chucked off the candidates' list and then rehabilitated when he set up 'Road Trip', which transported young activists around the country to campaign in key seats. Road Trip turned out to be less of a godsend to a party with an ageing membership than CCHQ had initially thought: it wasn't just a dating agency for young Tories, but a hotbed of furious infighting between activists who wanted to gain ultimate power over an organisation that few had heard of. Clarke, for his part, has denied allegations that he bullied Johnson (along with 13 other activists who were named in an inquiry by law firm Clifford Chance).

But one question that goes far beyond the complexity of a suicide is how did Clarke end up getting so much power – and how on earth was a man like him ever a candidate? A great deal of the answer to this has to do with the people who choose our MPs. They're not the general electorate, who decide between candidates, but a selectorate within a party. And those selectorates are often rather small and quite unrepresentative of the voting public.

The membership bubble

Clarke was chosen by a selectorate in Tooting. He managed to appeal to those party members, but the wider Tooting public had other ideas about his suitability for Parliament. He then tapped into an insecurity that the Conservative Party had about its activist base, which came about as a result of declining party membership.

The Conservative Party only tends to publish figures on how many members it has when it can report an increase. When things are going badly, CCHQ claims that it is difficult to collate the data as it is held by local associations rather than centrally. When things are going well, CCHQ manages to get around these impossible barriers with rather more ease. It last released figures in December 2013, when there were 149,800 members. Though other political parties have gained significant numbers of supporters since then, it is fair to surmise that the absence of any new data since 2013 means that the Tories have not conformed to this trend. In the 1950s, when party members pushed their politicians to go further on policies such as house building, they had 2.8 million members. Now Conservative Party conferences are far more about corporate visitors than they are about members voting on policy. Indeed, they often feature stands from upmarket department stores such as Harvey Nichols.

The Labour Party saw a massive surge in membership as a result of its 2015 leadership contest. It now claims to embody a 'mass movement' of some 517,000 members (official party figures released in March 2017, though various figures have since claimed that more have joined as a result of the 2017 snap election). In the 1950s, the party had over a million members, but that number gradually fell.

Similarly, the Scottish National Party gained so many members following the 2014 independence referendum that by July 2016 it had 120,000 members: impressive for a party that only stands candidates in one country of the United Kingdom (Scotland has a population of over five million people).

Meanwhile Liberal Democrat membership has fluctuated according to whether it is in government or not, with so many resignations following the party's U-turn on its tuition fee policy in 2010 that it took the organisation several years to process all the returned membership cards. As of March 2017, it had 82,000 members. The Greens had 55,500 members in July 2016, and UKIP had 39,000.[9]

Even parties with energetic new memberships like Labour have a way to go before they can really claim they are replicating the million-strong mass movements of the 1950s. Besides, 'mass movement' is not synonymous with 'representative movement'. The party members project funded by the Economic and Social Research Council and run out of Queen Mary University of London and Sussex University found in 2017 that 51 per cent of political party members are university graduates, 80 per cent are in the top three social classes known as ABC1, and 61 per cent are male.

Does it matter that party members aren't exactly representative of the wider population? Surely they can fight over who is in charge of various local political fiefdoms and leave the rest of us to get on with more rewarding hobbies? But party members have a particularly powerful fiefdom. They get to choose who will become their local constituency candidate, and in safe seats, this means they get to choose their MP. The stakes are even higher: the MPs they choose then make up the selectorate that chooses their party leader, and therefore the prime minister.

Council of despair

If joining a political party is a first and very small step on the ladder leading to Parliament, then working in local government represents the next step for many would-be MPs. Representing a ward on the town, district or county council entails many of the same activities: speaking in the council chamber, attending scrutiny committees, holding surgeries for people to bring their problems to. Of course, fewer people know who you are, and you don't get paid nearly as much as an MP (you receive an allowance, rather than a salary, which ranges from a few thousand pounds to as much as £20,000). And the job isn't always full-time, unless you become a cabinet member in your administration. But the MPs who have served as councillors say it gave them a realistic perspective about spending decisions, how to communicate with the public, and the intricacies of government.

The thing is, if you're an MP and you've served as a councillor, you're likely to be from the background that already dominates Westminster: white men of advancing age. The Local Government Association's Census of Local Authority Councillors in 2013 found that 67.3 per cent of councillors were male (down from 70.7 per cent in 2001), and a staggering 96 per cent were of white ethnic origin (down from, er, 97.3 per cent in 2001). The average age of a councillor was 60.2, while 46.6 per cent were retired and only

19.2 per cent in full-time work.[10] Council work is part-time but takes place in normal working hours, which makes it more difficult to juggle a full-time or even many part-time jobs. Additionally, meetings in large local authority areas are often held at times that make it impossible for parents of young children to attend. Though the start time may be a reasonable 9 a.m., the meeting might take place at the other end of the county to the ward that parent represents, which entails a childcare nightmare for someone who is not being paid a great deal in recompense.

So while local government might be a good tributary of politicians who have a better chance of understanding the mechanics of budgets, benefits and roads, the stream of parliamentarians it sends to Westminster isn't particularly diverse. Not for nothing are councillors often called pale, stale and male.

Asking the question

But what if someone who might make a decent MP has never really thought of going near politics? Gloria de Piero, who grew up in poverty, found that when she started applying for jobs in the Labour Party, 'I didn't recognise many people that sounded like me. I didn't go to Oxbridge and I thought you had to.' She struggled to get a job in politics, so moved into journalism before eventually being elected MP for Ashfield in 2010. But instead of basking in the affirmation of being elected, in 2012 she launched a tour called 'Why Do People Hate Me?', which asked ordinary people why they didn't like politicians.

She visited aerobics classes, bingo halls and pubs to find voters who wouldn't normally pitch up at her surgeries. A YouGov poll she commissioned asked those who wouldn't even consider standing for Parliament what put them off. Unsurprisingly, 41 per cent of them said, 'I don't like politicians and the way politics works', and 16 per cent said, 'none of the main political parties reflects my views'. But many identified with statements about themselves, saying 'being an MP isn't for people like me' (21 per cent), 'I wouldn't want the press crawling over my private life and my past' (31 per cent) and 'I couldn't afford to give up my job to campaign for election' (31 per cent).

De Piero also found a sizeable group of voters who, far from hating her, were actually quite interested in whether they could do her job. The YouGov poll revealed that 24 per cent of voters would consider standing as an MP if someone suggested it. But her conversations in supermarket cafés and elsewhere taught her something else: no one was making that suggestion. 'How do we do it, where's the job advert?' was the question people often asked her after she'd pointed out that if they cared so much about the problems in their community, they too should get involved.

How *do* people end up being asked to get involved in politics? Generally, they're already in a network socially or professionally that makes this more likely. The saying 'it's who you know' applies largely to old boys' networks, which are still alive and well in politics, but there are many other types of politically friendly networks, such as jobs with established links to politics, including the law. When the Equality and Human Rights Commission examined representation in Westminster with its *Pathways to Politics* report, it suggested that those from disadvantaged backgrounds were less likely to have been 'socialised' in politics; that is, that their family backgrounds and education meant they just hadn't come into contact with politics as a line of work, let alone politicians themselves. Worse, they weren't being 'sought out, encouraged, or "pulled in" by political parties or political institutions'.[11]

If it isn't suggested to you, then you're less likely to consider it. Even those who've dreamed of being a politician since a tender age will have been asked in one way or another – perhaps someone in their immediate circle made it clear that it was a possibility for them. This isn't just the fault of those in politics, though. Schoolchildren in deprived areas often grow up believing or even being told that certain jobs aren't for them. Some bloody-minded types ignore that. Many end up agreeing.

Can it really be the case that the best men and women for the job aren't even hearing about the chance to stand for it? This is no elegy in a country churchyard for those who were never asked to be MPs: this book will suggest they may have had a lucky escape. But it is an elegy for Parliament, which deserves to be fed by networks from across society, not just those connected to privilege.

Part I

HOW WE GET THE WRONG POLITICIANS

CHAPTER 1

GETTING IN

Brian Shaw is a three-time winner of the World's Strongest Man competition. At six feet eight and 415 pounds, Colorado-born Shaw must eat between 8,000 and 10,000 calories a day while training for the contests, which involve carrying fridges and heaving huge concrete balls known as Atlas Stones onto high platforms. He leads a disciplined life.

You'd be hard pressed to find many men like Shaw on the campaign trail. When he's pounding the streets, it's with a rope tied around his waist, pulling a truck, rather than clutching a bag of party leaflets and a clipboard. But Shaw and his World's Strongest Man competitors seem to have become a model for political candidates. The latter may not eat huge joints of meat to feed their muscle (endless takeaways and soggy service station sandwiches are more their fare), and most of them worry more about the cost of the petrol they're putting into their cars than the weight of the vehicle. But both candidates and truck-pullers are involved in what can be a totally pointless show of strength. Shaw pulls a lorry that runs perfectly well without him. Prospective parliamentary candidates (PPCs) pound pavements for two years and spend more of their own money than a strong man's daily calorie intake, only for voters to totally ignore their valiant efforts and reject their party because they don't like its leader and its policies.

Take Rowenna Davis. She was selected to stand for Labour in Southampton Itchen in July 2013. The party was just about hanging onto the seat with a tiny majority of 192 votes and the sitting MP, John Denham, had decided that 2015 was the year to retire from Parliament. Davis was a councillor in Southwark and a well-known political commentator and author. At the time, she was better known for her membership of the political class than her links to Southampton. But she upped sticks and moved to the constituency before the selection, and then flung herself into two frantic years of campaigning.

Davis and her team raised £150,000 through fund-raising events, donations from wealthy supporters and political groups, and recruited more than 200 volunteers to help. She posted half a million leaflets, got up early to follow the bin men around, and supported a successful community campaign to save an NHS walk-in centre from closure. Her friends from Westminster travelled to help her out at weekends. During the week, she worked full-time on her campaign, funded by what she describes as 'debt and generosity'.

She might have strong Bubble credentials, but there isn't a soul in the Labour Party who'll say a bad word about the way Davis ran her campaign, or the effort she poured into it. Campaign staff who were critical of other candidates thought her brilliant. Partly because of the high esteem she was held in by her Labour colleagues, and partly because of that existing network in Westminster, she appeared regularly in lists of 'rising stars' of prospective MPs who would make a big impact on the Commons when they arrived in May.

But Davis wasn't among those excited MPs clattering into Parliament for the first time on 11 May 2015. She never made it. In the final few days of the campaign, people living in homes marked on her party records as solid Labour were telling her they were voting either Conservative or UKIP. She went to bed as the polls closed feeling fearful – and tired after months of slogging her guts out. At 3 a.m., she was woken by her phone ringing. It was her election agent. She had lost.

Two years later, Davis watched another Labour candidate come within 31 votes of taking the seat from the Tories. Across the country, other Labourites who hadn't appeared to have even a splinter of the chance she'd had in Southampton Itchen were winning their seats. The 2017 snap election hadn't given anyone the time to embed themselves in a constituency like Davis and her comrades had done in 2015. But that didn't make any difference to who won.

Candidates in a planned, rather than surprise, election are forced to go through a strongest-man contest event while the judges – the electorate – are watching something else on another channel. In 2017, the Tory candidates who had resigned from their day jobs and leapt on the train to the seats they assumed they'd take easily from Labour found that actually those voters were sufficiently unimpressed with Theresa May to refuse them the chance. In 2015, voters couldn't even hear what candidates were saying about their two years of hard campaigning because they didn't trust Ed Miliband. Two very different elections, but the same pointless show of strength.

World's strongest candidate

That heavy lifting doesn't just involve a few weeks of knocking on doors wearing a rosette directly before an election. Standing for Parliament is, for many candidates, the most expensive and time-consuming job interview on earth. It's not just that you have to work hard to persuade voters to back you. It's that you have to work hard for free, for a number of years. Worse than that: you spend tens of thousands of pounds of your own money for the pleasure of working hard for free for a number of years – and without a guaranteed job at the end of it.

The cost of standing for Parliament is absurd. It is an embarrassment to Westminster, not just because requiring people to shell out a sum of money comparable to a deposit on a house naturally filters out good candidates who cannot afford this, but also because few of those in the Bubble acknowledge just what a problem it is. And as we shall see, being a candidate is costly not only financially, but also personally. Marriages break down, candidates develop addictions and mental health problems, and others end up sobbing on their kitchen floors night after night after reading streams of personal abuse over email and social media.

No one gets paid to stand for Parliament, even though most of those with a chance of winning a seat tend to give up their jobs or at the very least cut their working hours down significantly in order to campaign. And even before someone has the great honour of representing their party, the costs are mounting.

This chapter will show just how difficult it is for anyone outside the Bubble to enter Parliament unless they have a lot of money. If you're already working in Westminster in some capacity, for instance as a special adviser, then you've got a much better chance of having the contacts, time and understanding of the system to be able to stand.

You're unlikely to get much interest from a political party if you apply to be an MP without ever having attended a party conference, campaigned with your local party or joined a by-election campaign. Like any job application, parties are looking for signs of experience and commitment to the cause, so before you've even sent in your CV, you will likely have spent hundreds of pounds on party conferences and fund-raising dinners. The cost of attending the annual conference has soared in the past few years too: when registration fees, accommodation and travel are taken into account, four days listening to speeches in a windowless hall and eating stale vol-au-vents at fringe meetings costs around £700 per party member. You could enjoy a decent holiday in the Mediterranean for less. Swapping a week in Spain for the thrills and spills of conference season isn't something normal people do.

These are all silly little sums compared to the cost of being a candidate, though. For the Tories and the Lib Dems, it begins with an assessment day, known as parliamentary assessment boards and assessment days respectively. In Labour, anyone can apply direct to a constituency Labour Party (CLP) for selection, until the final months before an election, when the party produces a central shortlist for CLPs to select from before imposing candidates on seats that become free very close to the election.

The selection days generally feature an interview carried out by MPs and senior party figures to check a wannabe politician's eligibility, as well as tasks to make sure that you can manage your time, deliver speeches and handle local rows. The Tories previously ran theirs over a weekend 'to see what people were like at the bar', but they now take up just an afternoon. Candidates do fail this process, which is supposed to weed out the Walter Mittys, though the behaviour of some approved candidates in the 2015 election suggests it isn't failsafe by any means. One, Afzal Amin, was forced to step aside as a Tory candidate after a newspaper revealed he had spoken to the English Defence League about the far-right group announcing a march in the constituency where he was standing, so that he could take credit when the fake protest was scrapped.[1] Amin claimed that he never intended to deceive and said that the plan was an exercise in 'conflict resolution'.[2] A Tory MP contacted me during the row to tell me that this candidate was 'a well-known nutter' before this, but clearly even being a well-known nutter isn't enough to stop a selection day approving you as a potential candidate. Mark Clarke, whom we met in the last chapter as a candidate chucked off the list after his behaviour during the 2010 election, passed his PAB too. For sensible public servants and well-known nutters alike, the assessment process costs £250 for Conservatives and £50 for Liberal Democrats. Depending on where it is held, there may also be a chunky petrol bill or train ticket on top of that.

Once you're on the list of approved candidates, you need to persuade a constituency association to pick you as its MP. If your local seat has a vacancy and you've been trudging the streets with the party for years, this might be reasonably easy, though you'll still have to campaign for the nomination against others from all over the country. This is where the costs start to mount in a normal election cycle. Candidates can spend around £4,000 on glossy leaflets that they send to local party members persuading them to back them, while envelopes and postage costs can run to hundreds of pounds. If they're not local, they'll also spend hundreds of pounds travelling to the seat for meetings. Some people even move to live in a seat that they believe will become available soon. 'Available soon' includes an aspiring candidate judging that the incumbent MP may be likely to die before the next election. But of course, if they're not selected in that seat (or their prognosis is wrong and the MP lives a long and happy life), they'll do it all over again for another one. And another.

The parties don't just use their candidates list as a means of quality control. They also mine them as a rich seam of free labour, demanding help in by-elections and so on, regardless of a candidate's ability to afford to up sticks and trundle across the country to campaign.

Of 554 candidates from all parties surveyed about their selection for the 2015 campaign, 112 – 20 per cent – had applied for selection in other seats before being successful. There were 21 candidates who had applied for five or more seats, and six who had applied for 10 or more. One Tory who went for 10 selections says, 'It is incredibly bruising, as you have to go to two or three stages for each, with train tickets, hotel rooms each time.' The cost seems to disproportionately affect women, too: a survey of 3,107 Labour members by the Fabian Society found that 49 per cent of women who have stood for selection for Parliament, Europe or a devolved administration couldn't afford what they needed for their campaign. Just 27 per cent of men said the same.[3] Presumably this is because of the gender pay gap, and because the bulk of childcare responsibilities fall upon women, meaning they have less access to savings.

Polly Billington stood for Labour in Thurrock in 2015. After 18 years with a Labour MP, the seat had fallen to the Tories in 2010, albeit by only 92 votes. Billington was horrified when she first visited the constituency, because she couldn't believe her party had managed to lose a working-class seat. On first walking around Thurrock, she experienced a rush of emotion so strong that she moved to the constituency from Hackney, where she lived, and ran a campaign to be the candidate that cost her £10,000, including loss of earnings, rent, and leaflets to the local party. Fortunately for her bank balance, the party picked her, and saved her having to work out if she could afford to go through the same process in another seat. However, she then failed to win in the 2015 general election.

The selection process is just much easier to bear if you have financial support. That is especially true if that financial support comes from an organisation with a seemingly bottomless wallet, like a trade union. Trade unions used to be the way working-class people made it into Parliament: you started as a shop steward in your steelworks, and then rose through the union hierarchy before moving into party politics. But with the decline of manual jobs, 'working class' now applies to a rather wider range of occupations, including people who have worked for trade unions as lawyers (and can therefore afford to be candidates). Those in traditional working-class jobs are less likely to be unionised, and therefore have lost their route into politics.

Because the unions can spend a lot of money on their preferred candidates, it is in their interests for selection processes to favour the big spenders. And those processes tend to be drawn-out ones, which is why the Labour Party dropped what seemed to be a sensible policy of limiting selection campaigns to four weeks and returned to 13 weeks instead. That's a long time to be campaigning if you don't have any support.

If you are desperate to win a selection, there's a whole satellite industry of experts who, for a fee, will help you charm a local party. The Conservative Party expert Peter Botting helps candidates who can afford his services to write attractive CVs, prepare dazzling speeches, and understand a constituency using crib sheets. His success rate is impressive: over a third of current Tory MPs have bought his services. In 2010, he helped 34 Conservatives win seats, and in 2015, 20 MPs were elected thanks in part to this 'professional storytelling coach'. A number used his services repeatedly when applying for selection in different seats. He says his fees are a tiny fraction of the overall cost of standing, and he has helped the party select better candidates from outside the Westminster Bubble. But coaching is another way that someone with just a little bit more money can get much further ahead than their rivals.

Some argue that you don't need any of this professional help if you're standing in a local seat that you love. But if your home seat isn't up for grabs because the MP has been there for years, then you need to work out a way of convincing a local party in another seat that you'll do a good job for their area. And given that the local party will, quite understandably, consist of members who have fierce opinions about the town centre, commuter links and the distinct problems in different wards, you can't just bowl up and offer some vague platitudes about the lovely surrounding countryside. That's where the professionals come in handy: they can brief you on those local obsessions so that even if you've never driven along the A303, you will know all about the problems involved in its upgrade.

Other candidates adopt more inventive ways of suggesting links to a local area. At a Tory selection for Folkestone and Hythe, a remarkable number of candidates applied who claimed to have been conceived in the constituency. Chris Philp, now Conservative MP for Croydon South, applied to a number of seats before an association picked him. His candidate leaflet for each included a picture of him in a loving embrace 'with my horse Remy', and he told the primary for one seat that 'my horse is stabled locally', presumably to show his commitment to the area. Remy must have been relieved when the selection process was over – though his owner didn't win in the constituency where he was stabled.

The power of the panel

Remy the horse isn't the only one who needs to worry about the demands of candidate selection. The process is little understood by the wider public, yet it wields a great deal of power over the sort of politicians that we end up with in our parliament. Does it really find the right politicians?

Party selections usually involve a very small number of people: popular seats might have 250 members picking the future MP, while poorly resourced ones with demoralised associations might have a motley crew of just 15 hunched in a cold warehouse at the final meeting. And those party members are, as we saw in the previous chapter, increasingly drawn from narrow sections of society.

So a small group of people who are certainly unrepresentative of the country at large and probably even unrepresentative of their own constituency are responsible for picking the men and women who the general electorate must choose between for Westminster. And they are therefore responsible for choosing those who both design and scrutinise the policies that affect everyone. In *Who Governs Britain?*, Anthony King estimates that 'the twenty-six members of the House of Commons recruited to the cabinet by David Cameron and Nick Clegg in May 2010 had probably been selected as parliamentary candidates by a total of no more than about four thousand individual party members'.[4] That's a lot of power in just a few pairs of hands.

But even smaller groups hold huge sway over who gets to be an MP, and who doesn't. Though local parties are supposed to be the ones who select candidates, central parties and the trade unions get involved in various sneaky ways. Each constituency party has a committee of around five people that sifts through applications and draws up a longlist. At this stage, the central party gets involved. Either a small panel of party bigwigs tells the local chairman they are making a 'brave choice' by selecting so-and-so, or calls start coming from the leader's office suggesting an excellent former staffer. It's difficult for local party chairs to ignore the request of their national leader. So if you're someone with contacts inside the machine, you've got a much better chance of being shortlisted. That's fine if you've had the time and cunning to get in with the right people; less so if you've been busy experiencing the real world. And there's no evidence that those inside a party HQ have any better idea than grass-roots activists about what makes a good MP. Labour candidates need trade unions to endorse them to have a chance of getting a seat, but often the endorsement process is shrouded in mystery and would-be candidates aren't told who to contact, and when. It is far easier if you are an insider, whether from the party or a trade union.

MPs who were formerly special advisers are wrongly maligned in British political culture: they enter Parliament with a wealth of experience about how government departments actually work and an understanding of the system that enriches the way the Commons operates. We are relieved that our surgeon is a 'career doctor' who has performed this craniotomy thousands of times over his many years of service, but we would rather our politicians were as green as they come when they enter Parliament. The problem is more that special advisers are not the only people with the wisdom and ability to scrutinise legislation. They too are drawn from a rather narrow group of people who've had the good fortune to attend one of the top universities. They also have the luxury of being able to take time off to stand for Parliament without losing their career should the election not go their way. If you're from outside the Bubble, there are few luxuries when it comes to trying to get in.

What are these local parties looking for when they choose their prospective MPs? They'll read the leaflets and ask candidates questions at the final selection meetings, but many members may have already made up their minds. Unconscious bias can lead people to make snap judgements based purely on appearance. Anne Jenkin, the Tory peer who has campaigned for over a decade to increase the number of female MPs, says that at one selection, the local party saw three women, who all went down very well. But when the fourth, male, candidate walked in, the response was: 'But there's our MP.' Labour candidates describe the same response. 'What do people imagine when they try to imagine an MP?' asks one female Labour candidate. 'They imagine a bloke in a suit. So when you walk into their hall and ask them to make you their MP, you're already making them uncomfortable because you don't fit that deeply held impression.' These first impressions are the main reason the parties resort to some form of extra help for women. Coaching only your female candidates, as the Conservative organisation Women2Win does, might seem unfair on good men, until you realise that this may only give a woman the same chance as her male rivals. Women2Win even tries to help its candidates conform a little more to the mind's-eye impression of an ideal MP by offering fashion advice to those who want it. This might help at selection stage, but what it could do is create an illusion later on of a Parliament full of people who look and sound the same. One Conservative remarks that 'there's a terrible pressure to look posh in this game, and so the women who've come from humble backgrounds change themselves to fit in. You'd never guess, for instance, that Claire Perry [the Tory MP for Devizes, elected in 2010 and sometimes described using the mockingly posh term 'jolly hockey sticks'] was educated at a comprehensive.' Sarah Champion, a Labour MP elected in a by-election in 2012, was told by a local party member shortly after being selected that she had 'unparliamentary hair', which she eventually decided meant she wasn't a man.

Labour has gone much further than the other parties to get more women into politics, and introduced all-women shortlists (AWS) for some selections in order to force an increase in the number of female MPs. In the 1992 election, it compelled all selections to include at least one woman. Harriet Harman insists that these affirmative-action measures were the only option left after the party had tried everything else, and 50 per cent of women elected to Parliament have been chosen using an AWS. Prominent Labour women selected in this manner include Jacqui Smith, Rachel Reeves, Emily Thornberry and Stella Creasy. When the party dropped the policy for the 2001 election, just four new Labour women were elected, while 30 men managed to get in. Campaigners saw this as evidence that the temporary measure hadn't yet managed to change attitudes sufficiently to justify its demise, and so AWS returned in 2005.

One 2015 candidate who was selected by AWS was Great Grimsby's Melanie Onn. She says: 'I don't think I would have won without it. The retiring MP and his wife had supported another candidate who I beat by one vote and they did a huge amount of campaigning on her behalf. You just think if that candidate had been a man, then what would have happened?' But the AWS caused a huge row in the seat, and Onn found some voters complaining on the doorstep about a 'stitch-up' over the selection.

Women2Win, AWS and the Lib Dem Leadership Programme are all designed to increase the number of women in Parliament.

Labour's policy was the most artificial and has therefore made it the most successful party at improving the gender balance. But none of the measures outlined above can change the questions that the candidates who make it to final selection are asked. And when they are sitting in front of a local party in a draughty warehouse or Labour club, they find that if they're not a white, straight man, they can be in for a hard time.

One Tory MP who is openly gay was left so disgusted by the questions he was asked by one association at selection that he decided he would pull out of the seat even if they did pick him. 'They were innuendo-style questions,' he says. 'You know, stuff like "Have you got anything in your past that would embarrass you?"' Another party member who has sat on a number of selection panels says, 'You know when [the panel] think the person is a poofter because they start asking, "And will you bring your family here?" to a single man.' One MP, who has since served as a minister, was so anxious to give the right impression at his selection that he told the association that his girlfriend, who was present, was his fiancée. Activists watching recall that she wasn't especially taken with the unconventional proposal.

Women are seemingly punished at selections both for having families and for not having families. One Labourite was asked, 'Given you don't have children, how will you appeal to the family vote?' Others in all parties were asked repeatedly about how they would manage to juggle children and the job. No men interviewed for this book were asked about their childcare responsibilities, even if they happened to be significant.

The Fabian Society found that 22 per cent of the Labour women who stood for selection at regional and national level were asked questions that related directly to their gender. The problem was worse for women from ethnic minorities, with half of those surveyed saying this had happened to them.[5] Activists shouldn't be asking these sorts of personal questions at all, and the parties are trying their best to stop them doing so. But while the questions are declining from election to election, the fact that they are still being asked shows how far the parties have to come before they can say their selection process is really giving all candidates a fair chance.

Even when selection meetings aren't showing outright prejudice to some candidates, are the questions they ask really designed to find the right MPs? It doesn't seem so. Most selections seem entirely focused on how the candidate will campaign, and how they will represent the constituency in the House of Commons. Most local parties like the idea of having a minister representing them, and so they ask about ambitions for government. But no one has reported being asked about their ability and desire to scrutinise legislation. Local parties often ask applicants whether they would always put constituency interests ahead of their own ambitions and the party's interests, and whether they would be prepared to rebel. There's a reason Tory candidates pay Peter Botting for his constituency crib sheets: the local aspect is what members care about most when choosing the person to represent them at a national level.

Perhaps it's understandable that local parties only care about the local side of an MP's job. But their overwhelming focus on that one aspect means they do not know whether they are selecting the right people to be legislators. Constituency work is important, but MPs are not full-time social workers or campaigners. And yet their ability to carry out the bulk of the work that occupies them in Westminster is barely examined before they actually arrive there. And as for whether that candidate has the right personality to be a parliamentarian, well, the Tory selection process for the past two elections still ended up with Mark Clarke and Afzal Amin as candidates.

It's all about the money

Another question that all candidates should, unfortunately, be asked is 'Do you have any idea how much this is going to cost you?' If no one has mentioned this, then would-be MPs are in for a nasty shock after surviving the selection process.

You don't have to be rich to be a parliamentary candidate. But it helps. Ideally you should have several thousand pounds knocking about, or failing that, the ability to run up thousands of pounds of debt when you have no guarantee that you'll become an MP and earn £74,000 a year to pay that debt back. The parties raise money for your campaign, but they do not pay you to stand or compensate you for personal expenses such as accommodation or petrol.

Few in Westminster have paid much attention to the cost of being a candidate. The influential website ConservativeHome asked 37 of the party's candidates in the 2005 general election how much their fight had cost them personally, and came back with an average of £34,392. For winning Tory candidates the average cost was £41,550, and for those who lost, it cost £27,235. Both these figures included loss of income; when direct costs only were calculated, those elected spent £22,020 and losing candidates spent £19,045.[6]

The ConservativeHome study was the first of its kind. But it only gave costs for Tory candidates, from a relatively limited sample. My own cross-party survey (see p. 9) of 554 parliamentary candidates from the 2015 general election – the most extensive yet – found that little changed in the next decade, and that the main parties are just as bad as each other when it comes to expecting people to pay to become politicians. The survey asked candidates to calculate the personal cost of standing, including buying or renting a home in the seat, loss of earnings from leaving a job, and other costs.

For the 532 candidates who gave details of the personal financial cost of standing, whether in a safe seat, a marginal or as a paper candidate in a no-hope seat, the average cost was £11,118. This ranged from a £250 profit (one Monster Raving Loony Party candidate claimed the experience 'enabled my other work to become more profitable'. He didn't explain what his 'other work' entailed) to a £550,000 loss (as a result of a candidate quitting a very well-paid job and buying a house in the constituency).

Many candidates took huge personal financial hits. There was even a special elite club, the Six Figure Society, comprising 11 would-be MPs who spent at least £100,000 of their own money. These often incurred huge loss of earnings from very well-paid jobs.

All the main parties are guilty of expecting a huge personal outlay from their candidates. The average personal cost for a Tory who won in a marginal seat was £121,467. This is much bigger than the ConservativeHome average and is explained partly by the presence of Six Figure Society members. At least those candidates won: their colleagues who failed to win marginal seats still lost an average of £18,701. The Tories may be considered the party of the rich, but Labour, which prides itself on being the party of the people, still saw its candidates in marginal seats spending an average of £19,022 to win, and the considerably higher sum of £35,843 on average to lose. Their successful safe-seat colleagues still lost £13,617 on average. And while the Lib Dems like to think they've worked out a better way of doing things than the two big parties in British politics, that doesn't extend to the demands they placed on their candidates, who lost on average £26,608. The SNP managed to offer a budget election experience, with candidates losing an average of £9,700, but this is partly because many of them were selected late and rode one of the most extraordinary political tidal waves, which nearly wiped out the other parties in Scotland.

Why would you spend this much money on a job interview you don't even know you'll pass? Some candidates said they had no idea how much they'd lose as a result of standing for Parliament. Others were well aware. One MP elected in 2010 decided to stand when a relationship breakdown meant she no longer needed the deposit they'd been saving to buy a house. Some candidates stand, blow huge sums of money losing, and sit out the next election so that they can save enough to try again. And one successful MP refused to take part in the survey because she worried that 'if people know how much it will cost, it will put them off: they should just do it without thinking too much'. There speaks someone who has enough money not to worry about the cost of starting a new career.

Vikki Slade was one candidate who had no idea how high the cost of standing would be until it slapped her across the face. She stood for the Lib Dems in Mid-Dorset and North Poole in 2015, and was so confident she would win her seat that she scaled back her involvement in her family wedding catering business. The family survived on one salary and her allowance for being a local councillor. Eighteen months out from the election, she stopped taking bookings from couples for weddings that would take place after the election, because as far as she was concerned, she would be an MP then, and unable to honour them. 'It meant that the business started to fail,' she says. 'We then found that my desire to be an MP – and it was the source of many a family argument – was actually jeopardising the family's security and the ability to pay the bills.' She had to rely on the kindness of strangers to survive: the family eventually sold the business and kept up their mortgage repayments with the help of Liberal Democrat members. Another party member who Slade had never met offered to pay for childcare, and a local Lib Dem put the au pair up in their house for free. 'There wasn't anyone who didn't put themselves out for me,' says Slade. All of those people thought they were helping out the next Lib Dem MP for Mid-Dorset and North Poole. In the end, they were helping out someone who was unemployed for three months after being swept away in the storm that engulfed her party.

Where does all the money go? Andrew Atkinson was a window-cleaner who ended up being a politician after attending a Conservative Party meeting that he didn't realise was the selection process for local councillors. He enjoyed working as a councillor so much that he decided he should have a go at being an MP, in both 2015 and 2017. It wasn't just that he had to scale back his window-cleaning business, or that his wife took a small pay cut when they moved from Hereford to Wrexham to fight the safe Labour seat. It was also that at every event he attended, whether a constituency charity event, sports match or local fete, he needed to donate money or buy a ticket. He didn't mind, and enjoyed taking his young family to many of the events, but the tickets still amounted to a tidy sum at the end of months of campaigning. You can't refuse to donate to the local breast cancer charity at their annual fund-raiser on the grounds that earlier in the week you also bought tickets to the local football team's play-off, and donated to a youth club's appeal for a new minibus.

Many candidates discover that a surprising number of people in their local party, let alone the wider public, think they are being paid to stand. So explaining that you're broke and have maxed out yet another credit card isn't going to work either. 'Most people have no idea you're doing it for free,' says one failed Labour candidate. 'And when they realise, they think you are mad. Yet the party does little or nothing to support you through that or acknowledge the difficulties.' Indeed, some Labour candidates in 2015 complained that their party was still phoning them and asking them for donations, even though they were already working for free on their campaigns.

Most candidates end up spending a small fortune on petrol bills as they criss-cross their constituencies during the campaign. Ian Blackford, the SNP MP for Ross, Skye and Lochaber, had a slightly bigger challenge than just hopping in the car: at 12,000 square kilometres, his constituency is the largest in the United Kingdom and includes several islands. Canvassing involved not only miles of driving, but also chugging across the sea in a boat. And he had to stay in hotels several nights of the week when campaigning away from home.

Even for those who don't have to worry about boats and hotels, there's the mortgage, childcare and, as the election draws closer, the loss of income, which can be considerable. For candidates who work in the Bubble as advisers or trade union officials, it is much easier to take time off work and expect to return to your job if everything goes wrong on polling day. Those from non-political jobs have to give them up entirely, some a year or so out from the election. Some candidates raise enough money for their campaigns that they are able to draw down a modest salary, but this can cause a great deal of resentment with local parties, who believe scarce funds should only be spent directly on the campaign. Many rely on their own savings accounts. And to be able to rely on a savings account, you need to have been earning enough money to have something in that account. 'The total sacrifice was massive. Unrepeatable,' says one

Labour candidate who lost in 2015. 'Yet parties need people like me with life experience outside the political bubble.'[7]

It was indeed unrepeatable for a number of candidates who stood in 2015 and were given the opportunity of automatically being selected to stand again when the snap election was announced in 2017. But with thousands of pounds of debt still to pay off, a considerable number decided against it. Others were financially secure but hadn't quite got over the ordeal of losing last time. Some watched the candidates who replaced them winning the seat and wept, before wondering whether they'd actually had a lucky escape.

For any candidate, tens of thousands of pounds to get into Parliament is a lot of money. For many, it is prohibitive. It is fine if you are a barrister or a businessman who has earned enough to be able to take the hit. But the joining fee for the House of Commons is so high that anyone working in retail, or running a small business such as a corner shop, would baulk at the cost. It is simply unaffordable, and being able to afford to become an MP has absolutely no bearing on whether someone will do a good job once elected. Gone are the days of rotten boroughs, in which wealthy patrons paid their electors to get them into the House of Commons. That said, would-be politicians are still having to buy their way to a seat. No wonder Parliament doesn't look very much like the rest of the UK.

Yet it's not just about the direct financial cost of standing for Parliament, or indeed the visible loss of earnings. The demands on candidates' time are also so great that they must accept their career will either go slow for a few years or come to an abrupt end, even if they don't win their seat. So it's back to your boss, who may already have given you time off for selection, to ask for a sabbatical so you can stand for election, or to hand in your notice entirely. Unless, of course, you're already in the Bubble, where taking a few months out to be a candidate makes sense. It doesn't to many other people.

Dan Watkins stood in Tooting in 2015. He's affable and popular in his Conservative association: a neat contrast to his predecessor, Mark Clarke. He was selected in July 2013, aged 36. 'I've set up businesses, and taken them from start-up to medium-sized. I've been through all the growing pains of business, all the worries and stresses and strains of not earning anything and putting the money in and hiring staff and worrying every day if you're going to get paid, and despite everything I've been through, being a candidate was relentless, and even tougher than the toughest bit of starting up a business.'

What makes it so tough for those trying to win a marginal seat from another party is that the sitting MP has what is known as an incumbency factor. This means that they tend to be better recognised and better trusted than those standing against them, unless of course they have become the subject of a scandal, in which case the challenger candidate can have a field day. But most of the time, the job of being a candidate is to make sure that as many constituents as possible recognise their name and their party. That's why the parties start their selection processes so far out from an election: they need to try to establish their candidates in seats in order to overcome the incumbency factor.

To make sure someone is establishing themselves in a key seat, parties set targets for the number of voters a candidate must contact, and sometimes the number of mentions in local media. They enforce these targets by threatening withdrawal of funding, or even sacking a candidate. And what does voter contact involve? Public meetings and stalls in town centres are all useful, but most of the time it's just a case of knocking on as many doors as possible and giving voters a smile and a leaflet. This is time-consuming, and actually bothering to listen to voters, rather than talking at them while thrusting a leaflet in their face, takes up still more time. And after a hard day in the rain trying to encourage voters to like you, you come home to thousands of emails. Candidates also lose a lot of time attending rather inefficient events such as hustings, where many in the audience are either so politically engaged that they've already decided how to vote or are party activists who have come along to make appreciative sounds when their candidate speaks.

Hustings are the main opportunities for candidates to meet one another. Some become friends, giving one another lifts to the election counts, while other campaigns are so dirty that an extra minute in a room with a rival is too much. Scott Mann, a Conservative standing in North Cornwall in 2015, found himself helping out the opposition every day. In the mornings he would deliver the election literature of his opponents. In the afternoons he would deliver his own.

It wasn't so much that Mann was a charitable politician. He was a postman, and it was his job to deliver everything addressed to the homes he served, including mail shots from other parties. He knows better than most the dangers of the doorstep. Angry dogs, naked householders, and letter boxes with a habit of crushing fingers are just occupational hazards for postmen. But for that short campaign in an election, parliamentary candidates get an insight into the perils of being a postie too. And like postmen, if they don't deliver what they're supposed to, they get into trouble. The targets for the number of voter contacts per week ramp up as the election approaches, which is why people must leave their jobs and need to arrange for more childcare.

Some find those targets impossible to meet: both Labour and the Conservatives have sacked candidates who don't measure up. Others receive verbal warnings, and those considered regular underperformers are called into party HQ for a dressing-down.

These dressing-downs can be brutal, and often take place in front of many other people in order to 'test' the candidate. Several Labour Party officials told me they were unsettled by the 'dreadful' behaviour of general election campaign director Spencer Livermore. 'Spencer was the worst at this,' says someone who watched the senior strategist scolding candidates. 'He would humiliate people. There were these startling meetings with candidates where they were ripped to pieces.' Such behaviour didn't end at head office: with no warning, the party stopped resourcing some campaigns whose chances had receded, leaving candidates having to explain to devastated local activists that the race was effectively over with months left to go.

Those standing in no-hope seats are sent to other constituencies and used as free labour there. They have targets for the amount of work they do in those seats too, and are rebuked, sometimes rather clumsily, for failing to turn up enough. For some candidates, including Conservatives standing under the City Seats Initiative, in which the party places candidates who need to prove their worth in a seat they will not win, those targets are an important element in their future political career success.

Party officials often refer to their candidates as 'legal necessities': campaign fodder rather than people working for free and at huge personal cost. 'The position they all start from – without being too blunt – is "fuck 'em",' says one Labourite who has worked on various election campaigns. That attitude means pleas for a little humanity are ignored: one Labour candidate had frequent rows with HQ because their data on how many voters they'd contacted came in late every week. The reason was that Sunday night was the one time the constituency organiser had off. The party never agreed to make an exception for this, and remained in a stand-off with someone who had given up everything to try to win a seat.

Personal disaster

Often the controlling tendencies of the central parties are justifiable: not every local campaigner is really all that savvy, and some have funny theories about how to get attention. Labour HQ had to turn down a funding request from one candidate who wanted to launch his campaign on the back of an elephant that he'd procured from a local circus. But other decisions seem less reasonable. Kate Godfrey, the Labour candidate in Stafford in 2015, found that a line in her leaflets about being disabled and depending on the local hospital always seemed to disappear when it went through regional officials, whose job it was to make candidates conform to the central party standard. This might have been to protect Godfrey from negative attitudes towards disabled people, but she was demoralised by the constant editing.

It isn't just battles with the central party that run candidates into the ground. Local parties can be deeply unpleasant environments. Godfrey was one of those standing for Parliament who paid a personal price as well as a financial one. She hadn't expected to win her selection, and found herself in the middle of a furious battle between various factions in her local party. It began with one activist from the leftist Labour Representation Committee complaining that he'd seen her talking to another activist who he hated because that activist was a member of Blairite campaign group Progress. But after Godfrey refused to back a councillor who had been arrested for over-claiming on his benefits, things turned nasty. 'It was my turn to be not very popular,' she says. Not being very popular meant receiving hate mail. 'I used to get a copy of [page 3 of] the *Sun* with my face on it – it's always about your body, always the go-to thing. A couple of times I got [indecent] images emailed to me, and I hated them but I stored them. And I stored them when they said they were going to feed me rat poison.' She received silent phone calls in the middle of the night, and was regularly followed to her car over a two-month period. All of this abuse came not from random people on the internet, but from members of her own party whom she knew and whose numbers she recognised. She built a file of these threats and asked the Labour Representation Committee to investigate, but never received a reply.

Godfrey's misery may be extreme. But many others, particularly women, have reported struggles with their local party. 'Some members of my campaign team were difficult: I suspect there was a strong dose of sexism,' says one female Labour candidate.[8] Because candidates are selected so early, some try to carry on with their lives as normal. A number have children in the years between getting selected and the election, which brings its own problems, as some local parties aren't particularly keen on the idea of combining motherhood with elections. One candidate was scolded by her local organising committee for becoming pregnant without first telling them that she was trying – a ludicrous suggestion that would logically mean young female candidates warning their parties every time they sleep with their partners, or start taking folic acid in the hope of conceiving, even if nothing comes of it for months or years. There were comments from local party members, too, that suggested motherhood automatically meant a candidate wasn't serious about winning.

Those from minority groups have also encountered odd comments about their backgrounds, from inside and outside their teams. Ben Howlett, the Tory MP for Bath from 2015 to 2017, says one of his local Conservative supporters turned around to him and asked, 'Is it true, Ben?' Howlett was puzzled. Was what true? The man replied, 'That you're a gay!' He then claimed he'd been told this by someone knocking on doors on behalf of the Lib Dems. Meanwhile, Uma Kumaran, a Hindu, who stood for Labour in Harrow East, was attacked in leaflets issued by a local religious organisation for being part of a party that supported laws to outlaw caste discrimination. She says the leaflets were basically alleging she was 'betraying Hindu values', and condemned the literature during the campaign as 'gutter politics'.

Not every candidate is bullied. But many say they are horrified by the level of abuse they receive on social media. It isn't just their own experience of reading death threats, misogynist comments and libel on their Facebook and Twitter feeds; it is also what their children see. One candidate says that 'My three daughters found it difficult at times because of things they were reading about the campaign.'[9] Perhaps, given the online abuse directed at MPs, this is just a foretaste of what is to come for those who win. But people who can shrug off online trolling are not necessarily the sort we want in front-line politics: to be too thick-skinned is to lack empathy.

Similarly, do we really want people going into politics who don't mind risking their personal life in order to win? The impact on family and relationships was the biggest problem for candidates in my survey, with 35 per cent mentioning it in their responses. A number of candidates said they had lost partners and spouses as a result of standing. One claimed he lost two girlfriends in his (as yet unsuccessful) campaign to enter Parliament. And many complained that they received absolutely no personal support from the parties for whom they worked for free over a number of years. Indeed, when the Labour Party heard about the existence of a private Facebook group that candidates used to support one another, it shut it down immediately. This was perhaps understandable, given the party's fear that anything could be used against it in the media. But members of the group say they were offered no alternative support and that their one lifeline had been shut off. 'To be fair, there's a bit of risk there, but we had people who developed addiction problems, almost everyone got divorced, we were all isolated in our communities, and the Labour Party as soon as they found out about it, it was shut down,' says one of the members. Other Labourites complained that they were kept away from their fellow candidates so that they didn't work out that they were all experiencing the same thing. This might have prevented a moaning culture growing, but it also meant the party could pull resources out of seats without candidates working out that it was because they were writing a number of constituencies off, rather than because those individuals weren't doing well enough.

Is it worth it?

Most ambitious people make personal sacrifices to realise their ambitions. Soldiers spend months away from their families to fight for their country. Brilliant scientists can get wrapped up in laboratory work and damage their marriages. Barristers spend a great deal of money on their training and pupillage in order to get their dream job. Solicitors don't use their kitchens, because they eat at the office. Sometimes they don't even use their beds. Politicians aren't the only ones whose lives are turned topsy-turvy by the career they have chosen. The sacrifices of standing for Parliament can be worth it if it means you become an MP. And given the demands on an MP's time and personal life that later chapters will explore, anyone who is put off by having to work hard shouldn't apply anyway. But the question is whether the personal expenditure and time commitments are necessary for a candidate to win.

At first glance, even if you're the strongest candidate, you can only pull the juggernaut of a campaign so far on your own. You still need the party engine for the seat to go your way. And for Labour candidates in 2010 and 2015, and Tory candidates from 1997 to 2010 and again in 2017, all the tugging in the world wouldn't win them their seats when the national swing was going against them. Most newly elected Tory MPs in 2015 say they were only responsible for 20 per cent of their majority at most, with David Cameron winning the rest. So why make your candidates work so hard if what matters is your party's national campaign, its leader, and factors like whether voters trust you to handle the economy?

Anyone involved in campaigning for any party will tell you that they cannot simply scale back their contact with voters. Most parties aren't talking to enough people outside the Bubble as it is. Polly Billington, for instance, failed to win in Thurrock in 2015 because voters didn't like Labour. But she says she would have been much further away than the 536-vote gap between her and victorious Conservative candidate Jackie Doyle-Price had she been selected any later than December 2011. So the candidate must pull and heave the campaign in their seat to a certain point so that the party can drive them over the line. One will not happen without the other.

Yet there is still a difference between accepting that it will always be hard work to stand for Parliament, and saying that this means that candidates must always pay a high price in order to do so. The parties do not need to humiliate their candidates. And if they care about getting a greater range of people from outside the Bubble into Parliament, they cannot continue to expect candidates to shell out quite so much, both financially and personally, to become an MP – or in many cases, to fail to become an MP.

For candidates who win their seat, of course, the aftermath of the election is gloriously giddy and cheerful. There are interviews with the local paper and broadcast media, the trip down to Westminster for the first time, and parties and receptions to thank them for their hard work. But a candidate who isn't elected, and whose party loses, has debts to pay off and a new job to find. One hopped into her car and drove away from the count and her constituency and vowed never to stand again. 'We call them the drop-the-mic-and-out candidates,' says Kate Godfrey. A Conservative candidate who found work quickly after the 2015 election was pleased that for the first time in years he had regular payslips, which meant he could get a mortgage to buy a house for his young family. Then he realised he'd spent the deposit on his election campaign. Ironically, he'd made the 'party of homeownership' a key part of that campaign.

Some feel as though they've been bereaved. 'It took me a month before I didn't cry every single day,' says Vikki Slade, who only realised that she wasn't going to be an MP a couple of hours before her seat declared. For months afterwards she found herself trying to be polite to people who confessed that even though they'd put up an orange 'Winning Here!' sign in their front garden, they'd ended up secretly voting for the victorious Tory candidate. Speaking six months after failing to win a marginal seat, one Labour candidate confessed that 'I've only just stopped crying three times a week now' before bursting into tears again.

One SNP MP who did win in 2015 said he'd been lectured by his son before the election that if he lost, he wasn't allowed to spend three days weeping in bed as he had done after his side lost the 2014 independence referendum. But other candidates' children aren't ready for what is coming. They didn't choose their parent's career path, but have to watch a slow-motion video of their mother or father failing to get a job in the most public way possible. 'The emotional trauma of losing on my children has been considerable,' says one failed candidate. 'One needed counselling and the younger children were very confused by the whole experience.'[10] Another failed politico's child gave a presentation on the election to her class at school and ended up weeping while clutching a hand-drawn campaign poster that she'd made for him. Other candidates need to rebuild their personal lives. Some find themselves in the local job centre, trying to get a job, any job.

For many, the shock of losing is so great at the end of an exhausting few years that their friends grow seriously worried. 'I did worry after the election about some of my fellow candidates,' said one who stood and failed. 'I was fine and wasn't going to be the one who jumped out of a window, but there were others who I really worried about. They had debts, their relationships had broken down and no one seemed to be looking out for them.'

One Labourite who was in that very predicament, with tens of thousands of pounds of debt, no job, and a family to support, complained that no one got in touch from party headquarters to check everything was OK. Worse: 'Nobody thanked me,' she rages, her voice throbbing with emotion. 'Nobody even said sorry.' A number of other Labour candidates claim that they never heard from their party again after polling day, something those involved in the party's election review insist is not true. But the psychological impact of losing doesn't just extend to individual candidates: parties that lose elections they thought they might win end up demoralised and less motivated to help their foot soldiers. The Lib Dems were stunned to be so badly hit in 2015, which might explain why one of their candidates said, 'I believed the party would help me. How wrong was I. The party's collapse at the polls meant there were no offers of work, or even offers to help in terms of career support or recovery, and it was soon apparent I was on my own.'[11] Conservatives who lost in 2015 were so angry with the way their party forgot about them in its general excitement about winning a majority that they complained loudly; by 2017, the party had worked out that it needed to give its unsuccessful candidates careers advice, financial help and pastoral support.

Some candidates were left alone by their local parties too. The Carlton Club held a thank-you reception for Conservative candidates in the summer of 2015. But not all the candidates knew they were being thanked, as some associations had refused to share their contact details because they didn't want them to get invited to a nice drinks event. The losing contenders in World's Strongest Man would never be treated so badly.

At least for the Strongest Man competitors the prize is quite obviously something to covet. The victorious truck-puller gets a trophy and is feted as having the most powerful body in the world. But is winning your seat really a good enough reason to celebrate? 'It's not like the job is that rewarding at the end of it,' suggests one candidate, trying to console herself after losing. 'The more time you spend around MPs – it's not a happy life, is it?'

CHAPTER 2

STARTING OUT

For every new MP, whether or not they expected to win their seat, starting out in Parliament is a shock to the system. Nadine Dorries, who was elected in 2005, arrived at the Commons with no clean underwear, as she hadn't managed to work out amongst the rush of winning her seat what she needed to take down to London with her. In the ornate corridors of his new workplace, Wes Streeting, who was elected Labour member for Ilford North in 2015, stared at the cashpoint screen in front of him. He was on top of the world after taking his seat from a Tory. But his bank balance was at rock bottom. For the first time since being a student, the 32-year-old was about to take out his last £20. He had spent all the rest on getting elected.

Streeting knew he had more money coming: MPs earn £74,000 a year. So he borrowed some from his partner to tide him over, and carried on settling in as an MP. Unlike many of his Labour friends who had failed to make it to Parliament, he didn't need to worry about the cost of standing, because now he was being paid back.

Besides, Streeting and his newly elected colleagues had enough to be worrying about without thinking about money. Those who didn't live in London also needed to find a flat to stay in when the Commons was sitting, and work out where their families would live.

They also needed to set up offices, hire staff – and find their way around the strange building that was now their workplace.

The House of Commons is an utterly bewildering place to the outsider. Old hands claim it takes around seven years to know your way around, but this seems optimistic once you've spent a couple of months trying to find an MP's office in the North Curtain Corridor, meet a researcher in the Snake Pit, or direct a bewildered-looking policeman to the Yellow Submarine. All of these are real places inside the Palace of Westminster, which also boasts bars, restaurants, a shooting gallery, a florist (which, to add to the confusion, doesn't actually sell any flowers), a hairdresser, a post office, bathtubs, a gym (including a yoga studio, where Lycra-clad MPs try to make conversation with journalists in the middle of a downward-facing dog pose) and a nursery. It is also falling apart: shortly after the 2017 election, a piece of masonry from one of the buildings on the Parliamentary Estate fell on an MP's car.

Many employers whose staff work long hours have similarly well-stocked workplaces, ostensibly to help workers manage, but also to ensure that they don't have to leave the premises too often. Having so much available on site certainly makes it easier for MPs to stay in the Bubble, and that's exactly what their bosses expect of them.

New MPs who have just become big fish in their constituencies suddenly find themselves in a rather large pond with even larger fish. These include the party whips, who allocate MPs' offices, tell them where they need to be at certain times, and start to keep an eye (rarely a kindly one) on their personal lives.

Because the whips like to use offices as a way of wielding power in a party, just getting your feet behind a desk as a new MP is pretty hard. It takes weeks to divvy up the posh penthouse offices at the top of Portcullis House, which are reserved for the type of politician regarded in some way as a grandee, and to hand out the poky, almost underground offices in parts of the Palace to the more undeserving types. And while this happens, new MPs are herded into committee rooms, which act as temporary offices but feel rather like classrooms.

Not having an office so you can properly start work – or indeed, often, staff who can help you with that work – makes it much more difficult for MPs to settle into the job. True, they form good friendships in their temporary classrooms, but the first impression a new MP gets of his or her new workplace is that nothing really works very well. Imagine turning up on your first day in a job, bag packed neatly with a new diary and pens, only to find that you don't even have a desk and have to sit in the corridor for weeks before anyone does anything about it. Dame Joan Ruddock said she was 'treated like a new kid at school' in her first few weeks in the Commons.[1]

Even more confusing than not having a desk is not being told what your job actually entails. Of course, every newly elected MP will have honed a speech about what they intend to achieve once elected, whether it be world peace or a better deal for the dairy farmers of south Cornwall. But how best to accomplish it, and what else you're actually supposed to do each day, isn't set out. Most job contracts have a description of the duties the worker is expected to perform, and the hours they must keep. MPs have no such thing. The Speaker's Conference on Parliamentary Representation has tried to define what an MP's responsibilities are:

An MP has a number of responsibilities. The main ones are:

- as a legislator, debating, making and reviewing laws and government policy within Parliament; and

- as an advocate for the constituency he or she represents. The MP can speak for the interests and concerns of constituents in parliamentary debates and, if appropriate, intercede with ministers on their behalf. The MP can speak either on behalf of the constituency as a whole, or to help individual constituents who are in difficulty (an MP represents all their constituents, whether or not the individual voted for them). Within the constituency an MP and his or her staff will seek to support individual constituents by getting information for them or working to resolve a problem.

In addition some MPs will:

- take on an additional role as a government minister;

- take on a formal role within Parliament, supporting the Speaker by chairing committees or debates; or

- have a formal role to play within their political party; for example, being a spokesperson, coordinating a campaign or advising the party leadership on a particular area of policy.[2]

But there is no formal description setting out how an MP will perform these tasks, what proportion of their time they should devote to each activity or what happens if they don't actually do any of these things very well. Many MPs interviewed for this book complained that there is no formal appraisal system within Parliament. They might get turfed out at the next general election if they are a spectacularly lazy MP, but then again, if they're in a safe seat, they could feasibly get away with being spectacularly lazy for the rest of a very long parliamentary career.

This isn't a safe assumption to make, though, as the experience of Scottish Labour in the 2015 election proved. Some MPs representing seats in Scotland had become so used to their party being the dominant force in the country that they became deeply complacent about performing what would generally be considered the basic tasks required of them. When the nationalist tide swept across the country following the independence referendum, 32 Labour MPs lost seats previously considered so safe that one had joked to his colleagues that his method of canvassing was to walk down the main shopping street in his constituency town and make a tally of the number of people who smiled at him.

MPs in marginal seats are made very aware of what the public expects of them – and how many of their voters feel they are not living up to it. A number of websites keep an eye on MPs' activities, examining how many speeches they make in the Chamber, how they vote, and even how quickly they respond to correspondence. A surprising number of people castigate their MPs for their ratings on these sites, even if they aren't entirely accurate. For the general public, their MP is expected to be seen and heard a great deal in the House of Commons, but beyond that, it is a mystery to voters what he or she should actually be doing to best serve them.

The House of Commons currently sits on Monday afternoons; from 11.30 a.m. to 7.30 p.m. on Tuesdays and Wednesdays; from 9.30 until the afternoon on a Thursday; and on 13 Fridays a year. These hours are considered more family-friendly than the all-night debates Parliament used to stage, though how this is much help to an MP with a family in their Scottish constituency has never been clear. London MPs, or those who choose to bring their families to the capital, might have a sporting chance of making bathtime once a week, or dropping their children off at school before heading into Westminster. But even when little is going on in the House of Commons, an MP's diary can be stuffed full of commitments from dawn till dusk. In fact, the work that a member does in the Commons Chamber itself represents a surprisingly small proportion of their responsibilities. The Hansard Society, which studies Parliament in detail, found that only 21 per cent of MPs' time is spent in the Chamber, with constituency casework taking up the most time (28 per cent), followed by constituency meetings and events (21 per cent).[3]

What the hell am I doing?

An MP can choose what policy issues they focus on, and what sort of politician they want to be too. When I interviewed a charmingly eccentric Labour backbencher called Jeremy Corbyn in 2011, he told me, while wearing a curious pea-green sweatshirt from his local community centre, that all he cared about was his constituency work. Other MPs see themselves as campaigners, coming into Parliament to ensure that very specific injustices are corrected. But an experience common to all MPs when they arrive is disorientation about how on earth to go about doing what they want to do; and for many, that confusion extends to what exactly it is that they want to do too.

Most MPs wanted to go into politics to make the world a better place, but like the Miss World aspiration of achieving world peace, what this actually involves is rather more elusive. Some will have been so focused on getting elected and getting to know their constituency that they will not have given a great deal of thought to what they will be doing in Parliament, not just in terms of their overall aims and objectives during the five years they've been elected for, but in their day-to-day work.

Others didn't even expect to be in Parliament. I bumped into Tania Mathias on her first day in the Commons in May 2015. She was barely able to speak with shock, having unexpectedly ousted Vince Cable as the MP for Twickenham. Now, she was getting used to the strangest of new jobs in the strangest of buildings, having never imagined she'd be here at all (she only lasted two years before Cable got his revenge in the 2017 snap election and returned to Parliament).

The parties may train their candidates, especially those from under-represented backgrounds, to give them the best chance of reaching Westminster. But they do not train them in how to be an MP. Parliament itself is gradually getting better at welcoming new MPs. In 2010, the latest intake complained that they felt lost and totally alone when they arrived in the Commons. Now there are talks, daily meetings and briefings about votes, speeches and committees, as well as a buddy system for new MPs in the first few weeks as they settle in. But the people who have the closest contact with policies that will affect everyone else's lives are given no formal training in how to examine them, or how to introduce their own. Parliament is an unprofessional place, both in the sense that it is dysfunctional and in that there is no training or membership for MPs. They largely have to work out how to do things for themselves. Perhaps this is fine, given that they have been approved by the electorate as suitable for membership of the House of Commons. But perhaps it is also a hindrance to good government that the people paid to scrutinise it don't really know what they're doing. And by the time they have got used to the way the Commons works, they've realised that scrutiny really isn't a big part of their job.

In interviews with new MPs, I was struck by the strange tension between their shock at the long hours that they were working and the creeping realisation that it was possible to be very busy without achieving anything at all. There are always dozens of different things going on in Parliament that an MP can do, whether it be sitting in the Chamber listening to a debate; meeting constituents, campaigners, ministers or journalists; attending receptions and campaign launches; sitting on a select committee or bill committee; tabling parliamentary questions; writing articles for local or national press; or plotting with colleagues to influence party policy or cause internal political trouble. It is perfectly possible to end up choosing to do the least productive thing each time, partly because pressure from certain groups means the incentives for attending a reception or sitting through a particular debate in the Chamber are rather high, even if those activities move you no closer to achieving what it is you actually want to do. Websites such as TheyWorkForYou monitor how many times an MP speaks in the Chamber – but this can include obscure adjournment debates and totally pointless questions that waste everyone's time. In addition, time spent in the Chamber does not necessarily achieve the policy change or spending commitment their constituents actually want.

One Tory MP elected in 2015 told me: 'I have been surprised since coming in here at how unproductive it is. I have had weeks where I just feel so demotivated because you're just doing nothing but talking pointlessly. I don't find the Chamber very useful. This whole place is dysfunctional.'

It's difficult to find an MP who thinks Parliament is functioning particularly well. But those who seem particularly unimpressed are those who have worked in private sector companies before entering politics. They are shocked by the IT systems, the lack of accountability or performance review for MPs, and the dearth of HR support. Some MPs are managing staff for the first time, and find themselves effectively running small businesses without any guidance. This leads to some very unpleasant situations in which members don't know how to deal with a junior researcher who has developed a crush on them, for instance (something rather less scrupulous or more vulnerable MPs can end up taking advantage of).

Those MPs from business seem angry, while their colleagues who were lawyers appear dazed. Many former solicitors and barristers are quite used to long hours and travelling around the country for work. But even they are shocked by how hard the new life is. What seems to most unsettle those from a legal background is that they are now totally in control of their own time, and there is no real structure to each day, save the Commons votes and bill committees that the whips require them to turn up to. The advantage that lawyers have, of course, is that they are used to studying laws, unlike many of their fellow new MPs.

Naturally, the least dazed MPs in the first few weeks of Parliament are the former advisers, who already feel at home in the Bubble. They know how to find their way around the rabbit warren of corridors, offices and buildings that make up the Parliamentary Estate. They also understand the rhythms of the day, the long hours, and how to get things out of ministers – having sat in on many meetings between MPs and the ministers they once advised. But oddly, these ex-advisers also seem to be the ones most shocked by the impact that Parliament has on family life. Most of them have been used to having their family in London as they worked in Whitehall, but as MPs, many choose to move their main home to their constituency. This may help an MP build a strong local presence and understand the character and struggles of an area. But by and large it has a detrimental impact on their personal relationships, and ex-advisers in particular seem ill-prepared for this.

A shock for all new MPs, save perhaps those who were famous in another field before Parliament, is how exposed they feel once they are elected. Special advisers, accustomed to rising and falling with the fortunes of their bosses, are now responsible for themselves, and very aware that false moves can cost votes. Even people who were previously active in their communities remark on a shift that occurs on taking public office that makes you public property. This can be quite a boost to the ego: people whispering 'There's the MP!' as you walk through the supermarket can, particularly in the heady weeks after being elected, feel rather exciting. But it also means that it is less possible to have a fully private life, or to amble through the aisles without someone ambushing you about casework, or remarking on how much alcohol is in your trolley.

Snouts in the trough

New MPs also learn pretty quickly that being public property means apparently being fair game for abuse, particularly when it comes to expenses. It has been over a decade since an MP was elected under the old free-for-all system that led to the 2009 expenses scandal, but the revelations about that system have had long-lasting effects on the treatment of every politician, whether or not he or she had anything to do with it.

It was an open secret in Westminster that one of the ways MPs could compensate for their comparatively low salaries (far higher than the national average, but lower than the earnings of many of their similarly educated peers working similarly punishing hours) was by topping up through the expenses system. This allowed politicians to claim for home improvements, mortgage interest payments and employing their relatives.

That open secret remained a secret for many years, despite the efforts of investigative journalists and campaigners Heather Brooke, Jon Ungoed-Thomas and Ben Leapman. In 2005, they filed Freedom of Information requests for details of MPs' expenses, but these were rejected by the Commons authorities. In the ensuing battle, a picture of politicians spending taxpayers' money in an inexcusable fashion gradually emerged. By early 2009, that picture was already disgraceful. Conservative MP Derek Conway was suspended from the Commons for 10 days after 'misusing' parliamentary expenses to employ his son. A 'John Lewis list' revealed that MPs were allowed to claim up to £10,000 for a new kitchen, more than £6,000 for a new bathroom and £750 for a television on Parliamentary allowances. Jacqui Smith, then Home Secretary, was revealed to be claiming allowances for a second home while living with her sister.

When the *Daily Telegraph* obtained a set of leaked computer disks that had been doing the rounds in Fleet Street, Westminster was tipped into uproar. The disks revealed egregious claims for duck houses, moat cleaning and wisteria pruning. MPs were found to have been 'flipping' the designation for their second homes, enabling them to spend money on both their London and constituency properties at the taxpayer's expense. This story would have been catastrophic for politics whatever the timing. But it came in the middle of an economic crisis, just months after Britain's banks had come close to collapse. In the country, people were losing their jobs. In Westminster, MPs were buying swish new kitchens.

Deep in Parliament, Conservative leader David Cameron could be heard by those working several floors above his office shouting at his MPs who had filed particularly embarrassing claims. The air in Parliament was thick with misery.

MPs were ordered to repay £1.1 million to the taxpayer. But the bill for the inquiry into those claims was £1.16 million. So the taxpayer still lost out even when the scandal was said to be resolved. Six MPs and two peers were convicted for their claims.

Labour's David Chaytor, Jim Devine and Elliot Morley tried to argue that their actions were protected by Parliamentary privilege. Chaytor pleaded guilty to charges of false accounting and was given 18 months in jail. Devine pleaded not guilty and was found guilty of two counts of false accounting and cleared of a third. He was sentenced to 16 months. Morley pleaded guilty to two counts of false accounting and was sentenced to 16 months. Eric Illsley pleaded guilty to three counts of false accounting and was jailed for 12 months. Their colleague Denis MacShane was sent to jail for six months in 2013 for expenses fraud, admitting that he had submitted 19 fake receipts to claim £12,900 in total.

Labour MP Margaret Moran suffered a nervous breakdown as a result of her involvement in the scandal and was declared unfit to plead. She was therefore unable to receive a criminal conviction for the 21 charges against her, but a trial of issue went ahead and the jury found she had committed 15 counts of false accounting and six counts of using a false instrument over the claims for parliamentary expenses. She was given a two-year supervision and treatment order for false claims of more than £53,000. The judge acknowledged in his ruling that 'there will inevitably be feelings among some that Mrs Moran has got away with it'.

Two peers, Lord Taylor of Warwick and Lord Hanningfield, were also found guilty of expenses-related charges. Taylor was sentenced to 12 months' imprisonment, and Hanningfield was given a nine-month sentence.

Whether or not MPs were paid less than they deserved, they did not deserve to be furnishing their homes at the taxpayer's expense to make up for it. There is certainly no excuse for forgery.

What was most striking was that this had become an acceptable culture in Parliament to the extent that more than half of the House of Commons at the time had to make repayments of money claimed. When everyone is doing something, it can seem less dangerous, and more morally acceptable. Throughout this book, we will see how other cultures of behaviour damage Parliament's efficacy and politicians' personal lives. But nothing comes close to the fingers-in-the-till culture that developed in Westminster over expenses.

The expenses scandal naturally stained democracy, and that stain will take many political generations to wash out. MPs still endure constant abuse and suspicion from constituents about their expenses, as do their spouses. Many have found that they are instantly reviled merely for being a part of an institution that has disgraced itself.

The scandal led to a new pay and expenses regulator, the Independent Parliamentary Standards Authority (IPSA), which deals with and publishes details of all claims made by parliamentarians. New rules mean MPs cannot claim for mortgage payments, and IPSA also sets the pay of politicians. The reason for making pay the responsibility of an external body is that it was widely agreed that the expenses culture had come about as a result of MPs being too frightened to vote to raise their own pay. Handing it over to a quango would remove this.

Or at least that was the theory. In 2015, IPSA did the job it was set up for, recommending a 10 per cent pay rise for MPs, taking their pay to £74,000 a year. The regulator argued that there was never a good time to increase MPs' pay, but that it was lagging behind that of other public sector workers. Its consultation on raising the salary noted that MPs' pay was 78 per cent of the salaries paid to equivalent public sector professionals. For instance, a headteacher earned a £79,872 basic salary in 2015, while a human resources director in the NHS earned £91,984.[4]

While most people would, if offered a pay rise, agree that they deserved one, MPs tended to differ. David Cameron pleaded with the regulator not to award it. Labour grandee Alan Johnson said it would 'once again lead to the reputation of Members of Parliament being besmirched'.[5] His party colleague Gloria de Piero argued that 'If I were to accept a 10 per cent pay rise I would simply not be able to look the constituents I serve in the eye.'[6] Many MPs said publicly that they would not accept the raise. IPSA hit back, saying it had to award it, but that whether they donated the extra money to charity or not was their own business.

Some brave souls decided to argue that they deserved at least this pay rise, if not more. In a letter to the regulator, Tory minister Tobias Ellwood said that only those who were independently wealthy were turning it down (this was not true). He wrote, 'I never expected to be watching the pennies at my age and yet this is what I now have to do', adding:

> Without a competitive salary you will fill this place with rich people and not those such as me who have taken a salary cut to serve here.
>
> In addition, as an MP, I have no hospitality budget so when, for example, the Mayor of Bournemouth comes up for an annual lunch at the House of Commons, the bill comes out of my own pocket.
>
> I exhaust my car travel mileage, as I return to Bournemouth most weekends, and my wife exhausts

her rail travel allowance for the same reason. So we have
to pay all this extra ourselves.[7]

Ellwood quickly found out that even if most people – including
the journalists who reported his comments – would baulk at having
to shoulder so many work expenses themselves, they weren't prepared
to hear an argument for more pay for MPs. He apologised, saying
he realised his comments had 'underlined the perception that MPs
are out of touch'.[8]

Research by the Hansard Society in 2011 found that a third of
the MPs elected the previous year had taken a pay cut of £30,000 a
year or more to enter Parliament. Only 13 per cent saw their wages
rise by £30,000 or more, with Tory MPs more likely to see their pay
fall (65 per cent) than Labour MPs (39 per cent).[9]

Do MPs deserve to be paid more? If we disregard the crude
argument that they are all useless villains with their fingers in the
till anyway, there are valid lines of reasoning both for and against
high pay for elected members.

The argument against is that being an MP is a vocation and an
honour, much like being a vicar, or even a doctor, where the talents
and commitment of the person in question are immeasurably higher
than the remuneration they receive – but then so is the reward
for serving in this way. Doctors could put their talents to more
lucrative use by working for pharmaceutical companies or in the
City, but choose to care for the sick instead (though of course their
pay is hardly penurious). Vicars only earn a modest stipend for
their service (though they also have their accommodation, often in
a rather nice vicarage, arranged and paid for them by the Church).
MPs serve their community and get the personal reward of making
things better for that area. They are also prominent members of the

local community and have access to some of the most important and interesting people in the land. If they are more worried about the money, then perhaps their instincts are not suited to be an MP.

The argument for higher pay is that MPs work as hard as their public sector equivalents and must possess a skill set that is at least as diverse as theirs, if not more so. They already make huge personal sacrifices in order to serve their local area in Parliament, and a reasonable but not luxurious rate of pay that reflects this is as fair for them as it is for a headteacher or civil servant. If we are to attract people with brains, compassion and commitment into Parliament, then we cannot pay them a derisory rate. Even public-spirited people like to feel they are being rewarded for sustaining that spirit through the ups and downs of service.

It does seem as though those who say that a headteacher should receive a £70,000 salary but that an MP should not believe that an MP is worth less to the country than someone who runs a school. Surely both jobs are important: one changes the lives of children through education, while the other can change everyone's lives through legislation. Perhaps the reason some people oppose higher pay for parliamentarians is a suspicion that they aren't actually doing their job and are not changing lives.

The MPs who wanted to turn down their pay rise may have done so because they genuinely thought they didn't deserve any more money. But most I spoke to admitted privately that they made public commitments to do so because they were afraid of the reaction from constituents if they did not.

This is not a reasonable response. MPs are already held in terribly low esteem. According to a 2014 poll conducted for the University of Southampton, 48 per cent of people felt politicians were out merely for themselves, with 30 per cent saying they were concerned primarily with their party and only 10 per cent saying they were doing the best for their country. In 1972, 38 per cent of people believed politicians were out for themselves – in 1944 that figure was at 35 per cent, with 36 per cent saying they were trying to do the best for the country.[10] Anti-politics sentiment has risen over time. But it has always been high. MPs are already despised by the population. They are damned if they do and damned if they don't. Brave souls might conclude that they might as well continue to be damned and be paid a reasonable rate for being so.

How does this place work?

As they're waiting for their first pay cheque to come through, new MPs are working out how to speak in the House of Commons. They all have a maiden speech, in which they need to set out what sort of MP they would like to be, as well as some interesting facts about their local area and praise for their predecessor. And they need to learn how to ask questions and how to behave. At the start of a new Parliament, there are dozens of these first speeches, which are spread throughout the normal debates between MPs.

The Chamber can be an intimidating place, not just because it is a surprisingly small room for more than 600 people to sit in, but also because there are so many rules about how and when to speak that a newly elected politician can fall foul of.

You are not supposed to address another MP by name, instead referring to them as 'the Honourable Member for Islington North' or, if they are a member of the Privy Council (the group of ministers and opposition figures advising the monarch), 'the Right Honourable Member for Islington North'. MPs also speak through the Speaker of the House of Commons, who acts as a regulator of the proceedings, rather than directly across the House. And you cannot speak unless called to do so by the Speaker.

Unless you have a formal question on the Order Paper, which sets out the day's business, getting the Speaker's attention involves a special ritual all of its own, which is known as 'bobbing'. This involves standing up and trying to catch the Speaker's eye in between questions and speeches. It is often the only exercise busy and tired MPs get – and the less senior you are, the longer you will have to 'bob' before you get called. A backbencher can be bobbing for hours in long debates on legislation.

To add to the other-worldliness of the proceedings, you cannot clap to show approval in the House of Commons, something SNP MPs took exception to when they were elected in 2015. They went through a phase of clapping colleagues rather pointedly to show that they were different to those strange inhabitants of the Westminster Bubble who say 'hear, hear' to denote praise. But those noises are quite normal compared to some of the other strange cries that a new MP hears when they first sit down in the Chamber.

MPs can get rather carried away, particularly at Prime Minister's Questions, which is a tribal affair largely focused on showing which party leader is stronger and rallying the troops behind that leader. They can be heard roaring, screeching, bellowing, and even making strange mooing sounds at times. Some female MPs like to claim that if the Commons had a better gender balance, it wouldn't sound so much like a zoo, but having sat above them for enough years to be able to identify where the mooing and roaring is coming from, I can say quite confidently that the animal noises are entirely gender neutral. Two particular offenders from recent years are Labour's Helen Goodman, whose piercing shouts can be heard across the Chamber, and Conservative Therese Coffey.

Sometimes the MPs actually produce words as well as noises. Heckling is a fine parliamentary art, which, like sledging in cricket, can be done very well or very crudely. There are two types: the sort that is designed to wrong-foot a speaker on the other side but not be picked up by the dozens of microphones suspended above the Chamber; and the sort that, shouted into a pause for breath by a speaker, sends the Chamber into uproar.

Both main parties have professional hecklers who indulge in the first practice. It is particularly bad at the most political events in Parliament, which are Prime Minister's Questions and the Budget. Practised hecklers such as Labour's Michael Dugher sit on the steps alongside their colleagues so that the Speaker cannot see them, and shout insults across the Chamber to undermine ministers. Others will gesticulate at their opponents: Ed Balls was famed for a special 'flatlining' gesture to illustrate the state of the economy under the Conservatives. The Tories consider heckling such an important part of winning debates that they have organised squads to do it. Known as 'departmental support groups', these gaggles of backbenchers meet before a debate or question time and agree certain words – such as 'Weak!' – to shout at Labour shadow ministers as they speak. On some occasions, opposition MPs find themselves faced with a wall of noise as they try to respond to economic announcements. It is enough to wrong-foot anyone.

The second sort of heckling is an art, and only a few MPs are witty enough to do it. There are any number of backbench brutes prepared to shout mean words, but it is the quick one-liner spoken at just the right moment that makes the Chamber dissolve into laughter. The practice is ancient and its canon rich.

Some of the best heckles refer to a particular weakness of the speaker. When Liberal Democrat leader Menzies Campbell, who was often considered too old to do the job, stood up in 2006 to ask a question about pensions, Tory MP Eric Forth shouted loudly, 'Declare your interest!'

Responding to David Cameron's statement on his renegotiation with European leaders of Britain's relationship with the EU in February 2016, Jeremy Corbyn started talking about meetings he himself had been holding: 'Last week – like him – I was in Brussels, meeting with heads of government and leaders of European socialist parties, one of whom said to me . . .'

As Corbyn very briefly caught his breath, Tory backbencher Chris Pincher shouted into the silence, 'WHO ARE YOU?' The House collapsed into laughter. It was a perfect heckle because Corbyn was struggling to make his mark as an authoritative leader, and certainly did not have the confidence of his own party.

MPs can make all the strange sounds they like, but they can't get away with saying everything and anything in the Chamber. *Erskine May*, the weighty guide to parliamentary procedure, bans them from describing colleagues as 'liars' or 'hypocrites' – though you are permitted to say that someone has 'misled the House'. Other slightly more obscure banned words include 'git', 'guttersnipe', 'hooligan', 'rat', 'stoolpigeon' (police informer) and 'pecksniffian' (an insult derived from a hypocritical Dickens character).[11] The Speaker will call on an MP to apologise for such language, and may banish them from the Chamber if they refuse to do so. Veteran Labour MP Dennis Skinner was famously asked by the Speaker to withdraw an assertion that 'half the Tory members opposite are crooks'. His cunning remedy was to tell the Chamber that 'half the Tory members opposite aren't crooks'. The Labour MP for Bolsover has been ejected from the Chamber for describing the then prime minister David Cameron as 'dodgy Dave', and is also 'famous' (in the insular world of Westminster, at least) for producing a pithy one-line heckle during the Commons stage of the Queen's Speech.

New MPs might find the rules about language a little difficult to negotiate, but what many more of them struggle with is the atmosphere in the Chamber, particularly at Prime Minister's Questions. Those who have spent little time in Westminster can be utterly terrified by the wall of noise that this weekly session produces, and still more frightened when their name is drawn in the ballot to ask their first question. The House of Commons at PMQs is as forgiving to those who stumble over their questions as a boys' school dining room. Trembling papers, shaky diction and overly wild hand gestures to disguise nerves are the marks of many MPs who have sat in the Chamber for years, let alone their inexperienced new colleagues.

The Chamber can be too brutal for its own good. MPs coming out of PMQs often admit that they have lost control in the session, roaring in a manner they hadn't believed themselves capable of before entering Parliament. This loss of control leads to horrible clashes between overexcited MPs and those asking what turn out to be very serious questions. Labour MP Barry Gardiner was caught in a gale of laughter when he stood up to ask his question in March 2015. MPs had been chortling at someone else, but their giggles punctuated his first sentence, which was 'My father died of cancer.' He then added, to shamefaced silence from those opposite him, that his mother and sister had also died of cancer. The collision between question and behaviour elsewhere in the Chamber couldn't have been worse.

John Bercow, the Speaker of the House, frequently upbraids MPs for their behaviour, claiming that the public despises PMQs for its childishness. There is evidence that bears this assertion out. YouGov polling conducted for this book following the Prime Minister's Questions session on 22 February 2017 found that only 2 per cent of adults surveyed had watched the session in full, while just under a third said they hadn't watched this particular session but had watched PMQs before, and 54 per cent said they had never watched it.

Of those who had seen at least some of the session, 77 per cent agreed that there was 'too much party political point-scoring instead of answering the question'. The most interesting response was that 23 per cent of people claimed it had put them off politics – even though they were already sufficiently engaged to turn the TV on to watch the session in the first place.

Voters' attitudes had largely hardened since the previous poll, in 2015, just after Jeremy Corbyn had tried to change the culture of PMQs by crowd-sourcing all his questions to members of the public (a practice that fizzled out). In that poll,[12] conducted for the Hansard Society, a greater proportion of voters had either seen the whole session or watched clips on the news (47 per cent in total), and 46 per cent felt there was too much political point-scoring. But the session was strangely more off-putting: 54 per cent agreed that it had put them off politics, with 10 per cent disagreeing and 34 per cent saying they neither agreed nor disagreed.

But is the dim view of the Chamber that the public tends to hold really fair? Many critics of the Commons – including MPs themselves – claim that it is built as an adversarial Chamber, and that this damages our politics. Labour MP Chuka Umunna, for instance, argued in an interview with the *Evening Standard* that the Palace of Westminster should be turned into a museum and a new semicircular Chamber built in which MPs are grouped according to region to encourage 'less confrontational' debates. 'How can we continue with a Chamber that nurtures the ridiculous tribalism that switches so many people off?' he asked the newspaper.[13]

Umunna was, like so many other proponents of a change to the design of the Commons, conflating confrontation with tribalism. It is perfectly possible for two parties to hold debates about the merits of a policy without resorting to petty tribalism. Buildings can indeed shape the way people behave, but they cannot totally change personalities and cultures – something that is perfectly obvious to those working in other sectors, such as education. Schools that move into well-designed new buildings often see marked changes in pupils' behaviour, but without teachers enforcing a culture of discipline, those changes only go so far. Would a change to the structure of the Commons really stop the party whips from ensuring that their MPs fall into line in debates and votes? Would it really remove the power of patronage that encourages backbenchers to spend much of their time in the Commons sucking up to ministers rather than scrutinising their actions?

The circular Chamber argument comes up regularly. Winston Churchill faced down calls to rebuild the Commons along these lines after it was bombed in 1941. He told MPs that 'we shape our buildings and afterwards our buildings shape us', arguing that the oblong shape of the Chamber was a 'very potent factor in our political life' because it created a clear division between the parties.[14] As someone who had twice crossed the floor of the Chamber to join the opposing party, Churchill believed that those divisions were serious and should be maintained.

Debate and disagreement is the flint that creates sharp policy. Consensus can lead to laziness on the part of ministers who do not feel the need to argue their case or ensure that their policy works. Standing up in the Chamber to face someone just a few metres away whose job it is to ask whether you are really doing the right thing is a refining experience. When he was prime minister, David Cameron told me that 'At 11.50 on a Wednesday, I think, oh God, what am I doing? Why am I doing this?' Other ministers confess to feeling sick as they walk to the Chamber for the much tamer departmental question sessions that they have to face. As we shall see throughout this book, the Chamber is often ill-used. But it is not the shape of that Chamber that creates the problem; it is the culture of those who fill it.

What does shock even those who love a good fight in the Commons is the way their parties require them to behave. If your party is fortunate enough to be in government, you are expected to make life as easy as possible for ministers by being totally loyal in the Chamber. This means you can end up giving what appears to be a pointless speech in a debate in which you do not probe whether a policy is a good thing or not, or ask for changes, but merely fill the air with your words until it is time for the next speaker. This results in some MPs not appearing to know what they're voting on even when they've given a speech about it.

All MPs end up having to work these things out for themselves, since there is no proper induction process on how to be a good MP beyond directions around the House and how to address the Speaker and other parliamentarians in the Chamber. This wouldn't matter so much if new parliaments started slowly, but most prime ministers are anxious to use their first hundred days to make a mark, and introduce reams of complex legislation as soon as possible. Not only do new MPs have no idea whereabouts in the building they are most of the time; they also have no idea how to scrutinise the legislation pumped out by the government.

And this means that they are voting on measures that they may later find themselves having to criticise.

There was some wry amusement at a meeting held by the whips in 2015 for newly elected Tory MPs when Lucy Frazer, one of the youngest QCs in the country, stood up and asked, 'What is the point of me making a speech?'[15] She was trying to work out whether she was actually required to persuade anyone with her arguments, or just sound supportive. As a barrister, she was used to spending a year buried in a brief and trying to win over a courtroom. Though some of her colleagues felt she was being naive, her outsider perspective had helped her pinpoint a really important question. As we shall see, the real answer to 'What is the point?' isn't very satisfying.

CHAPTER 3

____

GETTING OUT THERE

One of the dullest accusations that people level at MPs is that they are 'out of touch' and never meet anyone who is struggling. You might be able to accuse parliamentarians of being venal, selfish, and overtly ambitious for themselves. But as we shall see, Members of Parliament meet more people in dire straits each month than the rest of us manage in a year, perhaps even a lifetime. And they are doing more and more of it.

Once upon a time, your constituency was just the seat whose name you bore when you spoke in the Chamber. MPs could get away with barely visiting the seat they represented in Westminster. Duncan Sandys, MP for Streatham and Norwood on and off between 1935 and 1974, boasted of his annual trips over the river to visit it. Winston Churchill rarely visited his constituencies either.

Now MPs often describe themselves as 'glorified social workers', and are expected to hold surgeries at least once a fortnight, if not more often. At those surgeries, they meet members of the public who live in their constituencies and help them with any problems they need solving. Sometimes a constituent wants a general chat about policy. More often, the person visiting the surgery is in crisis, at their wits' end, and carrying a heavy bag of papers to prove quite how bad things have become. The MP has no obligation to take on that crisis, and indeed they have no more formal powers than the member of the public sitting opposite them. But what they do have, as this chapter's tour of constituency surgeries will show, is a local and national reputation that means many organisations listen to them and take them just that little bit more seriously. In addition, they have staff who understand the complex benefits, housing, schooling and health systems in this country that are so confusing to the layperson.

A survey by Young Legal Aid Lawyers of the 2010 Parliament found that for 33 per cent of MPs, constituency work took up between 50 and 74 per cent of their time, with 35.7 per cent spending between 35 and 49 per cent of their time on casework. This study also found that 34 per cent of MPs received between 100 and 200 new casework queries a month, 29 per cent receiving fewer than 100, 20 per cent between 200 and 500, and 13 per cent saying they had more than 500 casework requests each month. Asylum and immigration were the most frequently mentioned topics for casework, followed by welfare benefits and housing.[1]

Voters consider constituency work to be an important element of the job for the people they send to Parliament, expecting their MP to spend two or three days a week working on local issues.[2] The expansion of constituency work as a central part of an MP's role seems to coincide with the growth of the state following the Second World War, and the breakdown of the two-party system, with the rise of the SDP followed by the creation of the Liberal Democrats playing an important part in the development of 'pavement politics' and local issues. MPs now largely regard the job they are elected to do as their primary occupation, and while many have second jobs, these take up only a couple of days a month at most, with the bulk of an elected representative's hours spent working as an MP, either in the constituency or in Parliament. Their salary has risen over the decades to reflect this move from amateur to professional – and so have the allowances for MPs' office costs.

The academics Philip Norton and David Wood, who have studied in great detail the relationship between MPs and their constituencies over the decades following the Second World War, believe that the real explosion of constituency activity came in the 1960s, when the elections in that decade 'brought in many new Labour MPs drawn from professional backgrounds', and that the growth of local radio and free-sheet newspapers in the 1970s further encouraged those new members to be more involved.[3] Former Commons Library official Oonagh Gay also believes that MPs have become more interested in constituency business as more and more of them have come into Parliament from the public sector, bringing with them an interest in how services really work for people.[4]

No matter what the cause, MPs today devote considerable time and emotional energy to constituency work. Most seem to enjoy it, finding the contact with people satisfying, the perspective those meetings bring useful, and the feeling of solving a complicated problem addictive. Their staff, even those who work in Parliament rather than in the constituency office, often rank the MPs around them according to how interested they really seem in their seats. Good constituency workers are as valuable as gold dust: MPs often cast around for workers – sometimes described as 'matrons' – who understand the many ridiculous bureaucracies that utterly bewilder and subsume their constituents.

I wanted to understand what it was that the MPs I saw every day in the ornate Palace of Westminster got up to when they were in their constituencies. Many would mention in conversation cases they had encountered, or tell me over a coffee about how they and their staff had cracked open a bottle of wine to celebrate solving a particularly thorny problem. Constituency work is rarely celebrated in the media. It is not what young aspiring politicians who practise their maiden speeches in the mirror imagine as being the most exciting part of the job. Yet it seems to hold such emotional sway for so many MPs that they not only give in to the growing demands of the people they represent, but also insist on meeting their constituents even when it puts their own safety at risk.

In recent years we have seen the brutal murder of an MP outside her surgery, and another seriously wounded in a stabbing. Yet none of the visits I made to constituency surgeries across the United Kingdom over a two-year period offered any evidence of MPs trying to remove themselves from the people they serve. Far from it: for all they complain about the 'glorified social work' that they are expected to carry out, they seem to regard that work as a sacred duty, rather in the way that a vicar believes in the importance of meeting his parishioners. And although as a rather grumpy political journalist I often mock the way MPs conduct themselves in Westminster, I struggle to find much fault in the way that they interact with their constituencies. The visits I have made to chilly church halls, leaky community centres and library basements have provided a more eloquent riposte to the out-of-touch charge than anyone could write on an MP's behalf.

A number of things stand out: first is that MPs have to be able to respond to people in severe distress, and to bounce from one upset and confused constituent to another. The second is that they have to be able to understand the exact nature of the mess that someone has ended up in, which often even the constituent themself doesn't fully grasp. The third is that an MP's headed notepaper is one of the most powerful tools a parliamentarian carries. As we shall see in the case studies below, it has the ability to open doors and close down cases.

David Cameron, Conservative, Witney

Even prime ministers hold constituency days. For David Cameron, going from being a backbencher to a shadow minister to prime minister just meant fewer surgeries, sandwiched between European Council meetings, and a rather more organised day involving more burly security men than your average backbencher might encounter. 'Constituency work is not quite the icing on the cake,' he told me, as we drove in convoy with his security detail between one engagement and another. 'But it's the thing that makes it all hang together. Like the eggs! Yes, there's a good *Bake Off* analogy.'

Cameron believed that the 'social work stuff' that MPs had to do was important. He dismissed the grumbles of some of his colleagues that MPs were facing too many constituency demands, arguing that quite often his office could solve a problem before he needed to see it himself. Often he took conversations that he'd had in Witney back to Whitehall: he told me that a key U-turn on the legal aid cuts was sparked by a conversation with a solicitor who came to his surgery and set out the problems with the dual-contract arrangements for criminal solicitors. When Cameron heard these arguments, he asked Michael Gove, then Justice Secretary, to change the system.

As with all the MPs I've shadowed, it was clear that Cameron enjoyed meeting his constituents and finding out more about what they did. I saw the same expression on every face as he came over to talk to people: a momentary freezing and a slightly goggle-eyed look of fear before they realised that the prime minister had indeed just asked them a question and they needed to answer. Cameron tried to relax everyone he met with gentle humour. He also planned questions to ask them, as he realised that often those he visited forgot to tell him important bits of information until he had gone and they had recovered their composure.

On a day that ran from visit to photo opportunity to surgery, the Tory leader had a small black folder with him containing a briefing on everyone he was going to meet – including me – to help him appear knowledgeable about each person. He had already put in five hours of work by the time the constituency day began at 10 a.m.: between 5 and 6 a.m. he was working on his prime ministerial box and taking calls from Gordon Brown about the EU referendum – which was a few weeks away and which would bring an end to his own political career, something he clearly didn't expect as we buzzed about Witney together – and the Australian prime minister about the kidnap of a British national.

Some of the residents of a local dementia care home were a little too relaxed about their special guest: one elderly woman grabbed the prime minister's hand and bit it before being gently restrained by her carers. Cameron was here because one of the managers at the home had visited his advice surgery to complain about wages and staff training. As they walked past bedrooms and sitting rooms, he asked her and her colleagues to tell him more about training requirements, Care Quality Commission inspections, and pay scales. He was interviewing them in as intentional a manner as any journalist. This was clearly part of his strategy to get the most out of each visit.

But there were also less constructive, more human moments. In one bedroom a woman was celebrating her 106th birthday, and Cameron opened her telegram from the Queen. 'I have never opened one of these before!' he exclaimed, showing it to everyone. The resident was thrilled too, though she was more interested in passing on her own message to Her Majesty, which was that 'She spoils her children.' Upstairs, a patient who was clearly in the advanced stages of dementia was shouting and swearing as her daughter, obviously upset but resigned to her decline, told Cameron: 'I know this sounds selfish. But this disease is much harder on the relatives than it is on the people with it.'

It might be possible to be an MP and lack empathy. But it must be difficult. It's not just in the care home that a sensitive touch is needed. When Cameron sat down in his surgery, he faced people who were talking about the saddest and most sensitive of times: the death of a partner, a terminal illness, the treatment of disabled children. Like the rest of his day in Witney, his surgery was very tightly organised. It was not a drop-in session. In fact, you wouldn't even have known it was taking place behind the closed doors of the West Oxfordshire Conservative Association. It was also no ordinary surgery in terms of the paperwork that visitors brought with them. There were no plastic bags full of pages to sort through. One woman had even laminated her notes. Another visitor made a presentation of slides to show the prime minister about Parkinson's care.

But the skills required were the same as for any MP: the prime minister had to jump from a discussion about life in the Middle East to talking about illness and disability, listening to complicated stories about the mess created by pension companies after someone's death, and about the fears of parents of Down's syndrome children that other parents-to-be were being talked into terminations. The last discussion required the most sensitivity, and as the constituents sat down, Cameron reassured them that he was aware that this was an incredibly delicate subject. He referred briefly to his late son Ivan as he talked, but the conversation remained gentle, again with little flashes of humour to relax everyone. The women sitting in front of him wanted his advice on medical testing, on charities advising parents-to-be, and on campaigning to change the law on late abortions. As he did at the end of other appointments, Cameron listed the things he intended to do, which included a conversation with the Chief Medical Officer. But he also gently advised the women that if they hoped to change the law concerning late abortion of Down's babies, they shouldn't focus only on contacting pro-life MPs, as this would hurt their cause. And before they left, he got to do what every MP is supposed to do, whether humble backbencher or prime minister: pose for a photo with an adoring baby gazing straight up into his eyes.

Karen Buck, Labour, Westminster North

Karen Buck had so many constituents waiting for her at her advice surgery in the library in Church Street that they were handed tickets and called forward when it was their turn. This surgery took place as part of Advice Plus, an event organised and part-funded by the local housing association, and included many different agencies and advisers, including tax, benefits and legal. Anyone could turn up, and this meant Buck had to spend some time during each appointment simply picking through the piles of paperwork that constituents brought with them, trying to work out what the problem was and who was at fault.

And the piles of paperwork came in all forms. Some of the constituents clutched plastic wallets stuffed with pages. One man had a brown envelope of documents arranged far more neatly than his account of what had happened to him, which was so confusing that Buck concluded privately he was probably more in need of help from a mental health professional than from an MP (she believes around one in five of her cases involve serious mental health problems). Another man held a mess of papers and envelopes, which he shuffled about as he tried to find the right document relating to his eviction for failing to pay service charges. The mess slowed up Buck's conclusion that he had been wrongly evicted, and that she should take up his case. But she added, 'I can understand if they get into a muddle.'

One of the most striking things about all the constituency surgeries I attended (aside from Cameron's) was the way piles of paper came to symbolise the mess that the state had left people in. Those piles of paper are baffling enough for an MP to sort through, let alone someone whose life feels very much on the edge. When I visited Buck's Labour colleague Tristram Hunt in Stoke-on-Trent, the carrier bags that people hauled in with them to explain their child support or eviction case seemed much heavier than they should. The state has huge power, not just to change lives, but to turn them into a teetering pile of papery mess.

Buck is a very forthright MP. And even though she was clearly horrified by some of the cases she saw in the two-hour session, she was always brutally realistic about how much she could do for the people sitting opposite her. One woman brought a friend with her, not because her English was poor, but because she grew too distressed during the appointment to actually speak. Her friend explained that she was at her wits' end, in an overcrowded flat with three children and a second bedroom so small that not even the government's official criteria for paying benefits considered it a bedroom. Poor repairs by the housing association had left the property in a state, and there was nowhere for the children to do their homework, let alone play. The immaculately made-up young woman sobbed repeatedly as she described the physical health problems she had developed as a result of the intolerable situation.

Faced with a sobbing, sick woman, it would be tempting for any MP to say that they would try and change things immediately. But while Buck was clearly moved by the story she was hearing, she was also firm, explaining to the woman that there was very little that could realistically be done for her. Unless the council's environmental health department decided that the flat was uninhabitable, she wasn't even near the start of getting a transfer to a bigger property. To qualify for a priority move, she would have to be severely disabled, with a mobility problem. The young woman obviously felt relieved that Buck had listened and promised to do what she could. But she still left looking utterly hopeless.

For another couple with a housing crisis, something needed to be done immediately. The woman was due to give birth the following day and they had been evicted without warning by their private landlord. Buck was again very firm, explaining that as the pair had moved to Westminster North from another part of the country, the local council had no duty to house them. But she was horrified that no one had taken into consideration the fact that the woman was about to give birth. She called the council's children's services department, and though it took a while to get through, by the end of the surgery the couple had temporary accommodation.

Half the problem was their lack of understanding of what a local authority was required to do for them. But the other half was a housing department not getting in touch with the children's services department down the corridor to warn them that a baby was about to be born homeless. While MPs need to manage constituents' expectations when housing is scarce and funding thin, they also need to be able to coordinate the many disorganised bureaucracies that those constituents are caught up in, even if it's just encouraging people in the same building to talk to each other.

Tim Farron, Liberal Democrat, Westmorland and Lonsdale

That ability to get people in the same building to speak to one another should not be underestimated. When I sat in on Tim Farron's surgery in the Cumbrian market town of Milnthorpe, constituents seemed remarkably relieved just to hear that their MP was going to write letters on his House of Commons notepaper to various organisations. One woman was despairing about the care that her elderly and infirm parents were receiving. 'It shouldn't work like this,' said Farron as he looked through the pile of documents she had handed him. 'But often when we send them letters it kicks them into action.'

Farron has a reputation in Westminster for being a cheeky chappie, and he did chatter a lot during his sessions, which took around ten minutes each. His approach to expectations management couldn't be more different to Karen Buck's firm way of talking. One man who had recently moved from near Buck's London seat to a rural Cumbrian village was disappointed with the local bus services. It had come as a shock to the former north-west Londoner that there weren't buses running on Sunday evenings, for instance. Farron didn't explain the difference between Cumbria and Kensal Rise, but promised to arrange a meeting with Stagecoach, which ran the buses, to see if they might be able to introduce more services. It seemed to be a way of setting the constituent up for disappointment, but presumably it also meant that Farron could argue he had done everything he could to pressure the bus company into listening to residents, even if they didn't do anything in response. And since his constituent was in a low-paid job and struggling to get to work, why shouldn't Farron tell him that he was taking his concerns seriously?

The thing that seemed to upset Milnthorpe residents more than anything else was parking. The two meetings on parking were the grumpiest ones I'd seen, with one man complaining that he had been waiting for eight years for the council to sort the situation out – and that he felt Farron wasn't doing enough. Farron explained that he had an ally in the local highways department who he felt responded well to his calls. And it was back to that House of Commons notepaper again. So much of the job of an effective constituency MP is about good relationships with the people you have to badger over and over again.

Alison Thewliss, SNP, Glasgow Central

Alison Thewliss's Glasgow Central surgery was another example of how powerful an MP picking up their pen or the phone can be. MPs can stick their professional spanner in the works before a small crisis for one constituent spins out of control, leaving that person homeless and without food all because of one mistake from one part of government. The SNP MP sees more immigration cases in her inner-city seat than most other MPs, and contacts the Home Office round 10 to 15 times a day.

It was a chilly morning in a draughty community centre as I watched Thewliss talking to two burly Glaswegian men who had both come to her with money worries. One had had his bank account frozen without warning and wanted Thewliss to intervene with the bank on his behalf. The other had suddenly been told he no longer had a right to live in this country, even though he had lived and worked here since he was four. He had had all his benefits stopped, he explained as he unfolded a set of documents proving where he was born. And he grew visibly ashamed as he said he'd been forced to visit a food bank. This was not what a hard-working man wanted to admit to. Once again, MPs need to be both technically adept and compassionate in order to serve their constituents well at the most worrying times in their lives.

Jo Cox

Most people are barely aware of their MP's surgeries, let alone the skills their representative needs to be a good constituency MP. But the local work they do came to the public consciousness in the worst possible way in 2016.

Jo Cox was one of those MPs who loved her constituency far more than she loved Westminster. She was bursting with pride when she rose in the Commons to give her maiden speech on 3 June 2015. 'I am Batley and Spen born and bred, and I could not be prouder of that,' she said. 'I am proud that I was made in Yorkshire and I am proud of the things we make in Yorkshire. Britain should be proud of that too. I look forward to representing the great people of Batley and Spen here over the next five years.'[5]

When I met Cox for lunch, we talked about her work as an MP and what she planned to achieve. She was one of the most energetic and determined MPs I had ever encountered, telling me quite directly that if she didn't feel she was getting enough done in Parliament in her first five years, she would have no compunction about going off to do something else. Living out her values in the most productive way possible was something she cared about deeply, and something that everyone who knew her, even vaguely, noticed straight away.

She only had the chance to represent the great people of Batley and Spen in Parliament for just over a year, because on 16 June 2016, Jo Cox was murdered.

As she walked into a library in Birstall, where she was about to hold a constituency surgery, she was attacked by Thomas Mair, who shot the 41-year-old mother three times, and stabbed her too. Witnesses said he had shouted, 'This is for Britain. Britain will always come first.' A local man, Bernard Kenny, was stabbed in the stomach as he tried to stop the MP's attacker. Cox pleaded with her office staff to 'let him hurt me, don't let him hurt you' as she lay in the road. She died shortly after arriving at hospital.

The following week, MPs broke down in tears in the Chamber as they remembered their colleague. They wore white roses as a tribute to the Yorkshire MP. One red rose on the Labour benches marked Cox's space. Her children and husband Brendan sat in the gallery above, listening to the tributes. At the end of the session, the whole house rose to applaud Cox. This in itself was unusual: clapping is normally frowned on in the Chamber. More unusual still was that the journalists above in the Press Gallery, who normally do not participate in proceedings in any way at all, also stood to honour an MP who many had grown to admire very quickly.

Cox made an impression on Parliament with her determination and kindness that most MPs fail to do over many years. She campaigned on Syria and on loneliness – a perfect example of how an MP can reach across the world while standing up for their own local area.

Mair was convicted in October 2016 of Cox's murder; of grievous bodily harm with intent for stabbing Bernard Kenny; possession of a firearm with intent to commit an indictable offence, and possession of an offensive weapon (the dagger he had used). The

53-year-old was given a whole-life tariff and will never be released from prison. In an impact statement read to the court, Brendan Cox said, 'The killing of Jo, in my view, was a political act and an act of terrorism.'

Jo Cox wasn't the first MP attacked while serving her constituents. A study in 2016 by the Fixated Threat Assessment Centre, which assesses security risks to high-profile figures such as members of the royal family, found that four in five MPs had been victims of intrusive or aggressive behaviour. Worse: half of the 192 MPs who responded to the survey, which was circulated by the chief whips, had been targeted in their own homes.[6] This means that their families were also suffering, even if they didn't share the parliamentarian's politics or help in any way with their activities. But even if spouses do hit the campaign trail, or children appear in campaign leaflets, no one deserves to be threatened in their own home. Likewise, it is often the staff who take the abuse aimed at an MP. They are the ones most likely to be sitting in a constituency office, or picking up the phone to the wannabe abuser. Most MPs have at least one story of their staff being screamed at down the phone; others have had to install panic buttons for constituency workers.

It is not just the constituency where MPs are at risk. Party whips regularly text their members advising them which exit from the Palace of Westminster is safest to use when a demonstration is taking place outside and things are turning ugly. On those days, the Commons security staff stand by the entrances reminding everyone to remove their passes as they leave, as even those make someone a target.

After Cox's death, MPs turned on their expenses regulator, IPSA, and demanded that it stop dragging its feet over security measures. Some had waited months for IPSA to approve claims for basic measures such as CCTV. Others, fearing copycat attacks, installed additional locks and intruder alarms at their constituency offices and homes. IPSA did not rush, leaving MPs fretting about the safety of their staff and their children.

Yet we cannot just blame IPSA for taking too long to approve funding for security measures. We have to ask ourselves how we have created this climate of politicians being forced to give the impression that they do not trust the people they live amongst. Politicians have long been held in low esteem by the public, but there now seems to be a cohort of people who think that a person's political beliefs or activities make them and their families a legitimate target for abuse and violence. It coincides with a general struggle in Britain to debate respectfully and fully, with even university students retreating into 'safe spaces' and 'no platform' policies simply so they do not have to encounter ideas they find uncomfortable. Arguing and disagreeing is too much effort: much better to hate, resent and, in extreme cases, abuse and attack.

Those threats might well put people off going into politics. It would be bad enough having to tolerate abuse and the risk of violence on your own. But add your spouse and young children to the mix, and the prospect of being an MP is too much even for genuinely public-spirited figures. Those who claim they could wear it and are tougher than our current parliamentarians should look no further than Jess Phillips, the Birmingham Yardley MP who moved from running women's refuges to Parliament and found herself having to install additional security at her home following death threats – not against her, but against her children.[7] Next time we ask why we get the wrong politicians, perhaps we should ask why any of the right ones want to put themselves in this kind of danger.

Stephen Timms, Labour, East Ham

One thing that MPs never seem to waver from, even as they install CCTV and more locks, is their belief in being able to sit across a trestle table from a constituent and listen to their problems. Stephen Timms has more reason than most to want to separate himself a little more from the public when they come into his surgery. On 14 May 2010, the Labour MP for East Ham was holding his regular surgery. His next appointment approached, smiling and stretching out her hand. But Roshonara Choudhry wasn't stretching out her hand to greet Timms. She was holding out a knife and stabbed the MP in the stomach. Choudhry, a student who had been radicalised online, told the police: 'I was trying to kill him because he wanted to invade Iraq.' She was found guilty of attempted murder and jailed for life.

Just three weeks later, Timms was back at work. And though his first surgery after the attack was attended by a police counter-terror unit and community support officers, the MP was insistent that he wanted to stay as close to his constituents as he could. Another threat was made against him, this time online, with a post urging people to finish the job that Choudhry had started. But though that first surgery back was 'a bit odd, after two or three appointments, you just get back into the swing of it'.

The police offered Timms a permanent knife-detecting arch for all of his surgeries, but he refused. 'That would change the way we relate to our constituents,' he said. 'I didn't want people to have to be scanned every time they walked into my surgery.' He didn't want to give the people he served the impression that he didn't trust them.

I met up with Timms the day after Jo Cox's murder. Naturally, his phone was buzzing constantly with messages from colleagues worried that the attack would trigger some extremely traumatic memories for him. Timms is not the most effusive character, and only shudders slightly when talking about his own attack. He did add a little extra security to his walk-in advice centre that morning, and the appointment-only surgery that I sat in on in the afternoon had a volunteer showing constituents into the room where the MP sat with his two case workers. And that was that: business as usual.

The surgery contained the same complaints and troubles as any other: a house with a leaking roof, an infestation of mice, and damp – and the children falling sick because of the squalid conditions; immigration difficulties, problems with schools, and struggles with the taxman – issues that feature in every inner-city surgery. At least one constituent broke down in tears. Everyone came in looking burdened, their voices tuned to a minor key as they set out their problems. And even though the only way Timms could help was either to write a letter on his headed notepaper to the powers-that-be, or to attempt to explain the tangled bureaucracy that his constituents had somehow become knotted in, most people left looking relieved that at least someone had agreed that what was happening to them was not OK, and that they were prepared to do something about it. Even when that offer was made in the same forum where an MP had been stabbed just a few years ago.

The Vly Be on the Turmut

Most MPs complain that their job makes them unhealthier and fatter. Not so Steve Baker, who faces annual humiliation in the town square if he doesn't stay lean. Every year, Wycombe weighs its local dignitaries, with a town crier announcing whether they have gained weight at the taxpayer's expense. The year after Baker was first elected as a Conservative MP, he was horrified to hear the crier shout, 'And some more!' to the waiting crowd of locals, meaning he had gained weight. The experience of clambering onto a rickety chair to be weighed in front of his electorate and discover that he had put on weight was enough to force Baker into a rigorous regime of running, swimming and counting calories. For the past few years, he's had the pleasure of hearing 'And no more!' shouted across the town square.

This ancient ritual, preserved by the shire town, may seem silly. Many other MPs have to endure similar strange, quirky British traditions. John Glen, the MP for Salisbury, has to sing a song about keeping flies away from the turnips from the balcony of a local hotel after every election. He took singing lessons in preparation for his rendition of 'The Vly Be on the Turmut'. As Tory MP for Oxford West and Abingdon until 2017, Nicola Blackwood practised her best over-arm lob in preparation for the celebratory bun-throwing in her constituency that heralds major events such as the Queen's Jubilee. Unfortunately, one year a constituent complained that Blackwood had hit her in the eye, and accused her of aiming straight for her. Bread-throwing is more common than you'd think. In another, similar tradition, John Healey, the Labour MP for Wentworth and Dearne, threw 100 bread rolls from the roof of a village church to celebrate his election in 1997. He insists that it was an important local tradition, not just his own over-exuberance.

Michael Fabricant, the always exuberant Tory MP for Lichfield, needs no encouragement to take part in his own strange local tradition. 'I am summoned to St George's Day Court,' he says excitedly. 'And if it's a day when Parliament is sitting and I cannot attend, I have to pay a fine!' He has also dressed up in a KGB costume, and smeared his face with ketchup and staggered and swayed like a drunkard, all apparently in aid of the local St George's Day festivities.

Why do MPs submit to these humiliating rituals? Some, like Fabricant, enjoy the drama and attention. Others feel they have no choice. But many feel that it's part of that quiet civic pride that crops up at events celebrating the local area and that propelled many of them into political life in the first place. And if nothing else, no MP should take him or herself so seriously that they can't bear a little bit of public humiliation.

Dating advice

Even constituency surgeries, normally solemn affairs, can be entertaining. Karen Buck was amused to take a break from sorting emergency accommodation for young families to advise a constituent that actually, helping with the costs of a wedding really wasn't the sort of thing she could do. She was also once asked for help returning a pair of trousers that didn't fit.

Tory MP Alun Cairns received a request to find someone to feed a constituent's dog while he went on holiday – and actually did arrange for help. But his animal-related endeavours were nothing compared to the battle that East Worthing and Shoreham MP Tim Loughton went through. One of his constituents enlisted his support in retrieving a bearskin rug that had been impounded by customs on the advice of John Prescott's office. The owner of the rug threatened to shoot two more bears in Canada – which he had a licence to do – unless his rug was released. Fortunately Prescott's office yielded in this instance: 'A Canadian bear is still walking around without a bullet hole in him,' says Loughton.

Despite the rather high divorce rate in Parliament, MPs are also often approached for relationship advice. Loughton was asked by one local for advice on how to make the man who had dumped her change his mind. Therese Coffey, more accustomed to dealing with pleas for help with housing in her Suffolk Coastal constituency, was asked if she could recommend a good dating agency.

Some MPs oblige with these ridiculous requests because they know they will forever have a grateful constituent. But this of course encourages more people to see them as general handymen who will get involved in any local problem, no matter how small. One MP was horrified to be approached by a woman in the supermarket who thanked him loudly for 'getting me my council house'. He told her very firmly that he was not responsible for her success in reaching the top of the waiting list, and privately prayed that she wouldn't go around telling her friends that she'd got a house thanks to her local MP. 'I could just see my surgery filling up with even more people who thought I could achieve the impossible for them,' he says. Even non-ludicrous problems are often the purview of a local councillor rather than an MP, but few people know who their ward councillor is, and anyway, that all-important parliamentary notepaper holds far more sway than a letter from the town hall.

This does mean that constituency casework is just growing and growing. Perhaps this in turn means that MPs are becoming more and more in touch with the ordinary people they spend so much time talking about when they are in Parliament. Perhaps it means that they are more likely to spot bad policies and help change the dysfunctional ways in which the state operates when they return to Westminster. But one northern Labour MP, who complained to me about how out of touch her own colleagues seemed, cast doubt on this idea. 'No,' she said. 'It's like doctors who are surprised when they themselves get ill. We kind of compartmentalise between the people in crisis who we see and the rest of our lives. It's all too easy to forget that life is hard even for those who don't turn up at our surgeries. Too many of us leave our constituencies, come back here, and get all worked up about the politics in Parliament.'

Other MPs worry that the growing demands of constituency surgeries and local events are undermining what they are supposed to do as parliamentarians. In 2015, Tory MP James Gray came under fire when he wrote:

> It may well suit the agenda of the government very nicely. The more we do in our constituencies (and in harmless, if worthwhile, pursuits like backbench debates, all-party groups and the like), the less we will trouble them.
>
> How wrong all of this is. The complexity of government is certainly no less today than it has ever been. Legislation has in fact vastly increased in numbers in recent years, and vastly decreased in quality. Why? Because we are failing to scrutinise it properly in Parliament. Why? Because we don't have enough time to do so. Surely we should be seeking to extend Parliamentary hours and scrutiny rather than shortening them?[8]

Perhaps Gray comes across as unfeeling. But isn't he right in the sense that MPs are creating a vicious circle for themselves in which they don't have enough time to scrutinise the very legislation that can near drown their constituents in piles of paper when things go wrong? If the people who have the power to stop the mess in the first place are too busy trying to patch it up once it has ruined things for a constituent, then that is a matter for grave concern.

How is it, for instance, that David Cameron only realised how messy his legal aid reforms were when he was sitting in his surgery and not in Westminster? Some of his backbenchers ended up red-faced when they complained to housing associations about increased demands for rent from tenants that turned out to be a result of a housing benefit cut that their own party had introduced, the consequences of which no one had really taken the time to notice until it was too late. Those MPs then found themselves busily writing to councils asking for a discretionary housing payment to cover the rent for a constituent who couldn't move from their social home because it had been converted for their disabled son, or – more often – because there was nowhere else to move to. They ended up spending a lot of time on a problem that they had devoted a very short amount of time to scrutinising in Parliament.

MPs take their constituency work very seriously indeed. But do they have the same seriousness about being legislators? If parliamentarians are not getting the balance right, they could be spending their time sitting in draughty church halls and community centres trying to unravel what they and their colleagues have unwittingly ravelled in Westminster.

CHAPTER 4

GETTING THINGS DONE

When biologists draw diagrams of ecosystems, the various nutrients, plants and animals that make up these complex natural communities look so neat and ordered. Everything seems as it is meant to be, even though the reality of the meadow, woodland or mangrove is so much messier and confusing than its depiction on paper. Parliament is the same: its rabbit warren of offices and corridors and strange conventions makes little sense to someone wandering through, but everything is supposed to come together in a complex, messy and often rather archaic way to make the laws of the land.

MPs leave their constituencies and work in Parliament for four days each week primarily so that those laws can make their way through the Westminster system. They are told by their parties when they must be in the Commons, and have to get permission from the whips to be absent. More than that: they are told most of the time by those whips how they will vote, not just on the big principles, but on every detailed aspect of a piece of legislation. So the Westminster ecosystem contains a large herd of animals whose behaviour is often rather predictable.

But the ecosystem doesn't seem to work as well as those mangroves and meadows do. Once they've recovered from the shock of their arrival in a sprawling palace infested with mice, new MPs are frequently astonished by how little time they, as legislators, spend actually examining laws – and how those who try to do this are rarely rewarded by their seniors. One new Tory MP told me rather miserably after a year in the job that he felt as though he was 'failing the country in my duty to it. I am voting on things that I don't understand, and this upsets me.' Many of his new colleagues agree, remarking variously: 'scrutiny is shocking', 'scrutiny of legislation here is very bad, the whole thing is a theatre', 'I don't think scrutiny is very good here', and 'the thing that I've been really disappointed by since coming in has been how bad the legislation side of things has been'.

Wes Streeting, a Labour MP elected in 2015, confesses that the quality of work that the Commons does on laws is so poor that, having previously been a staunch supporter of an elected House of Lords, he has changed his mind on Lords reform: 'I think the Lords is much better for scrutiny than the Commons,' he says. 'Patronage is so strong and the executive dominates [in the Commons]. We don't really have the time to look at legislation, we don't take ourselves seriously as legislators.'

That impression doesn't change as MPs settle in. Former ministers agree: 'Scrutiny in Parliament is terrible,' says former Liberal Democrat pensions minister Steve Webb. 'You definitely get bad legislation coming out.' On standing down in 2015, Frank Dobson told an interviewer: 'Over the years I've developed a lower and lower appreciation of the place in terms of effectiveness. Our record on passing laws that achieved what it was claimed they would achieve when a minister introduced them [is] absolutely pathetic, quite frankly . . . Even if you don't agree with the laws, at least the bloody things ought to work, and so frequently they don't.'[1]

Graham Brady, the influential chair of the Conservative 1922 Committee – a sort of trade union for backbenchers, which chooses the candidates to be party leader and pressures the top brass to change policies – believes that the way the Commons works 'infantilises Members of Parliament'. Former advisers to ministers who have been involved in drawing up laws agree that MPs do little to improve them. 'Oh, it's utterly terrible,' says one former aide to a Conservative cabinet minister, when asked if the Commons does a good job in examining legislation before it makes it onto the statute books. Another remarks that 'You can ram most things through the Commons: it's the Lords you need to worry about.'

Given that Parliament exists primarily to approve laws, it seems odd that those who work in it don't believe it is very good at doing this job. The Westminster ecosystem doesn't seem to be behaving as it should. What has gone wrong?

How laws are made

As with academic diagrams of natural ecosystems, the system for examining laws in this country looks really rather good on paper. Every bill that a government proposes must go through a series of stages of scrutiny in the House of Commons, something that take months to complete. Then the same process is repeated in the House of Lords. MPs and peers have the power to suggest changes to bills on two different occasions, and legislation even goes through a lengthy process of 'line-by-line scrutiny' in a smaller committee.

When a bill is published, it has its first reading in the House of Commons. This is merely a formality: a minister will announce the bill, and the date for its second reading. This next stage is the first chance MPs have to debate the law in the Commons, and is supposed to focus on the principles rather than the detail of the bill in question. Backbenchers can use the second reading debate to raise concerns about certain policies they hope ministers will change before the bill is enacted, and to make a bid to be on the committee of MPs who carry out the line-by-line scrutiny. The bill then moves into committee, with a small group of MPs who reflect the political balance of the Commons debating the legislation in great detail over a couple of weeks. At this stage, MPs on the committee can table amendments to the bill, which are then voted on individually. Once committee stage is over, it's back to the Commons again for the 'report stage', at which any MP can table more amendments, which the whole House will vote on, before the bill has a third reading vote and, if approved, moves up to the House of Lords.

This is how legislation is supposed to work. There seems to be plenty of time for scrutiny and many opportunities for MPs to raise concerns about potentially bad policies. So why do so many of those involved in law-making in this country think the Commons is doing a bad job?

The problem is not that there aren't enough formal opportunities for MPs to scrutinise laws. It is that they cannot, or will not, take those opportunities. It is like someone who pays a large amount of money for a gym membership, and attends that gym four times a week – but only to sit in the jacuzzi eating cream buns. The gym is there, the membership card is there, but it isn't quite being used as it should be.

The first – and biggest – problem is that the parliamentary whipping system and the way any defeats for the government are reported makes it very difficult for an MP to change a bill once it has appeared in Parliament using the formal channels outlined above. If ministers have time, or if the legislation is complex, they may subject it to 'pre-legislative scrutiny' in the form of a draft bill that a committee of MPs and peers examine in great detail. This happens particularly with intelligence- and security-related legislation. The draft Investigatory Powers Bill ended up being changed dramatically as a result of the recommendations of the committee examining it.

There are also consultation documents known as 'green papers' in which various policy ideas are batted around, only to be dropped when experts point out the obvious flaws in them. Labour's 2009 green paper on cutting housing benefit, for instance, posed all sorts of ideas for bringing the overall housing benefit bill down that the party was then told would simply not work. This sounds like a reasonable process, and on the rare occasions it is done, it does give experts an opportunity to pick apart bad ideas. But the range of experts who respond to these consultations is often limited, and they are frequently special-interest groups that do not always have a legitimate claim to represent the interests of those whose names they bear.

Once legislation is written in a bill, the ego of the government swells and it does not want to be humiliated by a defeat, even on the design of a policy that really should change before it becomes reality. MPs can use the second reading debate to flag concerns about aspects of the bill that they think need improvement, and a minister wary of defeat will listen to those concerns, perhaps meeting MPs privately and asking civil servants to draft amendments in time for the bill committee.

The whips from each party select the MPs to attend the bill committee for each piece of legislation, which means it is highly unlikely that an MP from the governing party who has a detailed knowledge of the subject area covered by the legislation and wants to make changes to that legislation will be selected. A well-known example of this concerns Sarah Wollaston, a GP from Devon who was elected the Conservative MP for Totnes in 2010. She wasn't all that impressed with the Health and Social Care Bill introduced by Coalition ministers in 2011, and wanted to join the bill committee in order to table a series of amendments that she hoped would improve the way that legislation would reorganise the health service she had worked in for 24 years. But when she approached ministers, she was told she wouldn't get a place on the committee unless she agreed to table only amendments that were acceptable to the government. Wollaston was furious, describing as a sham the 'new politics' that David Cameron had made part of his appeal when campaigning to be prime minister. 'You can't say you want to have "new politics" but not change the way the system works,' she said bitterly.[2]

Wollaston's colleagues endorsed her remarks, reminding David Cameron of his claim in 2009 that 'there are far too many laws being pushed through, with far too little genuine scrutiny from MPs. And excessive "whipping" of MPs by party hierarchies further limits genuine scrutiny. This, too, has to change.'[3] Like so many politicians who found this system frustrating when in relatively powerless opposition, Cameron clearly realised on coming to power that the flaws he wanted to change were actually a way of ensuring that legislation got through without much trouble for a busy government that had already made up its mind.

Other new MPs are shocked on entering the Commons at what is expected of them when they join a bill committee. 'The whole thing is this 18-day charade,' says one Tory backbencher. 'It is a theatre and everything you achieve comes from work outside the committee room, not inside, which makes it difficult.' Another newly elected Tory remarked after her first committee that 'It was fascinating but frustrating because I ended up agreeing with the Labour amendments but couldn't vote for them.' A minister who led a bill committee was amused to read the claims of one of its backbench members, who wrote in his local paper that he had listened carefully to all the evidence presented. 'I just thought, no you haven't, you are the Conservative MP on the bill committee and you are going to vote the way your whip has told you,' he chuckled. Former Conservative MP Andrew Tyrie considers the committees a 'pointless ritual',[4] while the late Labour MP Michael Meacher told a select committee in August 2013 that the way governments used only loyal MPs to ram through legislation in this way was a 'public scandal'.[5]

These committees are famous for being an opportunity to write Christmas cards while paying little heed to the arguments being presented. Indeed, former Labour MP Tony Wright told a select committee in 2013 that 'when I sat on ordinary bill committees, then that was the Christmas cards, then it was doing your correspondence, then it was the whips saying "Don't say a thing. Certainly do not start flitting about with cross-party amendments. Do not complicate the party battle that we are engaged in." It was a firmly, firmly structured process. Every new member – those with any kind of sensibility – is shocked by what they find.'[6]

The 1922 Committee chair Graham Brady also chairs bill committees in Parliament. 'I chaired a committee this morning about the Bank of England,' he said before the 2017 snap election. 'It wasn't massively controversial, but through the two hours that I was chairing, the only people who spoke were the two shadow ministers, the SNP's George Kerevan [no longer an MP], who knows what he's talking about, and the minister! And you know, it kept going until the government whip finally woke up and said,

"Shall we go for lunch now?" I'm sure it would have been exactly the same in the afternoon session. Why ten Conservative MPs and half a dozen opposition MPs should spend five or six hours sitting in a room doing nothing while only two people speak is a mystery.'

What's the point of joining a bill committee if it is so intellectually unsatisfying? It takes up several weeks of an MP's time, and though they can carry on checking their emails and writing constituency letters, it is hardly a productive use of their busy week. One ambitious but rather too honest Tory backbencher summed it up very neatly when I asked him how he had found his first committee experience. 'My job on a public bill committee is to assist the minister and get the legislation passed,' he said, adding rather more bluntly, 'It is a good career move for me as you've got the minister and the whip watching you and it's a real test of your ability to argue for the government.' In other words, those 18 or so days spent sitting in a stuffy room in Portcullis House or the Committee Corridor of the Palace are worth it not because they improve the legislation that you have been elected to scrutinise, but because they improve your chances of climbing up the greasy pole.

Anthony King and Ivor Crewe, in their masterful study of how governments manage to mess up big and important policies so often, argued that 'MPs on public bill committees almost always see themselves as partisan advocates, not as dispassionate lawmakers.'[7] There is no culture in Parliament that rewards dispassionate lawmaking. If you want to get ahead, you must be a passionate, partisan supporter of the law as you find it when you reach the bill committee, rather than trying to challenge it yourself. If you see a part of a bill that you think could seriously damage your constituents, the bill committee is not the forum in which to raise it, even though it seems that you have all the time in the world in which to do so.

If being on a bill committee for the sake of legislation is a pointless exercise for backbenchers in the governing party, it must be even worse for those in the opposition party, who do not have a majority and therefore will table pages of amendments to the legislation knowing that they will fail.

Some opposition backbenchers too see the committee as an opportunity for shining at an early stage in their parliamentary career. But others, while accepting that the exercise in itself very rarely produces any changes to a bill that the party can claim credit for, feel that they can make the case openly to a minister in a way that a government MP cannot about the need for something to change. Most of the time, the minister won't acknowledge their concerns, but he or she may make changes to the bill at the next stage of scrutiny – report stage – and claim credit for the government. It is a thankless task for the opposition, but it does have the potential to improve a bill. 'I think bill committees work well for opposition MPs,' says Tom Greatrex, who served as a Labour shadow minister for most of his five years in Parliament between 2010 and 2015. 'You can make points and push the ministers on things and see changes to the legislation, even if it is something they change back at report stage. But the government MPs, they do absolutely nothing. That's not one party or another; it's whoever is in government. You see the MPs turning up with letters to write, and their researchers come in and out with more things for them to do.'

Kevin Brennan is a former Labour whip and shadow minister who has sat on a fair few bill committees both in government and opposition. He says that 'There is no way that the government will ever concede anything in a bill committee', but like Greatrex, he believes that the opposition can use the sessions to good effect.

Louise Thompson, an academic whose grim job it is to study the workings of bill committees, has found that it is indeed rare for anyone in a non-governing party to make changes to the law in this forum. One of the reasons, she says, is the 'recognition that formal mechanisms are not the best means through which to achieve change to government bills'.[8]

In 2016, one shadow minister made more of an impact in a bill committee than any other for a long time when he decided it would be the best forum for his resignation from the Labour front bench. Rob Marris was so frustrated with the direction the Labour Party was taking under Jeremy Corbyn that he used a point of order at the end of a finance bill committee sitting to resign. He thanked those who had given evidence, his researcher and the minister, and then announced he was standing down and would not return to the committee unless there was a change of leadership in the party. There was an awkward pause, and then the chair thanked the MP before pointing out that strictly speaking this wasn't a point of order, but that the committee was grateful for the information.[9] A prosaic end to a frontbench career.

The report stage of a bill is where the real action happens. Anyone can table an amendment to the legislation, and well-organised rebels on the government side, or a clever opposition operation that embraces concerned government MPs, can send ministers into a tizz as they try to stop an embarrassing defeat on the floor of the House of Commons. Most sensible MPs who care about the law rather than about making a political point and humiliating the minister responsible for the legislation will try to have a meeting with that minister first in which they explain what they're particularly worried about. As at committee stage, the government may well take the credit itself by tabling an amendment, but as government amendments rarely fail, this is the best way of ensuring a change. It just means that no one sees you making the case for that change in public, as all the action takes place outside the Commons Chamber. This is one of the reasons why people who get annoyed that their MP isn't always sitting on the green benches of the Commons are demanding the wrong thing of their parliamentarian: often it is when a member is out of sight that they are doing their most valuable work.

But not all meetings with ministers work out. If a backbencher from the governing party tables an amendment, it is a sign of a breakdown between the executive and the legislature, and leads to a day of drama. The number of amendments tabled by previously ultra-loyal Conservatives such as Dominic Grieve to the EU Withdrawal Bill was a sign not just of Grieve's grave concerns about Brexit, but of Number 10's refusal to listen to him. The Immigration Bill of 2014 was another example where behind-the-scenes meetings didn't yield what Tory backbencher Dominic Raab wanted. He had been pressing for an end to foreign criminals' right to resist deportation on the grounds that they were entitled to a family life, but Theresa May, then the Home Secretary, refused. So Raab tabled an amendment to the report stage of the bill, which attracted so much support from his colleagues that the government went into meltdown.

In the hours running up to the report stage vote, ministerial aides sent out panicked 'dear colleague' letters, which are often used to try to persuade backbenchers to behave themselves. The whips were buzzing around so fast that Number 10 managed to instruct ministers to abstain on the vote at almost exactly the same time as Theresa May started attacking Raab's amendment in the Commons. In the end, the amendment failed, but it shows how dramatic and confusing report stage can be.

Another common tactic is to say that the government will make changes that address the MPs' concerns in the House of Lords, and if they could just help their beleaguered colleague out this once, they'll get exactly what they want in the long run. Sometimes the prime minister will get involved, holding meetings in Downing Street in which he or she tries to convince individual MPs that voting against the government is about so much more than this small amendment on the delivery of local health services or benefit cuts. Coupled with the threat of no promotions for ambitious backbenchers, rebellions can be whittled down to such an extent that even their leaders conclude there is no point in pressing the amendment to a vote – or division as it's formally known. But that's only if the whips have been effective.

Those involved in drawing up legislation often say that a clever tactic is to insert something in a bill that they know they will have to concede on in the Commons, in order to make MPs feel as though they have won a battle, even though that policy was never something ministers were that bothered by. A cut to housing benefit for people who had been on Jobseeker's Allowance for more than a year was widely regarded in the Work and Pensions department in 2010 as a useful lightning rod for opposition to the whole package of cuts, and so it was duly dropped when the legislation was published, giving campaigners a false 'victory'.

The way Commons time is allocated for debate at report stage means that while MPs can spend hours getting worked up about one particular amendment, others are dropped or voted on without serious debate. The government can table its own changes to legislation as it moves through Parliament, to the extent that a bill may not look at all like the set of proposals that appeared before MPs several weeks before. Steve Webb, the former pensions minister, says: 'You get so many amendments going through on the nod, you'd get an hour on one amendment, and then an hour on another, and then the rest of them just tabled at the last minute going through with zero scrutiny.'

Any MP worth their salt will know that to vote against the government is usually to vote against your own career prospects, which is why serial rebels tend to be rather eccentric characters ill-suited for life on the front bench (like Jeremy Corbyn, for instance, who rebelled against his own party more than 500 times). Each rebellion also diminishes your capital as an MP, so if you see a policy you feel uncomfortable with, you may raise concerns behind the scenes but will ultimately shut up and vote the way the whips tell you, even if there are no changes at all in the offing.

This means that bad policies are passed by the Commons because there is a culture in which joining the executive is more important than being a serious legislator. Every MP can think of legislation they voted on that they didn't feel fully comfortable with, sometimes excusing themselves by saying, 'We were promised changes in the Lords.' And when you do rebel in the name of better legislation, no one rewards you for doing so. You might get the odd admiring newspaper article, and jubilant congratulations from the opposition about a sinner that repenteth. But this admiration soon fades – and it is a lonely and boring business sitting in exile until your party leader decides to have mercy on you after a few years and gives you a junior ministerial job.

The whips also have another power that is rather less sinister than offering promotions, or patronage, as it is known. Since there is simply too much legislation for an individual MP to know what he or she is voting on, they need the whips to tell them which lobby to walk through in the five or six divisions that may happen in one afternoon as the Commons examines a bill at report stage. Whenever I'm having a drink or a coffee with an MP on the key Commons business days of Monday, Tuesday or Wednesday, and the division bell rings, I ask them as they jump up to run to the lobbies whether they have any idea what the vote is about. 'Not a clue!' most of them cheerfully reply. Unless you happen to be talking to a specialist on the particular day when a bill they are interested in is before the Commons, you're unlikely to glean much from the average backbencher about most bills: MPs learn pretty quickly that it is better to specialise and understand a few bits of legislation well, rather than drown under the sheer weight of laws that a government is pumping through Parliament at any one time.

Even serious legislators like Douglas Carswell, who defected from the Conservatives to UKIP in 2014, realise that there is just too much for one MP to look at. When he became UKIP's only MP in the Commons, Carswell had to work out how to vote on everything. There was no one there to tell him what to do, not that he'd bothered to stick to what the whips had told him when he was a Tory. So he hired a member of staff to help him out, and the pair held a regular UKIP Parliamentary Party meeting to discuss upcoming votes. Caroline Lucas, too, had to accept that she just could not be across all the issues in the Commons as the Green Party's only MP.

Therefore, the instructions on how to vote that whips send around by email and text message are invaluable to MPs so that they don't accidentally end up rebelling against the government, or damaging an opposition attack on a flagship policy. The whips can often get seriously bad policies through because a large number of backbenchers haven't noticed what they entail. And they have little sympathy for those who complain after the event. One Conservative whip admits: 'I think there could be better scrutiny of legislation, but that is down to the individual MP. They can choose whether to read the bill. They can find the time. Time management is a big issue in this place and people don't know how to deal with it.' Reluctantly, I find myself agreeing with this. As sympathetic as I am to MPs' complaints that they never have enough time to do anything, most of them can normally find an hour to have a coffee with me in Portcullis House at reasonably short notice. If they thought scrutinising legislation was worth it, they would refuse my offer of a natter about who hates who in their party, and instead hole themselves up with a bill. But what's the point when the culture of the Commons tends to reward those with good media contacts more than it does those who understand the real implications of the clause they're about to approve?

The process of first and second readings, committees, report stages and third readings is repeated again in the House of Lords, and this is where bills can really change and the government suffer defeat after defeat. The role of the Lords is as a revising chamber, but the culture of the Commons means that all too often peers are not so much revising as doing the dirty work of MPs too anxious to stick their heads above the parapet. The political balance of the Lords does not reflect the government's majority, and to make matters even more difficult for ministers, it has a group of people missing from the Commons: non-aligned cross-bench and independent peers, appointed because of their expertise, who will vote according to each issue. Clever political operators will work behind the scenes with cross-benchers respected in a particular field to table amendments to legislation, as other cross-benchers will be far more likely to support a proposal if party politics appears to be absent from it. And the whips have no reach at all into this large herd of cats, which means bills can suffer multiple defeats in the Upper Chamber.

The Legal Aid, Sentencing and Punishment of Offenders Act, a piece of legislation so poorly designed that ministers have put almost more effort into correcting its flaws than they did into writing the original law, will crop up again and again in this book as an example of what happens when the system goes disastrously wrong. As a measure of how much it horrified peers, it suffered no fewer than 11 defeats in the House of Lords. The key ingredient in the majority of these defeats was the support of cross-bench peers. Unlike MPs, they see their sole purpose in the Lords as being scrutiny of legislation. They don't worry that they'll get into trouble if they point out that it's a bit hopeless and try to change it. And the culture of the Lords rewards considered discussion and argument, not partisan point-scoring.

Of course, the Upper House isn't a parliamentary paradise. It is an appointed, not elected chamber, which means peers can build up years of expertise, but also means that cronyism is rife. David Cameron became particularly notorious during his premiership for stuffing the Lords with chums such as 'bra queen' Michelle Mone and former staffers. Just lurking around in Downing Street for a little while made you eligible in the former prime minister's eyes for a gong or a peerage: his resignations honours list was blocked by the commission overseeing the appointments because it included Michael Spencer, a party donor whose firm ICAP was fined £55 million for its part in the 2012 Libor crisis. Liberal Democrat leader Tim Farron said in a press release that the list of peerages and accompanying honours for former Downing Street staffers, including many who had served on the failed Remain campaign during the EU referendum, was 'so full of cronies it would embarrass a medieval court'.

Yet every political leader is guilty of handing peerages to people who will make life easier for them, or whose eligibility to join the

Lords is dubious – and this includes the Liberal Democrats. Take Baroness Sheehan, who was given a life peerage by Nick Clegg in August 2015. No one in the party seemed to know why this party campaigner, who had served as a borough councillor for just four years, and had stood for Parliament – and lost – twice, was right for the Lords. Some said she was an inspiration to other women in the party; others described her as a hard-working campaigner. But two party figures who had worked alongside Sheehan moaned privately to me that she was 'one of the least qualified people I've ever encountered' and that her peerage was an 'example of cretinous box-ticking politics so odious and naked I am ashamed to be associated with the party'.

Like the Lib Dems, Jeremy Corbyn doesn't believe in the House of Lords – most of the time. When it suits him, however, the Labour leader will happily confer a peerage upon someone who has helped him out, as he did with Shami Chakrabarti. In 2016, the respected civil liberties campaigner took a series of rather odd decisions. First, she agreed to chair an independent inquiry into anti-Semitism in the Labour Party. Then, on the very same day she started chairing the inquiry, she became a member of said party, which seemed a strange definition of 'independent'. Later, after her inquiry published a report branded a 'whitewash' by some Jewish Labour MPs, she accepted a peerage from the party. She furiously denied that this was transactional, telling the BBC's Andrew Neil that this 'particular peerage' was offered to her after she had finished the report, while also admitting that senior politicians had offered her a peerage before.[10]

So the Upper Chamber has many figures who will happily do their party leader's bidding, whether it be for the public good or not. However, even though the recruitment process for the Lords is far less meritocratic than even that for the Commons, it is widely agreed that when it comes to stopping bad laws, this part of the Palace of Westminster more than pulls its weight.

What it cannot do, though, is have greater weight than the Commons, which is the primary law-making chamber and has the ultimate say. So what to do when MPs have agreed a measure but peers vote it down? A bill has one final stage before it becomes law; this debate between the two chambers is formally called 'consideration of amendments', but everyone inside Westminster knows it as 'ping pong'. MPs vote on whether to accept a change passed by the Lords. If they reject it, which they often do because it is inconvenient to the government, it is then sent back for the Lords to offer an amenable amendment until the two Houses can agree on a compromise. The Lords can send it back to the Commons, and if both chambers are in determined mood, the changes can ping and pong back and forth a number of times – but they must reach an agreement eventually, or else the legislation will fall. That very rarely happens. Normally peers can be bought off with the promise of a twelve-month review of a policy or something similar that suggests the government will keep an eye on whether the dire warnings about its effects will indeed come to fruition. Though even if those dire warnings are proved correct by the review, ministers can still ignore them. At least peers will have done their level best to spot and try to stop bad policy. It's not clear the same can be said of the Commons.

The secrets of secondary legislation

An even better way of getting bad policies past MPs without them noticing is to whack them into secondary legislation. This sounds desperately dull but is in fact a sinister way in which the executive gets its way with very little scrutiny at all. Secondary legislation is supposed to include the detail of a bill: where the planned road will go, the precise rates at which a benefit will be paid, and so on. Depending on what type of secondary legislation is used, MPs will either debate the measure for 90 minutes on the floor of the House of Commons or in a smaller committee, or they will not debate it at all, with the legislation merely being laid before Parliament and becoming law all at once. In most cases, it is impossible for MPs to amend these laws, and so if they get a vote at all, they must either approve or reject the measure as a whole, rather than trying to improve it as they do with primary legislation.

This confusing system might sound like a scandal in itself until you consider the sorts of things secondary legislation covers. The River Mersey (Mersey Gateway Bridge) (Amendment) Order 2016, for instance, covers the provisions for charging drivers to use certain sections of just one road, and outlines which bits of the road the charge applies to. Even the MPs whose constituencies contain this road would struggle to make rousing speeches about such an order.

The problem with secondary legislation is that ministers can choose to put anything they want into this less well-scrutinised form of law, from boring roads to big changes to the way benefits are paid, to abolishing entire quangos administering government policy. There is nothing to stop them from, for instance, using secondary legislation to cut £1,000 from the tax credit income of some of the poorest families in the country. Even though this was a very controversial policy announced by George Osborne in his 2015 summer Budget, it was only given 90 minutes for debate in the House of Commons as a statutory instrument (a particular type of secondary legislation). Because few MPs had cottoned on to what they were supporting, and because Labour was in total disarray just days after electing Jeremy Corbyn as leader, the measure passed with a gravity-defying majority of 35 when the Conservative government only had a working majority of 12. It then moved to the House of Lords, where after a rather more furious debate, peers took the highly unusual step of voting the instrument down. As a punishment, the Tories introduced a number of reforms designed to stop the Lords being so insolent ever again.

MPs often don't know what the content of the primary legislation they are voting on is. They are even less likely to understand the regulations that are put to them either in the Commons or in a committee. Committees approving these laws are not selected on the basis of experience or expertise: quite the opposite. And that is why ministers make so much use of secondary legislation. Research by the Hansard Society found that between 1950 and 1990, the number of statutory instruments produced each year was rarely higher than 2,500. From 1992, it has never dipped below 3,000. And Parliament only scrutinises on average 1,200 of those regulations.[11] This keeps the executive powerful, as it can make big changes to policy without anyone noticing.

One such big change was the decision to axe maintenance grants for poorer students. Most people would imagine that approving the conversion of these grants to loans would be something that MPs would debate at length in the House of Commons. But they didn't. Just 18 MPs had the chance to discuss and approve this measure – formally known as the Education (Student Support) (Amendment) Regulations 2015 – because it was delegated legislation. A number of the Labour members present complained about the decision of the Conservative government to sneak it into secondary legislation. Ilford North MP Wes Streeting protested: 'This is not a usual statutory instrument that involves some tinkering with thresholds or levels, or amends an existing policy framework in the way that statutory instruments normally do. This is a major change in government policy, and this committee has no business discussing it. This should be debated on the floor of the House of Commons, because the result of the regulations that the government are railroading through Parliament today is that students from the poorest backgrounds will graduate with the highest levels of debt. How can that possibly be fair?'[12]

Perhaps the policy was the right one: the Conservative members of the committee either thought it was or thought it best to keep quiet about it, as they dutifully voted it through. But surely Streeting was correct that all MPs should have had the chance to examine it. Of course, his faith in the ability of his colleagues to scrutinise things better in the Commons is quite touching, given that the same culture of taking legislation far less seriously than other considerations prevails as much in the Chamber as on the Committee Corridor. But at least in the Chamber debate is encouraged, whereas most MPs want to zip in and out of a committee as quickly as possible.

If MPs believe bill committees to be a waste of time, they take an even less respectful attitude towards secondary legislation. The committees approving regulations rarely last their allocated time, with whips telling MPs to shut up and it'll all be over quickly. 'You turn up to them and the whips say, "Right, we can get this over and done with in five minutes if you keep quiet",' says one disappointed new MP.

Most of the time the keep-quiet strategy works. But it failed on 10 September 2012 when a group of MPs trundled into a committee room to approve two regulations: the Draft Victims of Overseas Terrorism Compensation Scheme 2012 and the Draft Criminal Injuries Compensation Scheme 2012. The newly appointed Conservative minister responsible for these schemes, Helen Grant, made a short speech explaining that the changes would 'remove payments for minor injuries and focus payments on seriously injured victims of serious crime'. At this point, the normal format of a committee examining statutory instruments would involve the opposition grumbling about the changes, the government MPs replying to emails and sorting out their diaries for the coming day, and a quick vote approving the new policy. What unfolded instead was uproar from the Tory members of the committee, who had realised very quickly that they were being asked to cut compensation for postmen who had been attacked by dogs, shop workers who had been assaulted, and other people left vulnerable in the course of their work or by terror attacks overseas.

As the session drew on, four Tory MPs – John Redwood, Jonathan Evans, Angie Bray and Bob Blackman – became increasingly agitated. Blackman argued that the changes risked 'sending a signal to say that some violence towards shop workers is acceptable', Bray claimed the work undermined what the government had been doing on dangerous dogs, and Evans fretted about the impact on postal workers. Normally backbenchers from the governing party don't make speeches in these committees. But Evans spoke up, declaring that he felt he had to say something about what was being proposed. He outlined his concerns about the cuts, called the policy a 'hospital pass' from Grant's predecessors in her department, and urged her to reconsider. John Redwood was still more blunt. 'My Hon. Friend is being very persuasive. I have never been shy about saying that I would like us as a government to spend less overall, but I have never once thought that it had to be done by cutting something so sensitive or giving a worse deal to the disabled, the poor or the most vulnerable. I hope that the government will think again.'

With Redwood, a famed deficit hawk, opposing the measure, it was clear that the government needed to beat a hasty retreat. Grant was saved by the division bell, which summoned all the MPs to the Commons to vote on something else, and when they returned, she was able to withdraw the motion, saying the government would think again.[13]

Was this a victory for victims of attacks? Well, momentarily. Two months later, a group of MPs trundled into a committee room to approve the Draft Victims of Overseas Terrorism Compensation Scheme 2012 and the Draft Criminal Injuries Compensation Scheme 2012. None of the gang of four – Redwood, Evans, Bray and Blackman – had been invited back.

Grant made a speech explaining what the changes would entail, then mentioned what had happened in September when she first proposed them, adding, 'We have listened carefully to the comments made, but the fundamentals of the case for reform have not, in our view, changed. Against that backdrop, we have decided to proceed with our changes to the Criminal Injuries Compensation Scheme without amendment. We believe that that is the correct way forward.'

She said the government would add some flexibility to help those who were temporarily unable to work as a result of their injury. And then she allowed her fellow committee members to speak. What followed was what normally follows a minister's speech in a committee. The opposition grumbled about the changes. The Conservative members of the committee stayed entirely silent. And the measure passed, just two months later than planned.

A related trick is to take what is known as a 'Christmas tree bill' through the House of Commons. This is legislation that is so bare without the detail of secondary legislation that is later hung on it that it hardly makes sense, and it certainly doesn't give the parliamentarians who do take the time to scrutinise it much idea if the changes it will enable are good or bad. Though in fact to say that the secondary legislation provides the detail is inaccurate: in many cases it provides the bulk of policies.

The whips merely take advantage of the culture in Westminster that rewards those who aspire to the executive, not those who take their jobs as legislators seriously. If you are an ambitious MP who wants to effect change and rise up the political career ladder, why would you start kicking up a fuss in a committee that no one cares about? It would be the dullest form of career suicide imaginable, as no one would notice, let alone reward you for your pains.

Select committees

There is one job that does involve being a serious legislator, and that is sitting on a select committee. These cross-party groups of MPs are arranged by departments and topics, such as Treasury, Communities and Local Government, and Science and Technology, and can order inquiries on any topic, as well as scrutinise departmental accounts and haul ministers to special hearings for a dressing-down about a particular policy.

The most powerful of these committees is the Public Accounts Committee (PAC). Its membership is hotly contested – like all select committees, MPs must stand for election – and its chairmanship highly prestigious. The profile of the PAC rose under Margaret Hodge, who chaired it between 2010 and 2015. She adopted an aggressive form of questioning that made for great news reports and clips on political programmes, savaging the heads of multinational companies for not paying enough tax, and senior figures in HMRC for failing to collect the tax it was owed. On one memorable occasion, Hodge forced HMRC lawyer Anthony Inglese to give evidence to the committee after swearing an oath on the Bible. Few MPs can successfully mimic her headmistress style, but what Hodge has done is make it fashionable to be a select committee chair and to take that role so seriously that witnesses tremble as they wait outside your committee room.

Select committees have risen in profile over the past decade. Chairs are paid an additional £15,000 on top of their basic salary, and enjoy both media attention and respect in the House of Commons. This is one of the most positive changes in recent years, giving MPs some teeth. In fact, the most professionally fulfilled parliamentarians seem to be the ones who work on busy and high-profile committees such as the PAC.

The culture of select committees is fundamentally different to that of the House of Commons Chamber, in which MPs from the governing party are largely supportive of their government. Being a patsy is so badly frowned upon in a select committee room that only the dimmest of MPs attempt it. The rest take pride in being able to ask robust questions of ministers from their own party, and know that they won't face the usual repercussions from the whips and other more loyal colleagues for doing so. But there's always pressure from above when it comes to controversial subjects, with MPs fighting over the wording of critical reports and press releases.

A good committee will organise inquiries into proposed policies that are causing consternation in a sector – such as the inquiries run by the Work and Pensions Committee into housing benefit cuts and the Universal Credit programme (which, no matter how long this book has taken to write, will still take far longer to be realised as a policy that works) – and highlight problems with the policies before they are implemented. A government department is duty-bound to respond to a committee's report, though of course it isn't obliged to change its policies at all, no matter how excoriating the conclusions of that committee. But what good select committees with media-savvy chairs – like Margaret Hodge – are capable of doing is driving an issue up the agenda so that pressure increases on ministers to change tack. Not all changes in Westminster are wrought in a clear cause-and-effect manner. In fact, most MPs' achievements come about as a result of canny work on committees and in behind-the-scenes meetings, rather than by making a noise in the House of Commons.

Utterly Pointless Questions

As well as sitting on select committees, MPs can also hold ministers to account for policies once they're in place, or demand changes to the law in the House of Commons at departmental question sessions. These happen on a rota basis every day of the week, with each department up for questions every four weeks or so. Members must submit their questions in advance – or they can be drawn in the ballot for 'topical questions' at the end of the session, and spring up with any question they fancy. Most of these questions sound rather anodyne and are worded in a certain way: it is actually in the supplementary question that the MP is entitled to following the minister's answer where someone can really make their point.

But even those supplementary questions are not particularly probing or sharp. Many of them are mere padding, designed to make the session easier politically for whoever is on the front bench of the party that the MP asking the question belongs to. And of course, the worst offenders when it comes to asking pointless questions are MPs in the governing party. Again, the culture in Westminster seems not to reward an intelligent questioner who has the temerity to point out that there's a problem with a certain policy. And some MPs can be too lazy to come up with the sort of really smart question that gets a decent answer from a minister without offending the government's mighty ego.

What MPs are instead encouraged to do is to take up valuable scrutiny time by asking ministers to join them in praising the great importance of motherhood and apple pie. Here is an example from a session of Treasury Questions in 2014, at which the Conservative MP for Colne Valley, Jason McCartney, used his topical question to ask: 'I do not know whether the Shadow Chancellor has been to Yorkshire recently, but if he does come up north, he will see that, in Colne Valley and Huddersfield, manufacturing is surging, whether it is Magic Rock brewery exporting to Australia, Camira Fabrics selling its textiles to the Los Angeles transit system or even Newsholme foods selling black puddings to Spain. Will the Chancellor please continue to reject the doom-mongering, mithering and class warfare from the Labour Party and continue with his long-term economic plan?'

All McCartney was doing was asking George Osborne to agree with him that Labour was wrong and to assure him that he would continue to do the right thing. Osborne replied: 'I was in Pudsey the other day seeing a very successful manufacturing business near to my Hon. Friend's constituency. What was interesting was that that business is now exporting to China, which is a total reversal of what we have seen in the textile trade over the last few decades. I am very willing to come and see my Hon. Friend and perhaps taste some of that delicious black pudding that the Spanish are buying.'[14]

What a waste of a question, allowing the minister to read out a press release instead of explaining why he was pursuing this policy, or agreeing to talk further with the MP about another measure that might help the businesses in his constituency. McCartney used local references as a cover to ask absolutely nothing at all using special language designed to hammer the government's message home: 'long-term economic plan' was the Tory slogan in the run-up to the 2015 election.

Perhaps McCartney had spontaneously thought up this question himself. More often, though, they are decided by 'support groups' of loyal (or brown-nosing, depending on your perspective) MPs, who meet with the frontbench team before a session to decide the line of attack. The parliamentary private secretaries to the ministers up for questioning will also suggest suitably friendly lines, and ambitious or self-loathing MPs will agree to ask them. When George Osborne's powers of patronage were at their height, his Treasury Support Group, which would also agree to heckle the opposition during Budget speeches and question times, had around 60 MPs in it, many of whom hoped they could advance their political careers by scratching the Chancellor's back. You be good to Georgie, and Georgie's good to you, went the Westminster saying – and he often was. Aides and loyal MPs who helped Osborne out often whizzed past their colleagues up the career ladder. It was much more interesting to ask MPs why they *hadn't* joined the Treasury Support Group: they were deliberately staying in the cold.

Other support teams are less well staffed: the Tories in the 2015/17 parliament had a bit of trouble attracting MPs along to help out with Scottish Questions, given that their one MP north of the border was also the Secretary of State for Scotland, David Mundell. But at each session, under each government, loyal backbenchers who want a promotion, and think that the best way of getting one is to be relentlessly positive about the executive, ask UPQs: Utterly Pointless Questions. Some MPs are repeat offenders: one such is Alan Mak, the Tory MP for Havant, who has the dubious accolade of having been scolded by his local vicar while campaigning in 2015 for claiming to attend his local church even though he had only turned up a couple of times. Since getting elected, he has thrown his heart and soul into ensuring that his Commons attendance record is quite different from his record at St Faith's, Havant. Reading through his questions in Hansard, it is difficult to find any that raise problems with a government policy, let alone contain criticism.

Mak skewers ministers at departmental question times with Jeremy Paxman-style zingers such as 'Ensuring students have access to the latest technology is key to raising standards in schools. Will the minister join me in congratulating Havant College on its pioneering partnership with Google, which ensures that every student has access to a tablet computer?'[15]

You have to admire the potent mix of utter pointlessness and media savviness that this question contains. Mak has managed to ask the minister to say he likes a nice thing as much as Mak does, while ensuring his office can send out a press release saying Havant College has been praised in Parliament, thus pitching for positive coverage in the local paper. Some questions are so nice that Mak has asked them twice, such as: 'Since 2010, nearly half a million fewer children and young people are in households where there is worklessness. Will the Chief Secretary confirm that the government will continue to help households into work and to cut poverty?'[16] It received such a good response (which, funnily enough, was yes, the government will continue to do what it's supposed to do) that Mak made some judicious edits and produced it again at Prime Minister's Questions the following week.

Mak is by no means the only offender. And his behaviour is, within the culture of Westminster, perfectly understandable. There aren't just rewards for saying and doing as you are told. There are also punishments for refusing to be a sycophant. Another MP who refused to take a suggested question from the prime minister's PPS (parliamentary private secretary, the most junior – and unpaid – position on the ministerial ladder) under David Cameron's leadership found that an envoy job that he had been in line for suddenly evaporated.

A better form of question is the urgent question, in which a minister is summoned to the House by a backbench MP or an opposition frontbencher on a specific matter. Such is the battle for power in Parliament that nervous governments will often organise statements on something that has gone wrong in order to avoid being humiliated by a UQ, or appearing reluctant to face scrutiny. This system fell by the wayside until John Bercow became Speaker, whereupon he seized on the opportunity to make the government as uncomfortable as possible by granting hundreds of urgent questions. He has helped Parliament become a little more threatening to the government.

Ministers sometimes try to dodge urgent questions by sending their juniors to answer them. George Osborne would famously send David Gauke in his place to defend any unpopular Treasury policy. Gauke had such a pacifying manner that Labour would struggle to use the urgent question to move the row on any further, and Treasury ministers and officials would 'uncork the Gauke' whenever a spot of bother appeared. But other urgent questions can force the government to announce a concession, because ministers simply cannot get through an hour in the Commons defending a dud policy.

The most pointless bills of all

If departmental questions seem a ridiculous charade, then just tune into Parliament on one of the 13 Fridays a year when it is sitting. Friday sessions are for private members' bills, which claim to be opportunities for backbenchers to introduce legislation. This sounds wise: it cannot be true that all the wisdom in Westminster resides in the executive. But even though the government is not the only fount of good ideas, it is true that most meaningful power in Westminster resides there, including when it comes to these backbench sessions.

These bills promise so much. They even have an important role in Britain's social history: in the 1960s, backbench legislation decriminalised homosexuality, abolished the death penalty and legalised abortion. Even if they are not proposing radical changes, backbenchers see these bits of legislation as an opportunity to show that they care about serious issues such as high hospital parking charges. They can make a song and dance about the importance of the issue, hook up with the relevant campaigning charity, and merrily send press releases about how they are introducing a new law. The press often writes these bills up as though they have a chance of becoming legislation. The reality is quite the opposite.

What happens when a private member's bill hits the Commons on a Friday is that a group of MPs who either oppose the principle of the bill or who dislike the idea of backbenchers being able to make law start talking. And they don't stop. This is an ancient practice known as 'filibustering' – talking out a bill until the end of that session. At 2.30 p.m., any bills that haven't reached a vote die. Even if the bill does get its second reading that day, it then goes into committee stage, where it is even more likely to be killed.

Filibustering is, in many senses, an impressive art. Serial talkers such as Jacob Rees-Mogg, Philip Davies and, when Labour was in government, Andrew Dismore have managed to cover topics as diverse as the quality of wine at the Garrick Club, Peter Pan, different types of shellfish, and bus routes.

The only way to end a filibuster is to gather together 100 MPs to vote for a 'closure motion' to stop the speaker and move on. This is a way of demonstrating that the bill has sufficient support to proceed. But it is increasingly difficult to gather 100 MPs together on a Friday. As we have seen, the demands on them to be in their constituencies are growing. And unless an MP is certain that enough of their colleagues will also turn up to make the closure motion a success, they won't see much incentive in neglecting their constituency.

Now, there are many, many private members' bills that are best kept miles away from the statute books. Some entail massive public spending commitments. Others contain policies contrary to the aims of the government of the day – the government that was voted in by the public. It probably should be the case that PMBs are difficult to pass. And just because the process for getting a bill through Parliament is complex doesn't mean that this process is bad. But the current system for PMBs is arcane and embarrassing. It sets the filibustering MP up as the sole regulator of what is good and bad in a bill, rather than allowing a proper verdict of the House on a day when MPs are performing their Commons rather than constituency duties. Far worse, it is a system controlled by the government. Serial filibusterers privately confess to me that they often come into Westminster for a Friday sitting merely because the whips have asked them to help kill an inconvenient bill.

The government has repeatedly dodged calls to reform these pieces of legislation. And so currently just one MP can kill off a private member's bill with a lengthy speech about nothing much. What would be far better would be a proper consideration of the principles of the bill, which can then be voted down because a majority of MPs have decided that it is a rubbish piece of legislation.

Pollution of the ecosystem

Private members' bills are also an example of how the political ecosystem is easily polluted. They often contain the pet cause of a lobby group, which the group then creates a very noisy campaign about, both in the run-up to the bill's second reading in the Commons, and afterwards when a cantankerous MP has slain it. Not only does the lobby group generally give a false impression of a PMB's chance of success; it also exploits the way in which slots for these bills are allocated. In order to give your PMB the best chance of getting heard in the Commons, you need to come top of a ballot of MPs. Most MPs enter without any idea of what bill they might put forward, and are then inundated with suggestions from charities and campaigning organisations of what they could propose when they do come top. A bewildered MP who hasn't had an original thought then ends up taking the pointless and expensive bill to the Commons, hoping to get a little bit of good press along the way before it dies the death of all poorly written bits of legislation that the government hasn't backed.

Lobbying organisations are both an important part of the way legislation is scrutinised and also a potential predator. They are often the first ones to alert MPs when a government bill contains a nasty policy. But they also have their own political agendas and weaknesses, particularly when it comes to the question of whether they are really representing the groups they purport to speak for.

The National Trust, for instance, is one of the most successful membership organisations in history, with 4.2 million paid-up members. It protects the heritage of England, Wales and Northern Ireland, and educates people about the past, as well as providing many families with somewhere nice to let off steam at the weekends. But it is also a formidable lobbying organisation, and has spearheaded opposition to planning reform, particularly by the Coalition and Conservative governments from 2010 onwards. In 2011, it joined forces with organisations such as the Campaign to Protect Rural England and Friends of the Earth to warn that the National Planning Policy Framework proposed by ministers – which was supposed to lead to a rise in house-building – was 'disregarding the impact that these proposals will have on open space in and around our cities, towns and villages', and that 'local voices will not be heard' in the reformed planning process.[17]

Open warfare between the National Trust and ministers then ensued, with accusations flying around that the – small 'c' – conservative organisation was in fact run by left-wingers. But the fight was so bruising for those in government, especially Eric Pickles, who was then Communities Secretary, and Theresa May, who observed it from a distance in the Home Office before entering Number 10 herself in 2016, that they privately vowed never again to have a serious stand-off with an organisation that represented so many people likely to vote Conservative. Consequently, ministers have dodged seriously considering reforms that could help build more homes and solve Britain's housing crisis, such as reviewing the protections for the Green Belt.

Another green and pleasant policy scuppered by a different sort of lobbying group was a 2011 plan to part-privatise the Forestry Commission, which manages more than 150,000 hectares of Britain's forests. Ministers insisted that protection for the forests would remain in place, but the plans to raise around £250 million from the sale caused a row that spread quicker than a forest fire. David Cameron hadn't noticed how potent the move would be – but he was made well aware of it when campaigning group 38 Degrees, which runs petitions on controversial political topics, launched a petition to stop the sell-off that was signed by more than half a million people. MPs were inundated, even if they didn't have any forests in their constituencies. Simon Hughes's office, for instance, received more letters about the forests than it did on any other subject that year, even though Bermondsey and Old Southwark had no Forestry Commission land at all. The government dropped the plan in the face of such fierce public opposition.

MPs complain about what they see as the malign influence of 38 Degrees and other organisations such as Change.org that drum up support for online petitions. Some say that their researchers spend a disproportionate amount of time replying to identical emails sent through the websites of these groups by people who have very little understanding of the bad thing they have decided they should oppose. Even if an MP subscribes to one of the research units attached to their party that helps deal with these petitions, the cost can amount to around £10,000.[18] The Transparency of Lobbying, Non-Party Campaigning and Trade Union Administration Act 2014, for instance, included a clause that limited the amount charities could spend on campaigns in the run-up to a general election. Ministers argued that it was to stop supposedly non-political organisations from pushing the agenda of one party without the usual election spending restrictions applying. But charities said it was a gag on their freedom of speech, and branded the policy the 'gagging law'. MPs' offices were deluged with calls from people demanding that they withdraw the clause but unable to explain what it was because they'd merely read about it in a generic email sent to them by a website on which they'd signed a petition about something completely different.

Yet it wasn't so long ago that petitions were the new, trendy way of staying in touch with the public. In 2011, the Coalition government launched an e-petitions system that would allow voters to get their concerns aired in the House of Commons. If a petition on the government website reached 100,000 signatures, it was eligible for a debate in Parliament. The then leader of the House, Sir George Young, said these petitions would be a 'megaphone' for voters. That certainly proved to be the case – though it turned out that being handed a megaphone didn't automatically confer wisdom upon someone. For instance, in 2015, MPs ended up debating a petition calling on the government to 'stop allowing immigrants into the UK'. Boasting 216,949 signatures, the petition declared:

> The UK government need to prevent immigrants from entering the UK immediately! We MUST close all borders, and prevent more immigrants from entering Britain. Foreign citizens are taking all our benefits, costing the government millions! Many of them are trying to change UK into a Muslim country![19]

The MPs who decided that this statement should be debated even though they vehemently disagreed with its sentiments (and perhaps its grammar) used the slot to explain *why* they disagreed. It was a neat way of giving those who had signed the petition a voice but not validation. Alternatively, it was a waste of parliamentary time.

A much greater waste of parliamentary time, which many more MPs took up as a cause célèbre, was a petition to ban then presidential candidate Donald Trump from the UK that attracted 586,930 signatures.[20] A three-hour debate in Westminster Hall duly took place, with plenty of grandstanding from backbenchers who were also aware that Trump had, at the time, said nothing about visiting the country.

What a lot of noise with no impact. This can be said not just of non-binding debates about petitions, but of so many of the debates in the House of Commons Chamber. This isn't just irritating to those who want to learn something and potentially be persuaded by discussions between MPs. It also means that MPs are not probing whether legislation really works.

So little of the motivation behind the activities mentioned above is about improving legislation. Instead, it is about getting attention, whether from an MP's own party hierarchy, a vociferous campaign group, or the media. The pressure on MPs more often than not is not to be an excellent legislator, but to stay out of trouble, in their party and locally. Better to get attention by participating in meaningless parliamentary activities than plug away at the boring work of examining laws properly. After all, you can always just take on more and more constituency casework when things go wrong – as they all too often do.

CHAPTER 5

GETTING ON

So if few MPs want to do a key part of the job they are elected to do, what do most of them really want from parliamentary life? Like most human beings, they want to do as well as they can with their skills, and because there is little or no reward in being a good legislator, the culture in Westminster is all about becoming a member of the executive as soon as possible.

Ambition is no bad thing: it makes us work harder and helps us take pride in ourselves. And given that we all adapt our behaviour according to the way we are rewarded or punished, it's little surprise that MPs see the most reward in being a minister rather than a lowly backbencher, and make that their ambition. You get more attention from the media and the sector that you cover, more people working for you, better pay (the pay rise in the 2016/17 parliament ranged from an extra £19,000 for a whip, through to £33,000 for ministers of state and £77,570 for the Prime Minister, on top of basic parliamentary salary), and better career prospects outside government. As we have seen in previous chapters, though, the attraction of being a minister means that MPs' minds are elsewhere when they are supposed to be ensuring that bad bills aren't making their way through the House of Commons. And even when someone realises their ambition of becoming a parliamentary under-secretary of state (the most junior minister), they quickly realise that Whitehall life isn't quite as satisfying as it's cracked up to be.

Building a profile

Smart MPs won't wait until they've found their way around Parliament to launch their bid to join the front bench. Some don't even wait until they are MPs. Just as it is much easier to understand Westminster if you have previously worked in it as an adviser, so it is easier to move up the career ladder if you already have established networks with your party's leadership. As mentioned in the last chapter, George Osborne famously used patronage to build support for himself, and the people he took the best care of were those who had worked for him before getting elected. Matt Hancock, Claire Perry and Greg Hands all moved far and fast as MPs because Osborne was making the case for them whenever David Cameron considered carrying out a reshuffle. There's nothing particularly sinister about promoting people who've worked for you, incidentally: it just shows that you rate them. But it does put those who enter Westminster from outside at a disadvantage.

What is more damaging to politics is the culture of promoting your friends. Often this can be indistinguishable from promoting your former colleagues, as those with the strongest Bubble credentials will have moved in the same circles from university onwards. David Cameron was notorious for thinking first of those he knew socially when arranging reshuffles, not just in terms of promoting them but in terms of protecting notable duffers from the sack. Gordon Brown preferred ministers with whom he could discuss football, which some Labour women felt left them at a disadvantage. All prime ministers have personal likes and dislikes that are little to do with whether someone would make a good economic secretary to the Treasury and which make the government seem rather more like an old-fashioned company than a meritocracy.

So how do you get ahead if you're not already thumbing through your photo album of beach holidays with the prime minister? We've discussed the ways MPs make themselves useful to the executive by being totally loyal. There are, however, other ways to climb the greasy pole. Robert Halfon made a name for himself and was subsequently promoted to the government by campaigning on a number of issues that affected his Harlow constituents. Those issues – including the price of fuel, tax on bingo halls, and beer duty – just happened to be issues that also affected readers of the *Sun* newspaper, and so the backbench Tory MP got many more name checks and glowing write-ups than other colleagues. Indeed, his campaigning was so effective that David Cameron dubbed him the 'most expensive MP in Parliament', due to the fact that he cost the Treasury so much in lost tax revenues. By focusing on popular concerns and being just a little bothersome to the government, the MP proved his mettle. This, of course, requires sustained effort, whereas asking silly questions that someone else has written for you merely burns a few calories.

Another Essex MP, Will Quince, who was elected in 2015, made one of the darkest moments of his life the starting point for a campaign. A few months before being elected, he and his wife had a stillborn child. The MP for Colchester gave a speech in the Commons that moved many of his colleagues to tears, before campaigning relentlessly for better rights for bereaved parents. In 2017, he managed to get a manifesto commitment to child bereavement leave, followed by a change in the way stillbirths and life-changing injuries during birth are investigated.

Halfon and Quince are MPs who worked out that a media profile counts for a lot in Westminster. Doing well on *Daily Politics* and getting written up as a rising star by newspaper columnists is the dream for an ambitious new backbencher. Of course, you're more likely to get invited onto political programmes and mentioned in columns if people have heard of you, and once again it's useful to have friends in high places who will tell journalists that you're 'one to watch'. Only a handful of reporters attend Commons sessions outside Prime Minister's Questions, key statements on European summits and the like, so it's often easy to become the 'one to watch' when no one actually watches to see if you're much cop. Meanwhile, hacks will want to have lunch with you to build a good relationship before you enter a ministry. If you're good company over lunch, they will warm to you and write you up as 'effective', even if this only means 'effective at gossiping and eating pudding'.

Other MPs, such as Boris Johnson, use their considerable wit to build a popular profile by going on shows such as *Have I Got News for You*. This only works if you are firstly actually funny and secondly able to laugh at yourself, as politicians are often invited onto these shows to be roundly mocked. But Johnson and Labour's Jess Phillips are MPs who have made themselves far better known than their colleagues simply by being able to work outside the Bubble.

Some MPs can grow bitter about this. Instead of finding an issue to campaign on, they shuffle around Parliament waiting for someone to notice their brilliance, without wondering whether they might need to do something in order to let that brilliance shine. In 2013, I was approached by a group of Conservative MPs who were grumpy that no one was writing about them. 'We're doing great things,' huffed one backbencher who had taken it upon himself to promote his colleagues (and himself). 'Why aren't you writing anything about us?' Evidence of these 'great things' was a little thin, though, beyond the odd constituency jobs fair and mildly interesting backstory before entering Parliament. Parliament rewards the noisy and determined, as it should, but there are far too many MPs who seem to think that 'great things' means just being their fabulous selves without lifting a finger.

A game that parliamentary reporters like to play is watching MPs file through the Commons during a vote. Evening votes often turn up parliamentarians in black tie or sweaty running kit. But they also seem to unearth MPs with such little impact that even the most committed members of the press gallery, such as Press Association reporters and sketch writers, are left thumbing through their ID books to work out which rare specimen they've managed to spot. These MPs, who may speak a tolerable number of times in debates and turn up as the whips ask, are not the stereotypical 'wrong politicians' who brag and cheat. Their voting records may make them appear to be reasonably diligent. But they do so little to improve Parliament that it isn't even as though no one would notice if they were gone: few have realised they are there in the first place.

These MPs do not get on, and that serves them right for being unimaginative about how to make the most of their precious time in Parliament. But others do.

The bottom of the greasy pole

For most ambitious MPs, the first step towards ministerial stardom is being appointed a parliamentary private secretary. Although this position is unpaid, it still puts you in the government. The job guarantees your loyalty in every vote, but it is largely about loyalty to an individual minister: PPSs are nicknamed 'bag carriers' in Westminster. The benefit of the job for a new MP is that it teaches them what a minister does and, depending on whether their boss is any good or not, how to do the job well. The benefit for the minister is that they have someone liaising with the rest of the party on important policies, and drumming up support when that minister ends up in a tight spot. Rob Wilson, the Conservative MP for Reading East, was Jeremy Hunt's PPS when Hunt was Culture Secretary and in serious danger of losing his job over his close relations with Rupert Murdoch. Wilson ensured that sufficient numbers of Tory colleagues turned up in the Commons to make supportive noises when Hunt gave a statement on the matter, so that what could have been a brawl turned into a relatively easy session, which Hunt survived.

Few want to stay a PPS for very long: indeed, a number of the 2010 intake of Conservative MPs turned down offers of these junior posts, claiming they deserved more high-profile roles. Notably, none of those who rejected these mini-promotions were doing so because they were worried they would be unable to perform their jobs as legislators. They just didn't want to be doing too much donkey work when they'd already had glittering careers outside Parliament.

The benefits of PPSs are clear: if you've been one, you've had a good introduction to ministerial life. If you have one, you've got someone helping you smooth the way for your policies in the Commons and watching your back personally. But given that this promotion forces an MP to be loyal to the government at all times or face the sack, and given that it takes them away from the Commons in order to serve a minister in a department, it is difficult to see what the overall benefits are to Parliament as it tries to produce good legislation.

Achieving stuff

When they move into official ministerial positions, MPs are often surprised by how little extra power they gain. Reshuffle day is exciting for a rising star. The weeks of speculation about who's in and who's out. That walk up Downing Street with the press watching. The ensuing profiles and hundreds of bids for interviews. Even the first red boxes – the official in-trays ministers take home with them to work on in the evenings – seem exciting to begin with. But as with all jobs, reality soon hits.

A month after a Conservative reshuffle, I had coffee with a newly appointed minister of state. She looked strangely harried. 'I feel as though I've been tagged by the Probation Service,' she joked, explaining that her time wasn't her own, and that no one really wanted to hear about the whizzy policy ideas she'd brought into the department. A few minutes later, a departmental press officer appeared at her elbow to 'help' us with the coffee we were having. Naturally, the whole meeting became somewhat pointless, as the minister felt as though she was being monitored and was careful about what she said. Over the next few months, little was seen of this minister, buried deep within the bowels of her ministry by an overbearing secretary of state who clearly didn't trust her.

Having only just worked out how to run a parliamentary office, ministers find themselves with a private office in their department to manage as well. They have more staff, more prestige, and more demands on their time. Most ministers find that their private office, if left to its own devices, will fill their diary from dawn to dusk with meetings with 'stakeholders' and other groups who want to bend their ear, regardless of whether the ear-bending will prove particularly useful. After a few months of tearing from meeting to meeting with no time to work on new ideas or keep an eye on existing responsibilities in their portfolio, many ministers wrestle back control of their diaries, or force their staff to ask them before booking meetings.

Even so, how much a minister achieves is dependent on whether their portfolio is something the prime minister is keen on, whether they're able to work the sector effectively, whether they know anything about that sector, and whether they have enough time in which to do anything useful before being moved on.

Of course, a prime minister being especially interested in a portfolio area isn't always a good thing for an individual minister. Downing Street or the Treasury getting more involved in certain issues can be a sign that those at the top of government are worried that policies could end up being too controversial for voters to stomach, or that they do not trust the minister in question. Prime ministers also choose to make certain policies their priority, which is flattering for the minister involved, but also means reforms can be rushed half-baked into Parliament. When Nicky Morgan was serving as Education Secretary under David Cameron, she was asked to push out a new bill before many of the reforms she had wanted to introduce were ready, which meant that as the Conservatives were writing one piece of legislation, they were already preparing for the next. This gumming-up of Parliament with bills does little good, and it also means policies are only half-cooked when they appear before MPs.

Cameron also learned the hard way that trust should be earned by your cabinet ministers, rather than doled out willingly. He left Andrew Lansley to his own devices in the health department, only to realise that the secretary of state had drawn up something so politically monstrous – the Health and Social Care Bill – that it dominated the political landscape for weeks. Lansley's successor, Jeremy Hunt, earned the trust of both Cameron and then Theresa May by staying loyal and keeping them up to date with any particularly tricky situations in the health service.

Hunt is one of the cabinet ministers who achieved a fair bit and survived an impressive amount of time in one department, partly because he knew what he wanted to do when he took on the job. He'd formed an impression of the NHS as a health service that was unusually unconcerned about patient safety, and made it his objective to change that. He used as his ministerial model Michael Gove, who took on the vested interests in the education establishment to call for higher standards and more competition between schools. Gove entered every government department with three strategic objectives for his time there, and focused on delivering those above everything else. As a result, he gained a reputation for being a radical reformer, even among those who despised his reforms.

Other cabinet ministers have had less of a serious focus on their brief. While Boris Johnson undoubtedly enjoyed the international exposure that being Foreign Secretary gave him, he struggled to grasp that this exposure meant that every comment he made could have serious implications. He failed to get on top of the detail of a case involving a British national, Nazanin Zaghari-Ratcliffe, who had been imprisoned in Iran, and ended up inflaming tensions still further by telling a select committee in 2017 that Zaghari-Ratcliffe had been in the country to teach journalism, something the regime instantly seized upon. Previously popular politically, Johnson had developed a reputation for being unreliable and thoughtless, despite his considerable abilities. His clumsiness also showed how powerful select committees can be in undermining politicians who come poorly prepared: it wasn't just that the hearing itself caused a furore, but the chair of the committee in question, Tom Tugendhat, then took every opportunity to press the Foreign Secretary on the matter in the House of Commons for weeks afterwards.

Johnson had enjoyed such a high media profile for years that when he finally took a serious job, there was much more interest in what he was doing than in what his predecessors had got up to. Many Cabinet ministers cultivate the media, especially journalists they hope will remain loyal to them, by feeding them gossip from the weekly cabinet meetings in Number 10. That gossip can range from regular complaints about how long Justine Greening might spend talking, to serious rows about the future of Britain's trading relationship with the EU. The cabinet is supposed to be a confidential forum for senior ministers to reach decisions on big issues. But such is the value of stories from the meetings that secretaries of state find it hard to stick to that confidentiality, to the extent that one minister under Theresa May received a furious call from one of her aides criticising him for 'disloyalty' after he raised mild concerns about a decision made in the cabinet room.

How much you can achieve does depend on whether your leader lets you do anything. Theresa May was already a notorious micromanager of ministers before she entered Number 10. As Home Secretary, she frequently cut her juniors out of meetings about their own portfolios by failing to send them memos that the meetings were taking place. As prime minister, she constantly demanded further details of policies before telling her cabinet ministers to water down ideas because they were unpalatable. But she was also, by the time it became clear that Johnson might thrive more in another department, too politically weak to move him without causing a ruckus among pro-Boris backbenchers. Tony Blair asked Frank

Field to 'think the unthinkable' as a minister examining welfare reform, before deciding that what the Labour MP came up with was best left just as a thought. Field is still smarting from that rejection today. Even within a department, ministers can be thwarted by their seniors. Nick Boles was an ambitious planning minister in Communities and Local Government between September 2012 and July 2014, but found his desire to shake up the system and get more homes built constantly thwarted by his boss, Eric Pickles, who was still recovering from his battle with the National Trust.

On the subject of planning, it is one of many policy areas with a system that is not fit for purpose, yet it suffers from all the worst flaws of Whitehall. Prime ministers seem unable to keep their promises on building enough homes, and housing ministers are replaced at every reshuffle. In the past 30 years, there have been 22 different ministers responsible for housing. Labour had nine in 13 years, while, at the time of writing, the Tories have managed eight in just nine.

This housing hall of shame has ranged from the noisy and media-savvy in the form of Grant Shapps, to a man nicknamed the 'invisible minister', Mark Prisk. 'Is Mark Prisk still alive?' one of his colleagues joked to me a few weeks before the then minister got the chop. 'We haven't seen him for months.' Prisk had made the mistake of knuckling down with the job, but not informing the media what he was doing. He had cheesed off the department's special advisers on arrival by telling them he wasn't interested in political knockabout, but instead wanted to work quietly on increasing housing supply.

One of the realisations that comes to most adults is that the people who make the most noise about how good they are rarely turn out to be the most talented. This is already obvious by the end of school, but it still seems to have passed Westminster by: there, if you're not noisy, you're politically dead, even if you are actually doing an excellent job as a minister. One special adviser to a former senior cabinet minister says he always panicked the most when his boss wasn't doing regular media interviews: it meant the prime minister might suspect him either of going to ground to plot against him, or of not doing any work, even though wooing the lobby is rather time-consuming. But impressing the right journalists with good chat (and, as already mentioned, good pudding-eating skills) means that you are able to create a reputation for being an effective minister, one that is sustained largely by writers who haven't got a clue whether any of your policies are actually working.

As well as being a good lunch guest, another way of appearing to be an effective minister is to meddle in your portfolio, thus creating headlines and debate about new and exciting policies you want to introduce. This can be regardless of whether your portfolio is broke and needs fixing: the important thing is that you are seen to be doing things. Then you become an effective minister while effectively messing things up as much as possible.

Ministers who mess things up may do so with the best of intentions but little understanding of what they are doing. Few are appointed as experts in their sectors. It is supposed to be the case that civil servants will advise politicians on the technicalities of the policies they want to introduce, while ministers focus on the overall direction. But civil servants aren't always bastions of wisdom. One of the first lessons a new secretary of state will learn on entering a department is that the clever reforms that smart civil servants suggest to them in their early weeks are actually silly ideas that will bomb politically – and which have been rejected by numerous predecessors. A good minister won't fall for these schemes. A good minister will also take time to understand the sector before trying to shake it up, because civil servants won't always tell them when they're about to make a mistake. If a minister is lucky, they will have shadowed the brief in opposition, or shown an interest for the subject on the back benches. If they're unlucky, they'll be given something they have no enthusiasm for, and no time to bone up on what they're supposed to be doing before the next reshuffle.

That ministers may know nothing about a sector before becoming its political overlord (or so they like to imagine, anyway) often shocks those outside Westminster. But it's surprisingly common. At any one time there will be a number of secretaries of state who have carefully avoided the portfolio they are then appointed to, in the hope that they'll never need to spend much time thinking about it. The late Tessa Jowell described her first day as a minister in the Department of Health thus: 'I remember the day I opened my first red [ministerial] box and looked inside. There was this great big submission, I think it was about antibiotic resistance. It was some incredibly technical public health issue. And I just looked at it and thought, "I have not the faintest idea what to do with this." But then you learn. I loved it.'[1]

Some politicians argue that not being an expert in an area is a good thing. In 2015, Chris Grayling managed to offend the few remaining lawyers who weren't already livid with his policies as Justice Secretary when he told ConservativeHome that not being a lawyer was 'actually helpful rather than a hindrance'. He argued that 'I think it enables you to take a dispassionate view. You're not cup-tied in any way to your previous career or your chambers or your former firm.' Turning the screw a little tighter, he added: 'So you don't arrive at a decision because you're a barrister and therefore you favour the bar or because you're a solicitor and you favour solicitors' firms.'[2] Perhaps the legal profession would have taken less exception to this had Grayling been an uncontroversial Justice Secretary and Lord Chancellor who sought to make few changes. In the end, a number of his most unpopular policies were reversed by his successor, Michael Gove, who was similarly active in wooing journalists but also made a point of trying to woo the lawyers too.

Even if it isn't necessary for a minister to have been a doctor before entering the Department of Health, or a teacher before becoming responsible for schools, it would be helpful if MPs weren't expected to become experts in so many different policy areas over such a short space of time. And if ministers were given time to understand an area before whizzing about making their mark with precious little understanding whether that mark will bless or blight the portfolio, then perhaps we wouldn't end up with quite so many confused policies.

Demotion

Reshuffle days are political journalists' favourites, and not just because of the news carnival they create. It is also that these are the few days in our careers when we find ourselves writing about a line of work with less job security and less meritocracy than our own. Ministers are sacked because it's 'time to give someone else a go', even if they've been giving it a pretty good go themselves. Mark Prisk, the 'invisible minister', was told he was being dropped from the Communities and Local Government department in 2013 to make way for someone younger.[3] It must have stung rather to discover that his replacement was in fact older than him.

There is always pressure on prime ministers to make their government, especially their cabinet, look as diverse as possible. This means that the most nervous and aggrieved characters on reshuffle days are invariably white middle-aged men. It also means that ministers aren't always appointed to roles because of their obvious aptitude. Caroline Flint, in her resignation letter, accused Gordon Brown of using her and other women as 'little more than female window dressing', consigning them to a 'peripheral role' while trumpeting his feminist appointments. David Cameron famously offered Chloe Smith the job of Economic Secretary to the Treasury because he felt he needed a woman in the department and had heard that she was an accountant. She had in fact worked for the marketing department of an accountancy firm, and was humiliated by her bosses by being sent on *Newsnight* to take a savaging from Jeremy Paxman for being 'incompetent' in the aftermath of the so-called Omnishambles Budget in 2012.

Politics could do with more women in senior roles, since they do after all make up more than half of the population and at least half of the collective wisdom of this country. But it does gender equality – and their own abundant skills – little service when they are clearly appointed to tick a box. Male ministers are watched less closely for signs of competence than their female counterparts: prime ministers who genuinely care about the advancement of women in politics should think as carefully as they can about appointments.

No minister wants to be sacked, but some might find in time that their demotion to the back benches is a blessing in disguise. Constant reshuffles don't just undermine the way Whitehall works from day to day. They also undermine accountability for failed policies. By the time it is obvious that a reform isn't working out as planned, the minister responsible for introducing it will be in a new job, or may even have left Parliament entirely.

We rarely know at the time a minister is doing their job whether they're actually much good at it. Many policies take decades to bear fruit. The Teenage Pregnancy Strategy, for instance, was introduced by the Blair government in 1999. It was only 15 years later, when the number of teenage girls falling pregnant had halved, taking the rate to its lowest since the 1970s, that the policy – which involved educating young people about contraception, dealing with the pressure to have sex young, and the realities of parenthood – was deemed a success. By that time, all its architects had left not only government but also Parliament. Satisfying, perhaps, for them to see an old policy working so well. But think of all the ex-ministers who feel relief that their policies that didn't work so well are only proving to be awful long after they have left office.

There is precious little accountability for ministers who do bad jobs. You might have been sacked or promoted regardless of your aptitude, but unless something blows up when you're in office and you are summoned to the Commons for an urgent question or hauled before an angry select committee, you can get away scot-free with having introduced poor policies.

Revenge

Of course, anyone who has just been sacked won't take much consolation from the fact that they have escaped a scolding for introducing terrible reforms. Once a reshuffle is over, the hunt for the bitter ex-ministers begins. Such are the personality types in politics that there are always a handful of demoted men and women who do not accept their fate well, and who act out their disappointment in public. Take Tim Loughton, who was so shocked that he had been dumped as Parliamentary Under-Secretary for Education in 2012 that he went on a rampage of bitterness that culminated in him telling the Education Select Committee, four months after he had lost his job, that his portfolio 'was a declining priority within the department', that 'the children and families agenda has been greatly downgraded since the reshuffle', and that 'there has been some neglect with children and families'.[4]

There's something about the Education Department that breeds bitterness. Nicky Morgan was unceremoniously dispatched from the secretary of state role in 2016 when Theresa May took over as prime minister. Her revenge was to become a rebel against May's plans for Brexit and to take a personal shot at her leader's fashion choices. The new prime minister had appeared in the *Sunday Times* wearing a pair of £995 Amanda Wakeley leather trousers, which Morgan took exception to, claiming that 'I don't think I've ever spent that much on anything apart from my wedding dress' and that the pricey garb had been 'noticed and discussed' in party circles.[5] As well as it being spectacularly unsisterly for a senior politician to criticise another woman's clothing, Morgan's sniping backfired, with the *Daily Mail* pointing out that she owned a Mulberry handbag worth £950. She later apologised for the comments.

Some sacked ministers bide their time quietly, hoping to return to government after a period of humility on the back benches. Others decide to seek revenge by becoming rebels, causing trouble for the prime minister who had the poor judgement to sack them. They join colleagues who are bitter that they were never promoted, MPs who revel in being rebels and would sooner leave Parliament than become a minister (until 2015, that group included one Jeremy Corbyn), and a very small handful of backbenchers who are happy to vote against their party whip when they fear a policy could do more harm than good.

Because the legislature and the executive are an overlapping group of people in the Westminster political system, voting against a policy is seen as rebellion rather than an attempt to improve a policy. Rebelling is like losing your virginity: the first time is terrifying, but after that it's quite easy to troop through the 'wrong' lobby again and again. Each rebellion involves a political calculation that it is worth expending capital on this particular matter, rather than the belief that the matter itself is wrong and therefore does not deserve your approval. Serial rebellions can make you as popular as the boy who cried wolf, even if in legislative terms there really are a lot of wolves stalking Westminster.

The culture of the Commons means that people who serially point out problems with laws are regarded as oddballs. Consequently, only oddballs tend to become serial rebels, and a vicious circle is created where no seriously smart would-be scrutineer wants to take that route. Instead, the smart people want to become ministers – and why wouldn't they, when that is where all the rewards lie?

CHAPTER 6

GETTING CAUGHT

'I don't know what all this talk of shagging is,' said one MP when I asked him why so many marriages broke down in Parliament. 'I've certainly never had any.'

That MP's marriage was still intact, though he was telling me at the time that he wished he had stood down at the previous election because of the damage parliamentary life was doing to his relationship. He was lucky: of the 666 MPs elected between 2010 and 2015 (some in by-elections in the middle of the Parliament), 12 per cent got divorced while serving as an MP. Of the 307 Conservative MPs elected, 32 lost their marriages, while 9 per cent of Labour MPs' marriages broke down while they were in Parliament. For the Lib Dems, it was 12 per cent, and for the 6 SNP MPs elected in 2010, 66 per cent of them split up with their spouses while serving.

This isn't particularly out of step with the general population, but what is significant is how many people cite parliamentary life as the cause of their split. It is more difficult to quantify the extent of general relationship breakdown in Parliament: marriage is a public declaration, but long-term partners can stay out of the public eye almost entirely. And many marriages have survived against the odds, including those beset by humiliating sex scandals and the drip-drip of misery that comes from being apart so much.

Parliament isn't responsible for every marital disaster. Some relationships end for reasons that existed long before one partner entered Westminster. Some marriages may already be on the rocks before someone becomes a parliamentary candidate, and find themselves under further strain during the gruelling years of campaigning to win a seat. And then, suddenly, unless you are an MP representing a London or south-east seat, your family is in one part of the country for half the week, and you are in the other.

Some MPs prefer to base their family in the constituency, or at least they feel pressure to do so, because living in London would make them part of the Bubble and not interested in the community they represent. Others don't want to come home to an empty central London flat at least three nights a week, and choose to make the capital their home, travelling to the constituency for Fridays and Saturdays. Neither is an easy option. The burgeoning demands of constituency life are such that it's very difficult for anyone who represents a marginal seat to breeze in and out on a Friday: people expect you to be on call all weekend, visiting community events on a Saturday and local church services on a Sunday.

Having your family in the constituency is seen as a sign that you're truly committed to the area, but it can end up making the logistics of family life very difficult. Local papers ask candidates and new MPs where their family will live as a matter of routine, and even other MPs, who really should know better, needle their colleagues over choices they've made about what's best for their spouse and children. During the Clacton by-election, for instance, which was prompted by Douglas Carswell's defection from the Conservative Party to UKIP, his former colleague Greg Hands took it upon himself to repeatedly highlight on Twitter that Carswell's family lived in Fulham, rather than in the constituency.[1] Perhaps

Hands, whose seat was just down the road from Parliament, had forgotten how difficult it can be to juggle family, Parliament, and constituency life.

That juggling can turn marriages that felt strong and happy into very miserable, distant relationships indeed. One MP whose marriage broke down within a couple of years of getting elected says: 'I thought my marriage was rock-solid. But I had so many people warning me that you should absolutely not do this unless your spouse is 100 per cent supportive. I thought, well, mine is about 90 per cent supportive, when in reality she was 50 per cent supportive and that went quickly down to 30 per cent.' Another whose other half had worked in politics for years and who knew the score says his partner said shortly after the election that 'I've got to be honest, I'm frightened about the impact this is going to have on your life and what this means for our relationship.' He was right to be frightened: Parliament is not the place to go if you want to improve your marriage. Some MPs walk into it with their eyes open, but most assume they will be fine – until they realise what the life really entails.

A spouse or partner might be as overjoyed as the MP themself when they get elected. But after a few months, the reality of living apart half the week, as well as a parliamentary culture that involves a lot of drinking late at night in bars with a number of single people who seem extremely taken with the aura of someone who holds elected office, starts to take its toll. In 2015, the Tories held an event for the partners and spouses of MPs who had been elected six months earlier. It wasn't just a way of saying thank you to them: it was also a chance for those people to talk to one another about the shock they'd experienced at how much the Commons had changed their relationships, often for the worse. Theresa May's husband Philip also set up a club for female MPs' husbands to share the challenges they encounter as a result of being a parliamentarian's partner.

Former Ilford North MP Lee Scott had already seen the toll that Parliament had taken on his friends when he entered the Commons in 2005: 'I had a lot of friends who were MPs and I had seen that in 60 per cent of their cases their marriages had broken up. And you sort of thought to yourself, "Why is that?" And then you realise that you're with a lot of people and you can be quite lonely. Voting late, sitting in your office on your own.' Scott made a vow to himself that he wouldn't get sucked into this culture: he employed his wife as his secretary so they could be together as much as possible, and didn't get involved in the social side. 'Every evening, I came home to my wife and family.'

However, you still have to wait around to vote before you can go home to your family or whoever else is waiting for you. On Monday nights, MPs are cooped up in the Commons until 10 p.m. waiting for the final vote of the day. Some filter down to the terrace for a drink and to gossip. Others carry on working, or start drinking in their offices with fellow MPs they are friendly with. Sometimes the drinking continues long after the last vote. And as a parliament wears on, the drinking can become more frequent, too. One MP told me: 'At first I was only late home one night a week, when I had to vote, and at home all the other nights. By the end of my five years, I was only home on time to see my husband one night a week, and out all the other nights.'

Sometimes relationships grow out of those drinking sessions, and not only between single MPs giddy as university freshers at the prospect of spending so much time with like-minded people. There have been many liaisons between married MPs, some reported, some kept entirely private. They are no more our business than the private arrangements of our doctors, teachers and other public servants, but what is particularly tragic about the effect of the Commons on so many relationships is that it's not just love rats who are vulnerable to infidelity. It's everyone, including those who cannot imagine themselves ever doing such a thing when they first enter Parliament.

There is of course a risk that an MP's private life stops being private. When you stand for public office, your life becomes public property whether you like it or not, and whether that is fair or not. Some MPs tempt fate by boasting about the importance of family in their election literature, thereby making themselves fair game in the eyes of journalists when they're discovered in another parliamentarian's bed. Others turn out to have amusing sexual peccadilloes that may be equally prevalent among the general population, but which become incredibly interesting when they belong to someone wearing a political rosette. The humiliation can be total: Tory MP Brooks Newmark decided to leave Parliament after a young male journalist posed as an attractive female Conservative activist and, using direct messages on Twitter, enticed him into sending shots of his genitalia and his paisley pyjamas. Among the whooping and cackling at the middle-aged man's foolishness was utter horror and sadness from his colleagues, who saw an unwell MP whose marriage, career and dignity had been flung onto the rocks for a titillating story.

Parliament is notorious for its sex scandals. Of the MPs who served between 2010 and 2015, 27 of them were revealed to have been involved in illicit sexual liaisons. Many others go unreported. Two Tory MPs, Jack Lopresti and Andrea Jenkyns, had an affair that Lopresti was forced to reveal to his wife after a tabloid newspaper told him it would be reporting the story, complete with pictures of the pair canoodling together at a railway station and wearing matching Christmas jumpers. David Cameron was furious at the time, muttering that it was no one else's business, though his party took another affair that cost one participant his marriage rather seriously: Mark Field MP had a nine-month affair with Liz Truss before she was an MP, which led to her local association trying to remove her as a parliamentary candidate. But the Tory whips consider all these incidents their business: in autumn 2017 they were revealed to be giving Theresa May regular updates on what they called 'the ins and outs'. Apparently the prime minister would roll her eyes before expressing frustration that her colleagues couldn't just get on with the job. But not everyone manages to keep their private and political lives as well separated as May does.

Other MPs end up with their researchers, who are often much younger than they are. In 2016, 39-year-old Tory MP Justin Tomlinson announced that he was in a relationship with his 25-year-old aide Kate Bennett. The *Mirror* surprised the 37-year-old girlfriend of Morecambe MP David Morris with a picture of him canoodling with his 23-year-old staffer, Alexandra Swann. 'Oh… it doesn't look good, does it?' said Katherine Antcliffe when she saw the photo. 'David is a really decent guy, I'm shocked.'[2]

When two SNP MPs, Stewart Hosie and Angus MacNeil, were revealed to have had affairs with the same journalist, Serena Cowdy, *Daily Mail* columnist (and wife of Michael Gove) Sarah Vine took a rather strong line in her piece for the paper that week. 'I mean, look at her,' she wrote. 'Honestly. That pose. That dress. She's not exactly backwards about coming forwards, is she?' Vine argued that Westminster was a 'hotbed of young, single women, often straight out of university, their brilliance almost as distracting as their skirt length'.[3]

Many thought this a rather unsisterly approach to a woman who, after all, was not the married party choosing to enter these liaisons. But Vine was expressing a not uncommon frustration among Westminster spouses, even those as powerful and gifted as she is, and did put her finger on something, which is that it is easy to cheat in Westminster, and easy to find someone to cheat with. Attend any party, and you will see rather average-looking middle-aged male MPs surrounded by considerably younger and more attractive young women. Even special advisers notice that their new roles don't just bring long working days and interdepartmental battles: a side effect of the job is attention from women, and a lot of it. Spouses and partners can certainly spot the danger: one remarked to me that 'some of them stop when they find out that he's married. Others don't care at all.' One MP who fancied himself as something of a Lothario was finally dumped by his on-off girlfriend for possessing what she described as a 'conveyor belt' of women.

Perhaps some of those young women on the conveyor belt have grown used to not being taken seriously in an environment where cheap insults like 'totty' can still be heard, and where smart women often feel as though they have to appear twice as serious as the blokes before they get a hearing. Perhaps some of them are dazzled by the power and confidence that even a backbencher has, compared to the self-confidence of the average 23-year-old man. Perhaps some of them see a powerful man and hope, even if they do not realise it themselves, that they might make him less powerful as he falls for them. Either way, not all of these flirtations at parties end by the bar. Some continue – but that is the choice of the married MP as much as that of the young researcher. In fact, the MP is the one with the power professionally, even if their sexual allure is rather less evident.

Even those who correctly diagnose the problems with Parliament aren't immune. When he was Tory Work and Pensions Secretary, Stephen Crabb told one young woman that 'Most MPs are risk-takers to one degree or another. Usually in the areas of money, sex, political opportunism. Add in the adrenalin, the attention u get, and the time away from family . . . toxic mix.'4 He was spot on, as it turned out, about himself too, as he later messaged the same woman that he wanted to kiss her 'everywhere'. No one can escape from the pressures that Parliament places on relationships.

Those who work in the Westminster Bubble are a little less shocked that these situations arise. It's not just the time away from your spouse every week that creates the problem. It is also the availability of young, attractive, often slightly adoring researchers who tend to work alone in your office and sort out your every problem. More widely, it is the crowd of young, attractive, often slightly adoring staffers from think tanks and other political organisations who appear at Westminster parties, hanging on your every word.

'One of the things about being a candidate,' says one former candidate, 'is if you're half decent at it, you do pick up groupies. I remember asking one new MP friend of mine how he was enjoying his first few months in Parliament. He said, "If you're the sort that plays the field, there'd be almost unlimited sex." He'd just got serious with his girlfriend and I think I detected a slight wistfulness in his observation.'

Aside from the wistfulness, a culture of 'unlimited sex' and regular adultery makes it much easier for politicians who want to cheat (I must confess that I have found more male MPs than female who have either confessed to me about an indiscretion, or whose indiscretions have been passed to me in the course of this book) to avoid taking responsibility for their actions. When everyone else seems to be at it, it just seems less serious, and more as though this is the best way of dealing with the misery.

Power and control

Some politicians had also long avoided taking responsibility for behaviour far more serious than the personal mess of a consensual affair. But then the global sexual harassment scandal broke in late 2017. Allegations such as those about Hollywood producers like Harvey Weinstein quickly spread to every industry, and Parliament was certainly not immune. Scores of MPs were alleged to have acted inappropriately towards both women and men, including considerably younger researchers. Michael Fallon resigned as Defence Secretary after journalist Julia Hartley-Brewer revealed that he had touched her leg during a work lunch many years previously. Her revelation, which he apologised for, prompted other women to come forward with their own stories, including another journalist, Jane Merrick, who told Downing Street that Fallon had kissed her when she was a junior political journalist. Writer Kate Maltby alleged that Damian Green, then First Secretary of State, had touched her leg during a meeting about her aspirations to break into politics, before sending her suggestive texts about a newspaper feature in which she had worn a corset. At this point, someone thought fit to leak to the papers that police had found 'extreme' pornography on Green's computer when they raided his parliamentary office in 2009. Green eventually had to resign after it was found that he had lied about the existence of this pornography.

The scandal quickly turned ugly. Tory researchers circulated a list of falsehoods, inaccuracies and aspersions about MPs that had made it into the public domain. Some of the inclusions in this 'dirty dossier' named the wrong MP. Others put people's private consensual relationships alongside claims of sexual assault, as though all sex in Westminster was now wrong. It muddied the waters, conveniently for those who wanted to dismiss the whole situation as being a storm in a teacup.

But it wasn't a storm in a teacup, not as far as the women who had been seriously assaulted and harassed were concerned. One activist, Bex Bailey, bravely waived her right to anonymity and informed the BBC that she had been raped at a Labour Party event but told not to complain as it might harm her political career. Other complaints had as much to do with prolonged indifference from the political parties as they did with what had actually happened.

What stung victims the most was that the parties had known about the incidents for years. Some of the complaints stretched back longer than a decade. And not only was it well known in Westminster that there were sex pests in the corridors of power; it was also acknowledged that there was a culture in which women, particularly younger women, were treated as lesser beings, sex objects who deserved comments ranging from the smutty to the obscene. Women also swapped tales on who to avoid and who wasn't 'safe in taxis'. One set of allegations against Labour's Ivan Lewis included staff in the department where he had worked warning young female staff to stay away from him because of his reputation.[5] He denied all the claims against him, but apologised for making women feel uncomfortable. But the tale of the warnings has been told about many other MPs, and shows how far young women were expected to change their conduct in Westminster just to avoid inappropriate behaviour. It was expected that the woman would simply have to deal with it, rather than the man changing his ways.

I'd had my own brush with this culture when in 2016 I complained to the whips about an MP who I knew very vaguely and only in a professional capacity calling me 'totty'. Frustrated that a small group of dinosaur politicians thought they could get away with using language that was clearly unacceptable and demeaning towards the women they worked alongside, I tweeted about my complaint – without naming the MP – in order to let the other dinosaurs in the flock know that women actually didn't want to put up with this stuff. I didn't want to name and shame the MP – though I was offered a fair bit of money to do so by some media outlets – because he was merely part of a culture, and because I didn't want it to become about one person.

The defence that some people mounted, that the term was a compliment, didn't stand: whereas most of us are perfectly happy to be told that we are looking nice, for instance, that sort of language objectifies women as sex objects. I had encountered the MP as I was about to go on television to talk about the SNP, and had never marketed myself as a sex object. If he hadn't worked out that 'totty' wasn't the sort of word he should be using, it was because he didn't care enough to check, and the only reason someone wouldn't care enough to check would be if they felt there were no repercussions for showing disrespect to someone else in their professional sphere.

A fortnight of debate and gossiping ensued, during which it became clear that I was being blamed for my response at least as much as the MP was being blamed for his behaviour. This does reflect our wider culture, not just the one in Parliament, in which women are criticised for how they respond to the unacceptable actions of men, from how they deal with an abusive husband right down to how they complain about sexist comments. 'Why doesn't she just leave him?' and 'Why didn't she just take it as a compliment?'

seem much easier for most people to say than 'Why doesn't he stop abusing her?' or 'Why hasn't he learned how to treat women with respect?'

The reaction to the incident was far out of proportion to what happened. I had naively thought that pointing out that it is not OK to call a woman 'totty' was a necessary statement of the obvious that might help a few other women. I did not consider it the worst act of sexism I had ever encountered. It was certainly not the worst thing a man had done to me. It was a minor irritation; rudeness that I suspected I would not have witnessed had I been a man and the MP a woman. I have never found occasion to tell a male MP in a studio green room or reception that he was a 'hot piece of ass', for instance. I merely tweeted about the complaint that I had made and got on with my working day. Others decided to turn it into an enormous political row. I now realise that this was because it served the purpose of those who wanted to play down serious sexism: they could claim that women couldn't even take compliments, thus undermining the credibility of others who complained. By focusing on cases where there is some debate about 'flirting' or 'taking a compliment', opponents of equality try to belittle suggestions that there is a powerful culture of sexism that goes all the way from telling a woman she's a sex object to telling her she shouldn't complain about a rape because it might harm her political career.

Unlike many women in politics, I had a fair bit of power to do something about the incident. I was on good terms with the whips. I had a supportive boss. I had been working in Westminster for a sufficient amount of time for most people to trust me and know I wasn't an attention-seeker. I didn't need anything from this MP. All these factors helped me, but they are absent for so many women who face terrible sexism and far worse. I was struck by the number of private messages I received from former advisers and researchers who were grateful that someone had taken a stand even on low-level sexism, because they had never felt able to complain about far worse incidents.

The Lord Rennard scandal, in which women in the Liberal Democrats who were hoping to become parliamentary candidates claimed they were sexually harassed by the then chief executive of the party, highlighted this. Rennard was involved in candidate selection. He held a huge amount of power over the future of those he was alleged to have harassed. He denied any wrongdoing. To complain about what had happened to them, the women involved would have been turning over someone they needed for their own advancement. Worse, when they did complain to their party, which has long preached gender equality, they found that nothing was done. And worse still, they felt they were being smeared, both by Rennard and by the party machine.

Alison Goldsworthy was one of the women who spoke out. She waived her right to anonymity in disgust at the response to her allegations, which were that Rennard had put his hand down her backless dress, inside her knickers and past 'extremely intimate' areas. She didn't complain at the time because of the power that the peer had in the party, and she didn't want to be known for 'making a scene'. But when Channel 4 began investigating the peer, she joined other women from the party to describe the incident.

When the story broke, Rennard issued a statement saying he had conducted some research that had turned up 'devastating evidence' to undermine the claims being made against him. His alleged victims were terrified that he was going to reveal details of their private lives and previous relationships, which would have been both humiliating and irrelevant. But Goldsworthy also believes that others within the party were circulating rumours about her to the press, which the press did not report. She and her fellow members felt as though they were being blamed for complaining.

This pattern, where the victim rather than the alleged perpetrator is blamed, pervades society but seems particularly prevalent in politics. Perhaps this is because of the amount of power that perpetrators have. Perhaps it is also because women remain in the minority in top jobs. But there is a powerful culture of taking women less seriously in Westminster.

The problem is that, having failed to take complaints seriously for so long, the parties then responded to the tide of allegations – from both women and men – in late 2017 with utter panic. They were panicked not just by the volume of complaints, but also by the number of allegations that involved someone covering something up, or telling the complainant to get a grip. Some of their decisions about individual politicians smacked of guilt that they had only acted when a newspaper had called rather than when the incident had first come to their attention. And naturally not all their decisions were particularly measured or just.

MPs are a curious mix of powerful and vulnerable. They are naturally in positions of great superiority over their staff, especially those many decades their junior. A number of them clearly enjoy asserting their dominance in a way that goes far beyond the slightly insecure power trip that everyone recognises from their own workplaces: abuse, assault and harassment are all about power, and it's hardly surprising that in a bunch of insecure people, there are men and women who want to humiliate others. But MPs are also public figures who attract enemies and people who enjoy making spurious allegations. Because women had been ignored for so long, there was a release of pressure when the scandal broke that meant every allegation was at once treated as preposterous and valid. There were those who wanted to suggest that the women hadn't complained in the right way, or that they were trying to get attention by writing in the press about their experiences. But there were also those who decided to believe every allegation as soon as it was aired, regardless of whether due process had been followed in investigating those complaints. Defamation suddenly seemed less relevant than the ability to publish any accusation anywhere.

There were two suicides in the Labour Party, and while suicide is a complex issue, it did show quite how devastating these cases can be for all those caught up in them. Charlie Elphicke, a Conservative MP, complained that he had been suspended from the party whip for months following an allegation of sexual assault, but that no one had provided any details of what the claim was.

This mess was perhaps inevitable, given how long victims had felt ignored and dismissed. But it cannot be the case that every allegation is true, or indeed that every true allegation is as serious as the next. Those tempted to abuse their position and harass and assault those around them may already be thinking again as a result of this row. Westminster will only have really learned from the sexual harassment scandal, though, when it is clear that complaints are properly and justly investigated. This means that people can complain in confidence and feel listened to, but that those who are alleged perpetrators are not taken through a kangaroo court process or left in a strange limbo in which they have no idea of the allegations against them for an extended period of time.

The scandal also highlighted how poor Parliament's HR structures are, with victims unaware of who to turn to about inappropriate behaviour. Given that a large number of researchers join Parliament fresh out of university, many of them simply do not know what to expect from the world of work but have no one to ask for advice. Similarly, a number of the allegations were made against MPs who were well known not so much as 'pests', but as sad characters whose personal lives had been in a mess for years. The only people who might check up on them would be the whips, who hardly lack their own ulterior motives.

Many changes were made to Westminster as a result of the sexual harassment scandal, but one way of preventing situations arising between MPs and subordinates would be regular appraisals for both politicians and their staff. These would have to be carried out by the parliamentary authorities rather than the parties themselves, as factions within parties could weaponise an MP's personal problems against them. The appraisals would also have to include probing questions about whether the staff member felt comfortable in their work; whether there was anything they wanted confidential advice on, such as should their boss really be asking them to do a certain thing; and whether they were coping with the workload. MPs would be asked in these compulsory sessions whether they were struggling in their personal relationships or with their mental health. It cannot be assumed that disclosures on either side would be made proactively: often people who are suffering need to be given permission to speak out by someone they trust. Some might argue that this is hugely invasive. But the culture of Parliament has been so unhealthy for so long that we owe it to political staffers and their bosses to make big changes.

The representation problem

This culture has a number of consequences. The first is that women are less likely to put themselves forward for political office. I have been told privately that around a third of applications to be a Conservative candidate – the very first rung of the parliamentary career ladder – come from women. All the parties have poured varying degrees of effort into trying to find and coach top-notch women to be successful candidates. But if they do not take sexism and sexual harassment within their own ranks sufficiently seriously, they will continue to put women off.

It's not just sexism in the corridors of power that's unappealing. Women in politics are subjected to a level of vitriol online that would put many public-spirited types off. Every MP gets abuse, but it's worse and more personal and physical if you're a woman, and particularly bad if you are Jewish. We will return to this later in the book, but abuse in person or online is one of the major factors that voters cite when asked what might deter them from going into politics.

One of the things that gets to all MPs who don't have a constituency in London or the south-east of England is the struggle to juggle family life and work. It's not just their relationship with their spouse or partner, but the amount of time that MPs get to spend with their children. If your family are in the constituency, you only have half a week with them. If you decide to keep the main household in London, you're still away for at least a day in your seat. Of course, many other lines of work, including the military, see parents separated from their children not just for days but for months on end. It is hardly unusual that MPs struggle with this.

But struggle they do, and sometimes things their children say or do contribute to that struggle. One candidate who was standing again in an election found a voicemail from his young daughter on his phone telling him she hoped he would lose as then she would see him more. Hazel Blears described in an interview seeing a 'young woman MP, not long since had a baby, and the baby was on the other end of the phone, just gurgling and crying on the other end of the phone, and she just went to listen, and that was quite heart-rending anyway, to be in that position'.[6]

Liberal Democrat MP Jo Swinson gave birth to her son while both she and her husband Duncan Hames were serving in Parliament. She was shocked by how many people asked her how she was coping with juggling parenthood and Parliament, but how few ever mentioned it to Hames. Yet parliamentary fathers struggle with the same miserable feelings of separation from their children as mothers, and have the same dread of the train journey back down to Westminster on a Sunday night. It's just that everyone expects them to forget about their children when they arrive in Parliament. Tracey Crouch also gave birth as an MP, having suffered a miscarriage during the 2015 general election campaign. 'I've had people telling me I shouldn't be an MP because I was a mother,' she told me. Yet people seem to have coped with fathers being MPs for a very long time.

A number of MPs elected in the late 1990s and early 2000s received a letter from a man claiming to be the son of an MP. Helen Liddell, who was a Labour MP between 1994 and 2005, mentioned it in an interview: 'I can always remember, when I was elected, I got a letter from a man whose name I didn't recognise, saying that he was the son of a Member of Parliament, and that it had wrecked his life. And I've always borne that in mind, and been a bit cautious about the consequences for my children.'[7]

MPs' children can have a rough time at school, picked on either because of policies their parents have supported or because of the expenses scandal. One MP recalls his son's primary school teacher saying that when she asked him if he wanted to be an MP like his daddy, he told her, 'No, I could never do that to my family.' Of course, they are also immensely proud of their parents, and many aren't put off enough to avoid politics totally, as the stream of second-generation politicians trying to enter Parliament shows.

It isn't quite right to say that Westminster is a hotbed of sex pests. It is certainly seething with people whose personal lives are stretched, sometimes to breaking point, by the life they have to lead. And alongside those MPs in messes are people who want to make others' lives a mess too. What unites the two groups is that their parties and the wider parliamentary culture have been indifferent to their behaviour for too long. And both groups are sufficiently visible to the public that more balanced individuals who could be very good MPs wonder, as that politician's child above did, whether they could really do that to their family.

CHAPTER 7

GETTING ILL

One relationship that just grows stronger for MPs is that with the bottle. Few seem immune to another toxic culture in Parliament: drinking. It is unparliamentary for one MP to describe another as 'drunk', but that rule does not exist because MPs are never inebriated. Take Mark Reckless, for instance. He doesn't enjoy jokes about his surname – indeed, he once complained about a rare joke that Theresa May made in the Chamber about his suggestions for getting hate cleric Abu Qatada deported more quickly. The then Home Secretary looked ever so pleased with herself as she said, 'Dare I describe urging the government to break the law as a rather *reckless* step?' Reckless was not pleased, and complained to the Speaker about 'what some might describe as personal abuse'.[1]

But that doesn't mean that he was always a sensible soul. In 2010, the newly elected Conservative MP ended up missing a vote on the Budget because he had drunk far too much on the House of Commons terrace while waiting for the next division. Apologising to his Rochester and Strood constituents, he said: 'I remember someone asking me to vote and not thinking it was appropriate, given how I was at the time. If I was in the sort of situation generally where I thought I was drunk I tend to go home. Westminster is a very special situation and all I can say . . .

is given this very embarrassing experience I don't intend to drink at Westminster again.'[2]

Reckless, who became teetotal, was mocked roundly and criticised heavily for being too drunk to vote, but there was something touching about his honesty in saying that he didn't think it was appropriate to vote without knowing what was going on. As we have already seen, unless he wanted to cause problems for the government (he did later become a Eurosceptic troublemaker, eventually defecting to UKIP), he wouldn't have needed to know much about the vote, other than how to put one foot in front of the other as the whips pointed to the lobby he was supposed to walk through.

But the incident did raise eyebrows about Parliament's drinking culture, which was supposed to have diminished as a result of the appearance of cameras in the House of Commons Chamber, which could tell the public whether an MP was drunk far better than a colleague using unparliamentary language could. As the gender balance of Westminster has slowly improved, the old boys' club drinking culture has also started to weaken. And the 'family friendly' sitting hours (which will never be truly family friendly unless all MPs have their families in London) also mean MPs aren't waiting on the terrace late into the night for votes as often as they once were. Some parliamentary bars have closed: one is now a nursery for the children of those who work on the estate, and the glorious old press bar is now a rather draughty room where journalists, including me, have their messy desks. However, there is still a long way to go. Reckless was voting on the Finance Bill, which doesn't have a cut-off point for debate, and so votes still happen late into the night.

And late-night votes aren't the only reason MPs continue to drink a lot, even if they don't turn up drunk in the Commons Chamber. Given the pace of Westminster and political news, few ministers or journalists have enough time for long boozy lunches that mean they don't return to their desks. But it is still perfectly normal for MPs to drink wine over lunch – as it is for journalists. Former GP and Tory MP for Totnes Sarah Wollaston objected to this in 2011, telling a party conference fringe that some of her colleagues were 'drinking really quite heavily', adding, 'Who would go to see a surgeon who had just drunk a bottle of wine at lunchtime?' Her colleagues objected loudly to this, with many arguing that heavy drinking in Parliament was a thing of the past and that they had only rarely seen colleagues inebriated.

The problem is that once you've agreed that being actually drunk is a bad thing, there are still grades of under-the-influence that some would find acceptable and others would not. MPs do not need the complex motor skills of a surgeon. But they are scrutinising our laws, and if they're a minister, they are involved in drawing up those laws, which affect everyone's lives. Even if someone is not visibly drunk, alcohol can impair judgement and encourage an individual to make reckless decisions that they would not take when sober and more rational. Yet alcohol laps around Westminster every day from lunchtime until the close of play. Once the restaurants have emptied of their guests, the Commons reception rooms start to fill up with MPs attending a launch for one thing or another – and with more glasses of wine. Even if MPs aren't drinking until obvious drunkenness, most of them are able to put a fair bit away.

It is difficult for a journalist to complain about alcohol consumption: it loosens the tongues of many MPs, and our own world is not inured to the dangers of excess alcohol. But more prevalent now than reckless binge drinking in Parliament is alcohol dependency in one form or another. In 2012, Commons doctor Ira Madan told a staff meeting that she was concerned about the proportion of MPs she had seen with alcohol-related problems.[3] An Alcohol Concern survey of 150 MPs in 2013 found that 26 per cent felt there was too much drinking in Parliament.

Within a few months of entering the Commons in 2015, one MP confessed to me that he was worried he was starting to struggle with alcoholism, and that the culture made it easy for him to think that the amount he was drinking each night was perfectly normal. The late Charles Kennedy's wife was quizzed about his drinking habits on Radio 4's *Woman's Hour* when rumours started to emerge about the Liberal Democrat leader having an addiction. 'Actually, it is just a normal, fun life, really,' she said. This was just before the pair married, and long before Kennedy admitted he had a problem. Whether or not Sarah Gurling thought at the time that her fiancé was struggling with alcoholism, the culture in parliament will have made it seem far more normal than it was.

Kennedy's illness was serious enough to visibly affect his ability to do his job – and it cost him that job as Liberal Democrat leader, and eventually his life: he died aged just 55. He wasn't the only modern politician killed by the vicious illness of alcoholism. Labour's Fiona Jones died of liver failure when she was 49, after a lonely parliamentary career that ended with her losing her seat in 2001. Her husband observed shortly after her death that she could drink whisky in the House of Commons 'because nobody cared if she drank'. Her loneliness continued after her death: journalist David James Smith was disgusted by the failure of any MPs to turn up to her funeral.[4] Labour MP Jamie Cann died of liver disease in 2001. Iain Mills was found dead by the Tory whips in his Pimlico flat in 1997, surrounded by gin bottles. His life, too, had been lonely: in his examination of parliamentary drinking habits, the journalist Ben Wright argues that 'Mills died as he had existed in the Commons.

Alone, only noticed when he failed to show up for a vote.' Wright also reports that Sir Menzies Campbell thought it was loneliness as a 23-year-old newly elected MP that first drove Charles Kennedy to heavy drinking.[5]

The Labour MP Liam Byrne also suspects that many MPs end up 'self-medicating', a term psychiatrists use to denote someone who uses alcohol or drugs to treat a mental health problem that they may not even have acknowledged to themselves. 'MPs are just ordinary people, and if they don't come in here with the skin of a rhino, they'll find a way to self-medicate,' he says. Having been 'gobsmacked' by how many of his colleagues are children of alcoholics, Byrne wasn't quite so surprised to notice how many of them had their own alcohol problems and other mental illnesses. 'Remember, up to half of children of alcoholics will go on to become alcoholics themselves, so if you're the child of an alcoholic, you're three times more likely to contemplate suicide and about five times more likely to have an eating disorder.'

It's not just those who've had family problems with addictions who are susceptible, though. Former Tory MP Ben Howlett believes that 'Most parliamentarians have got an addictive personality. Mix that with alcohol and that ends up being a challenge.' Alcohol can numb the pain, at least temporarily. And there's a fair bit of pain in Westminster. It might be that your career is going nowhere and you are struggling to adjust to this after years of straining every sinew, savings account and relationship to get into Parliament. One MP told me in a tone of disgust about his neighbour in Portcullis House who was repeatedly passed over for promotion from the back benches. 'He's now a drunk!' he exclaimed irritably. It transpired that his irritation was not with what Parliament can do to someone, but with the amount of noise emanating from his colleague's office from mid-afternoon onwards, interrupting his train of thought. 'Each day the popping of corks and the clinking of glasses gets earlier, and then you start hearing his stupid drunken laugh.'

Perhaps you already have a mental health problem – including alcoholism, which is a mental illness, not a joke – before entering Parliament, and now you're alone in Westminster for a number of nights each week, and all your colleagues are putting away the booze with enough abandon not to notice that you can't get past a certain time without a drink.

What can Parliament really do about this? Surely if we think someone is capable of representing us in Parliament, they should also be capable of looking after their physical and mental health. Ben Howlett wonders whether receptions for MPs could just serve soft drinks, while Alcohol Concern has campaigned for Parliament to stop subsidising drinks sold on the estate. But other MPs and staff have argued that they are being penalised for the bad behaviour of a few drunken idiots.

What is clear is that Parliament is sufficiently mentally unhealthy for alcoholism to be just one of the manifestations of things going wrong for our politicians.

Mental illness

Mental illness is so prevalent in Westminster that the Commons now has its own dedicated team of doctors and nurses with access to funding for psychiatric treatment. As with relationship problems, some MPs will arrive in Westminster having suffered from mental illness for many years. Tory MP Brooks Newmark, for instance, whose cruel treatment was discussed earlier, had struggled with anorexia as a teenager. Others find that parliamentary life tips them from a previously healthy mental state into their first experience of anxiety or depression.

'If you are predisposed to having a weakness or a condition, Parliament will expose it,' says Charles Walker, who has seen many colleagues come to him with their struggles after he spoke out publicly about his own mental health problems. 'If you have a predisposition to alcoholism, Parliament will accelerate it. If your marriage is weak, it might have failed in ten years, but Parliament will ensure it falls apart in five. If you have an underlying disposition to a mental illness, which may have never developed, Parliament will ensure that it does develop. Parliament is a bit like a screwdriver that prises the lid off a tin of paint. It is very good at finding your weakness.'

Alcohol doesn't help with that: it is a natural depressant and also contributes to sleeping problems. Tired, depressed MPs trying to self-medicate with the wine on offer in the Commons bars won't find themselves getting any better. And just as loneliness can contribute to alcoholism, it can also contribute to other mental illnesses too. Your family aren't around. You might struggle to find real friends rather than political allies. 'Parliament is actually really quite a lonely place,' says Tory MP Tracey Crouch, who has spoken publicly about suffering from depression shortly after being elected. 'While you do of course have friendship groups, the fact is that every single person in that place has very unique challenges within their constituencies, they have very different family circumstances, some of them don't see their family for days at a time, all with a backdrop of the public watching what you're up to.'

The cycle of affirmation and seeking more affirmation that many MPs have been locked into for years before entering Parliament is one of the key factors in the mental illnesses that they then develop in Westminster, believes Walker: 'We revel in being needed and wanted. MPs as a group are very needy people, constantly craving endorsement and positive feedback. They seek that by being hugely engaged with their community. It's all these endorphin shots, and I think that's why they are more prone to suffering great upset at rejection.

'Despite the huge amount of work most of them put in, selfless work, constantly putting their constituents ahead of themselves and their families, when that is met with rejection because people are much better at being anonymously nasty, MPs don't wear that well. They end up thinking, "I must do more, then they'll love me more." It's a very destructive cycle.'

MPs also live a curiously peripatetic life. No one need feel sorry for someone with two homes, but having their belongings and food in two places does seem to discombobulate both MPs and their families. One MP's spouse told me that he was constantly trying to work out what was going off in which fridge, at different ends of the country. Other MPs confess that they just have no idea where all their pants have gone. These are very much first-world problems, but this book isn't about how MPs have the hardest life and how we should feel sorry for them above everyone else. They quite demonstrably do not have the hardest life. But as they are the people legislating on our behalf, even if we think they have it easy compared to us, we should hope that their minds are healthy enough for them to stop our lives becoming even harder as a result of messy policies from Westminster.

What many lonely MPs find instead is a constant stream of communication from people who want their attention. The problem is that these people aren't their children or their family and friends. They're online trolls, who for various bizarre reasons have decided to dedicate at least some of their spare time not to normal hobbies and socialising but to sending abusive messages to men and (particularly) women they've never met.

Politics excites strong emotions. MPs who make unpopular decisions must be prepared to answer for those decisions. But what they shouldn't have to be prepared for is a stream of rape and death threats, comments about their personal lives and appearance, and endless harassment. In 2014, Peter Nunn was found guilty of sending rape threats to Labour MP Stella Creasy, apparently in revenge for her supporting a campaign to put Jane Austen on the £10 bank note. In December 2016, Joshua Bonehill-Paine was jailed for two years for writing a series of anti-Semitic blog posts about Labour's Luciana Berger, which the Liverpool Wavertree MP said left her feeling 'under attack' and 'concerned about my personal safety'. Creasy and Berger were also targets of internet troll John Nimmo, who was first jailed for eight weeks in 2014 after he sent abusive tweets to Creasy, and then jailed again for two years and three months in 2017 after threatening that Berger would 'get it like Jo Cox' just weeks after the MP's murder, along with a string of anti-Semitic abuse. Women and those from religious or ethnic minorities seem to attract more abuse than others, but no MP is immune from threats. And after Cox's murder, many MPs panicked that the trolls they had come to associate with their daily lives online might suddenly appear in front of them physically and carry out the threats that they'd previously tweeted.

Beyond the threats of violence, obvious racism, anti-Semitism and misogyny are subtler bullying tactics. One MP told me that after a year of being in Parliament and on Twitter, she was starting to believe what the trolls told her every day about how stupid and useless she was. It is a similar tactic to the one that domestic abusers deploy, wearing down their victims with a constant stream of comments about what they are getting wrong each day, to the extent that the victim then agrees with them and believes they deserve the abuse.

Walker says, 'Some of my colleagues are obsessed with Twitter and it is driving them mad. It takes up so much of their time, but it's just the same 30 people.' Walker himself is not on Twitter. Some of his MP colleagues have stopped reading their replies or have activated such stringent filters that they can only see messages from people they follow. This is a shame, as social media was supposed to help politicians stay closer to their constituents. A vocal and unpleasant minority have made that much more difficult. Who can blame an MP who, in an attempt to preserve their sanity and stay focused on their job, decides it is best to stop reading tweets just in case a few of them contain vile abuse? But many others can't quite rid themselves of their social media addiction. One former member of Ed Miliband's team when he was Labour leader says that they kept trying to delete the Twitter app from his phone, only for him to reinstall it late at night to read what people were saying about him. Even Boris Johnson, who gives the impression in public of being comfortable in his own skin, went through a phase of reading the comments below the line on online pieces about him.

I often observe a spike in MPs replying to trolls late at night, which suggests that politicians are logging on to Twitter as they lie in bed. They're inviting the most unpleasant people in the country into their bedroom when most sensible folk wouldn't even stop to listen to them on the street, but I wonder how many of them do this because the Twitter abuse in some way confirms how they already feel about themselves. If you already think bad things of yourself, the vicious cycle that you get locked into when other people repeat it back to you – regardless of whether they are right, or indeed are sending the same message to dozens of other MPs – can be incredibly destructive.

Many MPs are also on edge about doing – or being seen to do – the wrong thing and being hounded by the press. And what if the 'wrong thing' is either something you haven't actually done, or something that has been twisted? Andrew Mitchell's encounter with the police in the 'Plebgate' affair is well known. But what is less well known is the effect that the allegations, which dominated the news agenda for weeks, had on the then chief whip of the Conservative Party. He lost a stone in weight and was so depressed that he found it difficult to get out of bed. Speaking to MPs and peers who have been caught up in scandals of far less intensity than Plebgate, I've noticed that they all go through the same mental terror, often feeling too sick to eat for days on end. Some of them are pursued for making slightly clumsy comments that are then twisted in the press to become something far more menacing. Even small rows feel intensely traumatic, as it isn't just one journalist trying to reach you for a comment but hundreds, and often several from the same outlet. MPs take flak from journalists for sounding like boring robots in interviews, but many of them are too scared to be sincere, lest one quote leads to a week of people shouting at them in the press, online, and in broadcast debates.

For a long time, the stigma attached to mental illness meant MPs were afraid to be honest about their struggles in the same way as others were about physical illnesses. They also found it hard to get treatment. Many felt uncomfortable about going to the doctor in their constituency and then turning up at the local pharmacy to collect a prescription for antidepressants in full view of their electorate (some MPs point out that they have the same qualms about buying treatments for constipation or diarrhoea). They also struggled to find the time to go to the doctor in their constituency or in Westminster – or at least this was a convenient excuse for anyone trying to avoid confronting how unwell they might be.

But in 2012, something extraordinary happened in the House of Commons. A number of MPs spoke in an apparently routine backbench debate, but their contributions were some of the most influential and powerful of that entire five-year session. Burly Labour MP Kevan Jones told the Chamber that some of his family didn't even know what he was about to say, but that he had been suffering from depression. 'We're also I think in politics designed to think that somehow if you admit fault or frailty, you're going to be, you know, looked upon in a disparaging way in terms of both electorate, but also by your peers as well.' Telling the Speaker that he was finding this difficult, Jones insisted that MPs had to talk about mental health and their own experiences of it. He was swiftly followed by Tory MP Charles Walker, who cheerfully told his colleagues, 'I am delighted to say that I have been a practising fruitcake for 31 years.' Walker suffers from Obsessive Compulsive Disorder, which he said 'takes you to some quite dark places'.[6] But he and the other MPs who spoke for the first time in public about their illnesses found the experience liberating.

This wasn't just a personal catharsis. The sight of highly functional and popular parliamentarians declaring that they, like one in four of the wider population, had mental health problems was a big step in reducing the stigma attached to these illnesses. It led to legislation allowing people who had suffered from serious mental illnesses to serve in Parliament, on juries and as company directors. It led to other MPs speaking out about their own battles with depression and other illnesses, now confident that the sky wouldn't fall in if they said they were taking pills for their head rather than another part of their body. By the time I suffered my own fight with the black dog in 2016, I didn't feel particularly brave talking about it. Walker, Jones and others had done the hard work for me.

Mental health has become a political battleground, though it has yet to catch up with physical health in terms of NHS spending. Those MPs showed tremendous bravery in talking about being fruitcakes. They also showed how much like everyone else parliamentarians are. They too fall ill. They too can be frightened.

The Commons authorities and party whips also took note, and mental health provision for MPs is now dramatically better. There are mindfulness classes, cognitive behavioural therapy sessions and consultant psychiatrists available to MPs in the estate. They can refer themselves to the mental health service, which is so well hidden away that if anyone does still fear being seen to be struggling mentally, it is reasonably easy to sneak in without being noticed. Treatment is carefully anonymised, with names removed from prescriptions and pill packets so that no one will be able to pick up a bit of rubbish that betrays a personal secret.

The whips now see pastoral care as one of their responsibilities, alongside snooping on MPs' indiscretions. One whip who deserves particular mention is Anne Milton, whose work to improve the support for Conservative MPs made a huge difference to a number of very serious crises on her party's benches. Milton was a gem of a whip, able to give naughty backbenchers a fearsome dressing-down but also the sort of person that a suicidal MP might call and trust. She was an unusual gem, though. By and large, MPs still rightly don't trust the whips.

Mental illness isn't the political weapon that it used to be, in that journalists would now turn their nose up at a leaked story about a parliamentarian popping pills. But some of the side effects or the factors contributing to mental illness, such as relationship breakdown, are very useful bits of information for the whips to have on record. Not only do they keep a note of such things when they come to their attention; they also seek out more dirt on backbenchers in order to compile as weighty a dossier as possible on each potential troublemaker. They may not ever use the information, but most MPs are aware that the whips hold details of their secrets and weigh up whether to rebel on certain matters accordingly. MPs are sometimes hauled before their chief whips to answer questions about their close friends' or flatmates' personal lives. Some relent and spill the beans. Others are disgusted that the whips have picked up on another item on the parliamentary rumour mill that just isn't true.

A number of MPs who I spoke to privately about their mental health problems mentioned the Westminster grapevine. There are constant rumours about each MP, many of which are not true (some of them merely miss the mark and accuse MPs of having affairs with the wrong people), but they become what is known colloquially as 'Westminster facts', often based on nothing more concrete than two people of the opposite sex being spotted talking to each other twice in a month. It's not just the whips who benefit from salacious gossip: it is political rivals, too. Which brings us back to the loneliness of being an MP: you are surrounded by people, but few of them are really on your side.

This is your problem, too

This chapter has been difficult to write, not so much because of some of the heartbreaking interviews I have conducted about the saddest times of parliamentarians' lives, but more because suggesting that

MPs have their own struggles is always met with snorts of derision. At the end of 2016, I took part in a Radio 4 discussion with Charles Walker about Parliament and mental health. When we came off air, we found that some people were mocking us for being 'too middle class' and for my suggestion that having two homes at different ends of the country might be disorientating. Being middle class does not provide immunisation against mental illness – though given the paucity of NHS mental health services, having money does make it easier to get treatment for depression or an addiction.

This endless hostility to MPs is partly the fault of their own kind: the people who lied and cheated and gave Parliament a bad name. But it is wearing for those who try as best they can to live up to their constituents' expectations. Being hated for doing nothing wrong can't do much for the self-esteem of an already oddly fragile population of people.

Even if you will never be able to feel empathy for MPs, you should feel sorry for yourself and others whose lives are affected by laws that they are too distracted by the personal disasters that Parliament intensifies and multiplies to be able to scrutinise properly. Anyone who has had a personal disaster of the order described in this chapter (which, given the general statistics on divorce, addiction and mental health, will be most people reading this book) will understand that it can diminish the capacity of even the strongest person for a while. Even if you couldn't care less whether an MP has a happy home life for his or her own sake, you might hope that they do for the sake of Parliament at large. You might also hope that Parliament isn't so dysfunctional that it doesn't put off even better politicians from applying.

CHAPTER 8

GETTING OUT

So what if you don't feel you're being rewarded properly as an MP? Well, no one asked you to be one, and as we've seen, it's not always the happiest of lives. Increasingly, people who go into Parliament don't see it as a job for life – and that's not just because formerly safe seats have come under threat in recent years. It's something to do for a bit before moving on and using your experience elsewhere, or at the end of another interesting career.

This means that MPs these days don't stand down when they think they've reached the end of their working lives, but rather when they feel they're done with politics – or that politics is done with them. If you've been sacked from government by a prime minister who isn't going anywhere, you might conclude that there's no point in sticking around. Or, if your family has taken more than enough as a result of your job, you might decide that it's time to stop being an MP before you stop being a spouse. Tony Benn famously joked that he was leaving the Commons to 'spend more time on politics', which makes sense given the many demands on an MP's time that have little to do with politics.

A survey of 184 departing MPs in 2006 found that the largest group of these were retiring. But 11 per cent were leaving the Commons in their forties and fifties to pursue another career, fearing that they would be too old to do so if they stayed for another term. Twelve former MPs also mentioned frustration with the House of Commons, variously describing a feeling that 'I was on a different planet', exhaustion after working 83-hour weeks, and irritation that 'constituency work was creating a "social worker" environment that could only get worse in the future'.[1] A similar study of those who left in 2010 also found that the majority (60 per cent) stood down because of age, followed by a desire to spend more time with family (25 per cent) and that familiar gem 'personal reasons' (10 per cent). But moving on to a new career was the reason for 17 per cent of retirements from the Commons, while disillusionment with politics (particularly following the expenses scandal) was cited by 12.5 per cent of respondents.[2]

The expenses scandal loomed large for this group of politicians, and those who had done nothing wrong felt most aggrieved. One MP told the authors of the study that her 11-year-old son was invited to stand up by the headteacher during school assembly and was asked, 'You look really smart today. Did your mother buy you those clothes on her expenses?' Interestingly, the study also suggested that female MPs were choosing to leave Parliament sooner than their male colleagues, and that family was a major factor in this, with 43 per cent of women saying they wanted to spend more time with their partners and children, compared to 15 per cent of men.

I can't be bothered with this

Aside from the personal strains that Parliament places on MPs, there's also the apparent misery that being a backbencher can cause some formerly high-flying politicians. Remember that the culture of the Commons does not reward those who just want to scrutinise legislation. So if you lose your job in the government and return to the back benches, this isn't just a change of job. It's a demotion to a less high-profile and apparently less rewarding life. Why is it less rewarding? Well, if you've grown used to being praised for your performance in government, for your media appearances and your political games, then you will quickly feel hungry for attention that just doesn't come when you return to the back benches. Yes, you might manage to find success as a select committee chair, as Margaret Hodge, who served as a minister when Labour was in government, did under the Coalition. But beyond that, the rewards of the Commons are few and far between when it comes to your profile.

Many high-flying politicians just cannot take this fall from grace. At the 2015 election, a number of MPs who had left government in the 2014 reshuffle stood down. William Hague, Andrew Lansley, David Willetts and Greg Barker all left, despite being much younger than their colleague Ken Clarke, who stood again in both 2015 and 2017 and who continues to speak out as an independently minded backbencher who couldn't care less what the prime minister thinks of his contributions, other than that he expects her to listen to him. Those men could have provided a wealth of experience and expertise from their time in government departments, but instead they moved on. You can't blame them individually: they are all bright, and their experience makes them invaluable to many organisations inside and outside the political world. Why wouldn't they want to stretch themselves in another job, rather than retreat to the back benches?

Yet they were formally elected as legislators, not ministers, and Parliament feels the loss of such experienced people keenly. Without them there are fewer voices on the back benches to point out that policy A has been tried before, or that there is a very good reason for not introducing policy B. Ken Clarke may have proved a thorn in the flesh of his pro-Brexit colleagues, but he brought so much expertise to it that he required ministers to sharpen up their arguments, and sometimes even think again.

David Cameron had always made much of his desire to stay on as an MP once he was no longer prime minister. When I spent the day with him in his constituency in April 2016, we spoke at some length about his commitment to public service and his desire for there to be more experienced hands providing wisdom from the back benches. He mourned the number of former ministers who had departed at the 2015 election, and suggested that you could do other things alongside being an MP if you did fancy a little bit more income to make up the ministerial salary you had lost. 'John Major is a better model than Blair,' he told me, as we discussed what sort of ex-prime minister he wanted to be. John Major resigned as Conservative Party leader upon losing the 1997 general election, but did not leave the Commons until 2001 and did not embark on an ostentatious spree of earning a great deal of money as Tony Blair had done after stepping down as both prime minister and MP for Sedgefield.

Cameron's plan seemed so admirable; clearly he had been intending to leave on his own terms. Instead, just weeks later, he found that he had accidentally taken Britain out of the European Union in a referendum he had held merely to try to solve a problem with his own party. The *Sun* reported that the prime minister had told his inner circle, 'Why should I do all the hard s**t for someone else, just to hand it over to them on a plate?'[3]

It's a sentiment that most people might share when faced with something as colossal as the Brexit negotiations when they had never intended for there to be a Brexit in the first place. The difference with Cameron was that he had seemed so committed to doing the 'hard s**t' until he realised what it might entail. Theresa May, on the other hand, fatally wounded after the snap election she had chosen to call, and which had deprived her of her Commons majority, told her MPs, 'I got us into this mess and I'll get us out of it.' She promised the 1922 Committee, meeting on the first day the Commons returned after the election result, that 'I will serve you as long as you want me.' Quite a contrast to Cameron's desire to serve for as long as *he* wanted.

This desire extended to Cameron's life on the back benches. Having fretted about the number of ex-ministers who quit Westminster the previous year, the former prime minister then announced on 12 September 2016 that he was leaving the House of Commons. So much for his commitment to using his experience for the good of those who came after him. It was reported at the time that he was frustrated with the direction in which the Conservative Party was moving under Theresa May, and that he didn't want to become a distraction as he bristled with irritation on the back benches. But perhaps the reality of backbench life had hit him rather harder than he had anticipated. He and other former occupants of the great offices of state, including George Osborne, looked so much smaller as they strolled around Parliament with no entourage trailing behind them and no high-profile meetings to sweep into.

Perhaps they felt much smaller too, as Osborne proceeded to take on a succession of outside jobs, including the editorship of the *Evening Standard*, before concluding that he might not have a great deal of time to do any backbench duties at all, and quitting politics 'for now'.[4] That 'for now' suggested that he fancied a return to Parliament when the circumstances were more advantageous, and that backbench life was utter drudgery compared to being a newspaper editor. He was right: editing the *Evening Standard* is a much bigger deal than being an MP. But he and Cameron clearly didn't feel that the public service of a member of the legislature was worth as much as that of a member of the executive. Neither did Tony Blair, who still makes interventions in politics (not always the most helpful to the cause he supports), but from a distance while earning a great deal of money.

Life outside politics is clearly more satisfying for these former high-flyers, which is both a poor reflection of the current culture in the Commons, and a contributing factor to the Commons being a weaker force than it could be. The fact that politicians who are considered smart enough to take the highest office don't feel that the Commons holds anything for them afterwards says a great deal about the importance of legislating. It's not important, at least not to the people who are supposed to be scrutinising it, and that fundamental lack of seriousness about one of the most significant functions of an MP leads to the kind of disasters we'll encounter in the second half of this book.

Losing

At least Cameron and others who have held great offices of state know that once they decide to stop doing the 'hard s**t', they can earn some seriously hard cash. It's a rather different matter if you are a lowly MP who loses his or her seat.

While some might have greatness thrust upon them in an election, winning a seat by surprise and spending the next few weeks in a haze of euphoria, others encounter only misery on polling day. Candidates who fail to win a seat for the first time go through a fair bit of humiliation and disappointment. But an MP who loses their seat will have built up sufficient profile to make sure that everyone notices they have been made redundant, something most people like to keep rather private.

Of course, you live by the sword and die by the sword, and every MP – even those who are unaware they are about to lose until they see the way the votes are stacking up in the small hours of election night – concedes that it's hard to complain too much when they chose this line of work in the first place. Even 'safe seats' can stop being so. The electorate don't give you a job for life, so you shouldn't complain when they take it away.

Nevertheless, losing your seat isn't fun. It doesn't matter how philosophical an MP tries to be about it. They still have to stand, with the cameras focusing on their face, in a rather brutal line-up in a school gym, town hall or community centre, and hear it announced to everyone present that they have lost their job. Few of us would get through that unscathed. But it's worse than that: while you are losing your job in public, someone else is winning theirs. So as you stand, stony-faced, trying to look dignified about being made redundant, there are people cheering, jumping up and down and crying with joy. I spoke to one former Tory MP three days after he'd lost his seat in 2017. 'It was horrible,' he said, sounding flat. 'The thing is, you know you've got to go before the baying crowd. I just took the view that I was going to spend as little time as possible at the count, and say something dignified. I now need to make sure my staff are OK, that my office is wound up properly. It's the redundancies that are harder than me losing my job.'

Ben Howlett also lost his seat, as Conservative MP for Bath, in 2017. Though he had started the campaign knowing that it was going to be tricky to hold on, it was only when the exit poll came through at 10.30 p.m. on polling day that he knew he was done for.

'I was in the car on the phone to my mother, and she was saying, you know, you've done your best. The exit poll came through as we were speaking and I thought, "Oh, that's Bath gone." My heart sank at that moment. It was the realisation that it wasn't going to be pleasant. I had a real stomach-churning thought, that there was no point in writing two speeches [one for victory and one for losing].'

Afterwards, everyone went home, including Howlett's partner, who returned to London for work. And the ex-MP was left on his own. 'The thing that got to me in the end on the Sunday was the fact that I had had people all around me constantly, I was never alone. But that Sunday, everyone was at home. My team were back with their family, and there was a realisation that I was on my own. As someone who has had mental health issues in the past, to be on my own, literally broken, on my own with my thoughts, I just broke down.'

Lee Scott lost his seat in 2015. He wasn't expecting to, and neither was his party, so he spent time away from the constituency helping colleagues with their campaigns. When he was pounding the streets of Ilford North, he found himself up against vile anti-Semitism, including being called a 'dirty Jew', and receiving death threats. He attended some hustings with police protection. He and his wife still check under their cars every morning, more than two years after the campaign ended.

When it got to polling day, Scott knew he was in trouble in the seat, but still didn't think he would lose. Then it started to become clear that he was in a lot of trouble, the sort of trouble that involved office clearances and redundancy payments and concession speeches in front of a crowd cheering the person who just took your job off you. 'When it was obvious I was going to lose, I went to the leader of our group's office – and I don't drink – and I had vodka. And by the time we got to the result, I didn't know what day of the week it was. It didn't take much. I hugged him [Wes Streeting, the new Labour MP] and gave one of the funniest concession speeches you ever heard where, when he praised me, I said, "Well, if you'd bloody said that before the election, I would have got the lousy five hundred votes." And on the surface, I took it well. But I then went home and cried for three days. I was inconsolable.'

Scott said the loss felt 'like a bereavement'. 'I was depressed for ages. I was down for ages. I didn't show it, but I . . . I still get days when I'm down.' We were speaking shortly after the 2017 election, in which he stood again and lost, though he wasn't expecting to beat Streeting this time, and so was mentally prepared. Throughout our conversation, he insisted that he's not a man who cries very much. But losing his job made him cry a lot – just like plenty of people who lose their jobs without the full glare of the public eye on them. The campaign itself made him cry. 'It's going to sound like I cry a lot. I don't. I cried when my daughter was born; I cried when my mother died. I don't cry a lot. And I was in tears because of everything that had happened that day. People had said they wanted to kill me and I was a dirty Jew. I couldn't actually comprehend why my religion made any semblance of difference to anything. And I said to my wife, "I don't understand why I do it. What do I need this in my life for?" Now, of course, it's been taken away from me and I know why I do it: because I wanted to do it. It was my life. But yes, it was devastating. It still does affect us.'

A 2006 study of former MPs described emotions ranging from shock, anger and bereavement to failure and exhaustion on losing their seats. Two former MPs said the grieving process lasted between four and six years, and a quarter of those surveyed said they were still grieving.[5]

The next public humiliation is returning to Westminster to clear out the Commons office. They're generally easily recognisable, the ex-MPs who come back to do this. They move fast through the corridors of the Palace, and keep their heads down. Some have planned ahead: Nick de Bois lost his Enfield North seat to Labour in 2015, and had already emptied his office before the election campaign started. 'I didn't want to go in,' he says. '[The Conservatives had] just won a majority and I'd lost and it was a bit like they were having a party and I'd be the party pooper. I knew that if I went in there, they'd be, oh, sorry, mate.'

It's not just removing your books, family photos and the odd fold-up bed (one MP was very anxious about how to get this out of his office without anyone seeing). It's also making your staff redundant as a result of you losing. Every MP who has lost feels guilty about this. One felt so bad for his former employees that he secretly negotiated for IPSA to use his own pay-off as part of a bigger redundancy package for them. He has never told them this.

MPs get a loss-of-office payment, which has been cut down significantly in recent years. At the 2015 general election, MPs who lost their seats could receive up to £33,000 tax-free. As part of its overhaul of MPs' pay, IPSA decided to cut these payments so that losing MPs were entitled to double the statutory redundancy allowance, which takes into account years of service, age and so on. MPs had to have been in place for two years in order to qualify. So in 2017, an MP who had spent over a decade in the House of Commons before losing at the general election might have got around £17,000. An MP who had only joined Parliament at the previous election was entitled to around £3,000. IPSA will also pay the rent on an MP's London property for two months after the election while they sort themselves out.

Is this reasonable? A number of Conservative MPs who lost their seats in the snap election of 2017 didn't think so, though they were as annoyed with Theresa May for calling the vote as they were with the way the remuneration system was set up. Stewart Jackson, ousted after 12 years as the Tory MP for Peterborough, pointed out that the prime minister's chiefs of staff, Nick Timothy and Fiona Hill, who resigned as scapegoats for the election, were entitled to around £35,000 each as part of their government pay-off, even though they'd only worked in Downing Street for less than a year, which was far more than he would get under the IPSA rules.

You might argue that the redundancy packages are fair enough, given that MPs uproot their families to serve their constituents, and then face enormous upheaval again if they lose. But on the other hand, you might feel that the profile of having been a Member of Parliament is enough to ensure that the upheaval isn't really as terrible as it is for a steelworker in Redcar, for instance, who faces not only redundancy but also the prospect of no work suited to their skills in the whole of the region. Ex-MPs are probably going to be comparatively OK.

But are they? Howlett and de Bois were both fine, either getting a new private sector job that they loved quickly, or returning to their existing career. 'There's one huge ingredient that I had that not everyone else has, which is that I had an income. I wasn't forced to find a job,' says the former Enfield MP. But 10 per cent of those who lost in 2010 were still looking for work a year later.

It's easier for MPs who've expected to lose for a while, as they can spend a fair bit of time preparing their CVs. There was a stage in the 2015 parliament when every centrist Labour MP I spoke to seemed to be doing some kind of training course or other to prepare for losing their seat, or even leaving Parliament early because they expected their party to collapse at the next election. Their

Conservative colleagues were so worried about them that they sent kind messages of support as the 2017 campaign began. But in the end, it turned out that it was the Tory MPs who should have been brushing up on their employability. Theresa May felt so guilty about the shock losses that she promised to help former members with their finances, and the party paid for careers advice for MPs too. Labour MPs who lost in 2015 were offered nothing.

It's not just the financial adjustment, though. The mental health services that Parliament offers are no longer available to those who lose, meaning they have to fend for themselves like the rest of the population, who struggle to access psychiatrists and counsellors in a timely fashion. The parties have only recently started to cotton on to the fact that while there are many long-term advantages to not being an MP, losing your seat can be pretty traumatic. The personal support offered to losing Conservative MPs by their party in 2017 was surely as valuable as any redundancy package. Don't forget that many politicians are locked into a cycle of taking each vote as a verdict on whether they are any good as a person. Even the more philosophical types say 'I thought I'd done a good job', as though the electorate had decided that they hadn't, rather than that they just wanted a different party in government.

One Labour MP, defeated in 2005, told the authors of a 2007 study that he felt 'completely worthless. I told people that I didn't enjoy anything or look forward to anything.' Mental health problems were prevalent then, too, with 18 per cent of those surveyed mentioning mental issues as a result of their loss – and it wasn't just the MPs themselves. One said: 'My wife nearly died from an internal problem brought on by the trauma.'[6]

If you come from a political family, your whole life will be turned upside down by your spouse's or parent's job. You may have worked for that MP, campaigned for them, and certainly seen the highs and crashing lows of politics. Even if you'd like to see more of that person at home, the trauma of watching someone you love go through the public redundancy process is horrific – just as it is for anyone who has watched a family member crushed by losing their job.

Others have been so sucked into the Westminster Bubble for so long that the new world around them looks very daunting indeed. And rather lonely: one MP who lost in 2015 was discussing with some friends how exhausted and depressed he was. One of them suggested that going abroad for a well-deserved holiday might help. But the ex-MP replied dolefully, 'I can't. I don't have anyone to go with. All my friends are still in Parliament.'

Some try to float along as close to the Bubble as they can. Many of the happier ex-MPs deride their colleagues who do this. One former Labour MP believes 'There's something sad about the ex-MP lobbyist or freelancer who hangs around Portcullis House. There's a few who just never find anything else. I still try to avoid it other than occasionally, for that reason.' A staffer to an MP who lost in 2015 noticed that his former boss had rented an office in the constituency. 'I went to find out what he was doing there,' he says. 'All it seemed to be was him doing correspondence. Which he didn't need to do. Because he wasn't an MP any more.' The MP was hoping to return at the next election, which at the time he had assumed would be 2020, thanks to the Fixed Term Parliaments Act. He was in for the long haul with his correspondence, though, as he failed to regain the constituency in the 2017 snap election.

As with those who leave by choice, many losing MPs take with them a wealth of experience that Parliament could really do with. Their replacements will likely be as green and lost as those we encountered in Chapter 2. Some outgoing MPs offer the winning candidate any help they can give as they settle in, but others want nothing to do with the person who made them unemployed. Some make the offer but find they just can't bear to sit down and discuss the constituency they once served with the person who has taken over from them. If an MP is chucked out at an election, clearly the voters don't want their experience in the Commons. But Parliament and the parties could still try, as part of a stronger support package for losing MPs, to glean tips and advice to pass onto the new bunch so that the Commons isn't stuck in a cycle of new MPs taking a few years to learn the same lessons as their predecessors.

What happens next?

What do the MPs who decide to escape the Bubble – or who are unceremoniously ejected from it – end up doing? A surprising number take a long time to find work. Career changes are difficult for everyone, but MPs have profile, contacts and skills bursting out of their ears. Or at least that's what most disgruntled backbenchers will tell anyone who'll listen. So many MPs have assured me over the years that they could be earning at least twice as much outside the Commons that I wonder why they stay at all. But it turns out that while ex-ministers seem to have no problem moving on to smart, well-paid private sector jobs, it's not so easy for backbenchers to land something so lucrative.

Many MPs do more than one thing. My analysis of those who lost their seats in 2015 and 2010 shows that the majority kept at least one foot in the political world. The 2015 losers were most likely to go into public affairs or consultancy (17 instances), stand again in the 2017 snap election (15 ex-MPs did this), move to local or regional politics (11), or become a chief executive or board member of an organisation (8). There were six instances of former MPs going to work in sectors for which they had held ministerial or shadow ministerial responsibility, five returned to the law at least part-time, four became special advisers or kept up advisory positions in national politics, four took up work as 'talking heads' on TV and radio or as after-dinner speakers (such as Ed Balls), three went into single-issue lobbying, and three became peers.

Max Wiltshire is a recruitment consultant specialising in communications, and has spoken to a fair few ex-MPs in his time. He doesn't seem to have emerged with a particularly good impression of them. 'MPs have an odd ratio of self-esteem to actual ability,' he says tactfully. 'They have a genuine and sincere belief that they are cutting-edge rainmaking people. The truth is, most of them are just people who have managed to convince their association to make them candidates.' In 2015, he found a number of former MPs looking for work. 'Initially I was quite excited. I thought, these are actual parliamentarians, they've sat on the green benches. Surely they are going to be the perfect people to engage with government and Whitehall. But when I met them, all they'd done was have a private office function which allowed them to bang their own personal drums on a small policy issue. They tended to have done that via a very process-heavy and frankly pretty ineffectual method such as private members' bills, early day motions.' These backbenchers hadn't distinguished themselves in Parliament, and they hadn't served on the front benches of their parties either.

So Wiltshire had to have some 'pretty frank conversations' about what was possible for them in terms of a career in communications. This didn't go down very well. 'I got some pretty pissy feedback from a couple of them,' he says. But he was right: none of the MPs he met went on to do anything in his sector, and only one got a 'reasonable job earning about the same as he would have done as an MP'. Many of them, he suspects, had looked at friends who had worked as special advisers and imagined that their own experience in Parliament would have the same attraction to employers as someone who had been closely involved in running a government department. But if all you have to your name is an exemplary but dull record of speaking in debates, then there is little you can offer the world outside Westminster (some might wonder what you offered Westminster itself). Wiltshire observes that 'The spads [special advisers] that I've worked with have been without exception very impressive and have all gone on to prestigious jobs in the sector. There is a frustration that they express about the rather less impressive backbenchers with whom they have to engage.'

So if the quality of backbenchers emerging from Parliament is pretty poor, doesn't that suggest that the quality of person going in isn't tip-top either? Parliament can't deskill someone so much that they become unattractive to the outside world purely by sitting on the green benches for a few years.

You could argue that an MP's employability outside Westminster is irrelevant to whether Parliament itself works. Someone might be so well suited to being a legislator that other jobs would require a new skill set. Perhaps. But then again, isn't it useful to have people in Parliament who are well suited enough to the outside world that they might notice when a law that affects that outside world is badly drafted? MPs legislate for everyone else, not for themselves.

One group of people who benefit enormously from an MP losing his or her seat is their family, who have often seen far less of their spouse or parent than they'd like. Many ex-MPs confess that when they lost their seat, they kept their marriage. Others who chose to stand down did so because they felt it was, in one ex-MP's words, 'time for my family to have stuff, rather than me'. Plaid Cymru MP Elfyn Llwyd, who stepped down in 2015, said that though his wife had always supported him in politics, she suddenly turned around to him and said, 'Would you consider not standing next time?'[7] Liberal Democrat MP David Heath reached an agreement with his wife in 2010 that he would serve just one more term, after she reached the end of her tether with the strains that the job was putting on family life.

But many ex-MPs still ache for Westminster. Lee Scott says he doesn't want to go back, but it's obvious how much he yearns for the Commons. 'I loved every day of it and I still miss it,' he says, managing to smile and look incredibly sad at the same time. 'I'm not going to pretend that I don't miss being an MP. I miss making a difference, actually being able to do something.' More than half (53 per cent) of those surveyed in 2007 missed being at the centre of things, and 51 per cent also said they missed being able to influence events.[8] Suddenly, those MP letterheads and the ability to say whatever you want in the Commons (so long as you don't care about the consequences for your potential career in the executive) seem far more valuable than when you were actually there, muttering darkly about no one taking you seriously and the continuing mouse infestation.

Part II

WHY WE GET THE WRONG POLICIES

CHAPTER 9

THEY JUST DON'T GET IT

So do we really get the wrong politicians, or the wrong culture in Parliament? And does it matter anyway? After all, we have seen how unpleasant working as an MP can be, so if a strange bunch of people end up going into that line of work, at least the rest of us are spared the discomfort. As with undertakers, someone's got to do it, but it's fair enough if not everyone wants to.

The problem is that even the personal problems detailed earlier can have an impact on the way Parliament functions. And as its primary function is supposed to be to ensure that the government of the day is passing laws fit for public consumption, even a small spanner in the works can have very serious consequences. The first half of this book looked at the life cycle of a politician, from the initial thought about running to the day they finally wheel that folding bed out of their Commons office and start a new life. That life cycle is characterised by dysfunction, from the selection process that decides who our potential MPs will be, to the way MPs often don't scrutinise laws at all. This second half will show how this dysfunction doesn't just give us the wrong politicians, but the wrong laws too. We will take a grisly tour of the real and serious mistakes made by governments of all hues in recent political history, and find out why those mistakes seem to recur so often.

The principal reason why politicians keep making the same mistakes is not because individually they are fools, but because the system at large is in a tremendous mess. It starts with the selection process, which as we saw in Chapter 1 invariably means Parliament is still dominated by middle-aged white men who have earned a fair bit of money or had at least one foot in the political door for many years. There is nothing intrinsically wrong with a middle-aged white man, nor with someone who has a good lump of savings to spend on being a candidate or who has worked as a special adviser before being elected. It's just that a homogenous group can struggle to have a decent perspective not just on life, but on the impact of the policies its members are working on. The 'out of touch' accusation can often be far wide of the mark, given the number of people politicians *are* in touch with, both while campaigning and in their regular constituency work. But the simple truth is that if you all have similar instincts as a result of your background, you may not spot the consequences of a policy until it ambushes you in your constituency surgery as a crisis.

Out of touch

A homogenous group lacks insight, and this lack of insight means that even superbly bright types can cook up extraordinarily poor policies. This book has shown that Westminster is a profoundly odd world that attracts more than its fair share of people who, if not officially weird, are at least from one particular social group, who then socialise with that same particular group, and who find it easy to think that the world is divided merely into the people who turn up in their constituency surgeries in a crisis, and everyone else who is doing just fine. Shut them in a room with some similarly highly educated civil servants, and policy debate becomes about the academic beauty of an idea rather than its practical implications.

The poll tax is one famous example from history, cooked up by a homogenous group of people in secret, and examined by another homogenous group of people before turning into one of the greatest policy disasters, contributing to the downfall of a prime minister but not, it seems, teaching Westminster many lessons about how not to mess up. The 'community charge', as it was officially known, was drawn up in 1984–5 and dropped in 1991, and yet politicians have continued to fall into the very same trap that Margaret Thatcher's government went headlong into. The reason for this is that the system hasn't changed, and while the profile of MPs has become a little more diverse, Westminster and Parliament still contain too many people who wouldn't have recognised the practical implications of trying to collect the poll tax in Brixton, let alone the problems with the policies they find themselves looking at today.

We have seen how difficult it is for someone who is still 'working class' to make it into Parliament today. Yes, they might have been born in Brixton, but to be able to afford to become a politician, most people from low-income backgrounds have to end up working in Westminster or earning a good wage in a professional job first. This means that even those who would like to call themselves working-class MPs may have lost touch with their roots by the time they first sit on the green benches. The more similar the perspectives of the MPs who turn up in Westminster, the less likely they will be to spot a problem before it hits the public.

George Osborne, for instance, was a canny Chancellor of the Exchequer, and far cannier than those involved in the poll tax in that he didn't try to collect the taxes that caused him the most grief in his tenure as Chancellor. He dropped them before he faced the wrath of the public, but not before he had embarrassed himself in front of Parliament. What let him down was his failure to balance his own blind spots by consulting those with a different perspective, something he did repeatedly.

In 2012, he announced a Budget which he claimed would ensure that 'together the British people will share in the effort and share the rewards'.[1] One of the ways he would reward the people would be by simplifying the tax code, which in an academic sense was a jolly good plan. The tax code in the United Kingdom is fiendishly complicated. It is longer than the Bible, and has more loopholes in it than a Red Arrows display, something clever accountants can exploit on behalf of their wealthy clients to drive their tax bills down. Simplifying it made sense.

But there is a vast gulf between something making sense on the pages of a Whitehall memo and it making sense in the pages of a newspaper. Sometimes it takes a policy to be implemented before its idiocy is revealed. The 2012 Budget, though, fell apart within a few minutes.

Shortly after Osborne had finished his Budget speech with a triumphant flourish, lobby journalists filed out of their gallery overlooking the Commons into a 'huddle', which is quite simply a crowd of journalists around a minister's adviser, who explains the fine detail of an announcement and takes questions. In that post-Budget huddle, it became clear that the slogan that David Cameron and George Osborne had trumpeted – 'We're all in this together' – wasn't quite true in practice. Simplifying the tax code actually involved a number of changes that would either seriously hamper working-class voters, or at least cheese them off on a fairly regular basis.

In fact, the Budget seemed to have been written to annoy the readers of one newspaper in particular: the *Sun*. And the *Sun* isn't a newspaper with a tiny circulation or a gentle way of putting things.

There was a simplification to the tax on hot takeaway food that meant food such as Cornish pasties and sausage rolls that were sold hot would receive the same 20 per cent VAT levy as food cooked in a restaurant, thus clobbering people who enjoyed a hot snack from Greggs. It seemed a small tweak, but it quickly became known as the 'pasty tax'. The *Sun* sent a model dressed up as Marie Antoinette to stand outside the Treasury delivering pasties. Desperate to show that they were more in touch with working people than the Conservative-led Coalition government, Labour leader Ed Miliband, his Shadow Chancellor Ed Balls and Shadow Chief Secretary to the Treasury Rachel Reeves went to Greggs (with a photographer) to buy delicious pasties. They were no less members of the political class than Osborne, but they wanted to suggest that they knew the joy of a sausage roll as much as the next working man.

Sun readers couldn't even escape when they fancied a holiday, as Osborne had also levied a 20 per cent tax on static caravans. And then there was the 'granny tax'. Introducing this to the Commons, the Chancellor said: 'So over time we will simplify the tax system for pensioners by doing away with the complexity of the additional age-related allowances for anyone reaching the age of 65 on or after 6 April 2013 and I will freeze the cash value of the allowance for existing pensioners until it aligns with the personal allowance. This will protect the existing level of allowance pensioners have, while introducing a single personal allowance for all. It is a major simplification. It saves money. And no pensioner will lose in cash terms.'[2]

The problem is that the change, which threatened up to five million older voters (and older voters have a tendency to go to the polls in large and angry numbers), turned out to leave many pensioners worse off. Ros Altmann, the director general of Saga, described the measure as an 'outrageous assault' and 'an enormous stealth tax for older people'.[3]

All these measures, along with a 'charity tax' and a 'church roof tax', were eventually dropped when Osborne realised the scale of opposition and ridicule he was facing. The policies and the subsequent U-turns they prompted led to this Budget being dubbed the 'Omnishambles Budget', and was probably a significant factor in the Chancellor getting booed by a stadium of cheery spectators at the Paralympics later that year. (Osborne subsequently overhauled his image in order to deal with his unpopularity as Chancellor, and future economic statements were evaluated according to whether they were palatable for the *Sun*'s readership.) As he dropped the policies, he grudgingly gave the *Sun* a quote, saying, 'I've listened to *Sun* readers.'[4] He must have wished that he'd started by doing that, rather than listening to civil servants. Indeed, shortly after the Budget row blew up, former Treasury aide and spin doctor for Gordon Brown Damian McBride claimed that many of the measures had been suggested as 'fast ones' by civil servants to previous ministers when Labour was in government, but unlike Osborne, those ministers had spotted the obvious political problems with them.

Osborne is an incredibly bright man. He is one of those people who cannot hide their intellectual curiosity, with an excited grin breaking over his face whenever he comes across a historical artefact. He is also a warm, empathetic person in private, able to remember not only colleagues' names, but the names of their wives and any personal problems they are struggling with (David Cameron was notoriously hopeless at this). And while this book has gone to strenuous efforts not to berate politicians for their accidents of birth, it is a fact that Osborne's own accident of birth is a very fortunate one. He is the heir to a baronetcy who was educated at St Paul's, one of London's top day schools, before studying modern history at Oxford. Critics of politicians mistakenly claim that it is their privileged backgrounds that make them flawed people who are unable to improve the lives of vulnerable or 'ordinary' people. This is not so: Margaret Thatcher famously 'lived above the shop' but managed to introduce the disastrous poll tax. William Wilberforce was the son of a wealthy merchant yet campaigned to end the slave trade.

What Osborne failed to do – and what those who drew up the poll tax failed to do – was to address the weaknesses of his personal perspective by consulting those who lived differently. A *Sun* reader could have told him very quickly that taxing pasties and caravans might not be the friendliest political move. Some Tory backbenchers from more humble backgrounds could also have pointed this out, but they weren't admitted to the tight clique around Osborne and Cameron, which was largely drawn from their school and university circles. The Tory leadership had also lost someone who could have told them how *Sun* readers would react to things: former *Sun* editor Andy Coulson, who had already resigned over the phone hacking scandal. Couple that with the socio-economic background of the civil service, and you've got your latest policy failure plastered all over the front pages of the tabloids.

Now, everyone makes mistakes, but clever people don't make the same mistake twice. In May 2015, Osborne managed to stumble once again on a measure that made him appear out of touch. In his post-election Budget, the Chancellor announced cuts to working tax credits that turned out to hit the very 'strivers' he and David Cameron claimed they stood for.

By this point, Osborne had garnered a reputation for laying elephant traps for the opposition parties, briefing sympathetic journalists about how clever his traps were, then falling into them himself. The tax credit trap was a symptom of his 'cultural disconnect'⁵ in two ways: the first was that he hadn't thought through how much hardship a cut of this size could cause. The second was that he was sufficiently disconnected from the life of a person who needed working tax credits to think of the cut not in terms of how much pain it would cause but in terms of the political game he was playing. He hadn't made the same mistake again – this was a benefit cut, rather than a tax change – but it was the same old problem. Eventually there would be another U-turn.

Out of sight

Another effect of politicians largely hailing from one social group can be that they fail to see the urgency in addressing glaring problems afflicting a different section of society. Once again, MPs are not deaf to social problems, even if they represent some of the richest constituencies in the country, because they encounter people in crisis every week in their surgeries. But collectively they can fail to create enough of a political head of steam for those problems to have a chance of being solved. The problems can feel sufficiently out of sight of Westminster for its inhabitants to never quite manage to get round to dealing with them.

The media plays a part in this too. It is no coincidence that there was a bigger row over the loss of child benefit for higher earners than over any of the examples cited below – save the Grenfell disaster, which only got its row once the residents of that west London tower block had burned to death. Political journalists tend to look like the politicians they follow. Many of them studied together at the top universities and kept in touch until they ended up in Parliament together. They can whip one another up into a frenzy about the interests of their own social group, including the fact that that social group was about to lose its child benefit payments. Other crises felt far less personal for everyone in the Westminster Bubble.

Take temporary accommodation. This is used by councils for housing families who have become homeless, including women who have fled domestic violence. It isn't quite as 'temporary' as it sounds, with families spending months in B&B rooms that are so poor quality that no one would voluntarily pay to stay in them. Some are insecure, and women lie awake at night terrified that either the man who abused them or someone who has noticed their vulnerability will break in. Others have mouse droppings on the floor and mould on the walls.

By the end of 2017, around 128,000 children were living in temporary accommodation in Britain, according to housing charity Shelter, with no space to play or do their homework. Yet it is rarely mentioned in Westminster. Labour MP Siobhain McDonagh is an honourable exception: she has used a number of her slots at Prime Minister's Questions to complain about families being housed in totally unsuitable converted office blocks in her Mitcham and Morden constituency. But her complaints are rarely heard beyond PMQs: temporary accommodation has never become a huge political row despite its terrible impact on people's health. It is an out-of-sight crisis involving people with quiet voices leading lives astonishingly different to those of the politicians who speak on their behalf. Only a handful of MPs will know people who have lived in temporary accommodation. They may see these people weeping in their surgeries, but they know there isn't sufficient political interest for the government to bother looking into why councils are using such unpleasant properties to house the poor and the vulnerable.

Similarly, the underrepresentation of women in Westminster, in both the Commons Chamber and its press gallery, has led to a strange indifference about matters of basic dignity. It cannot be a coincidence that only in 2018, when Parliament was finally a third female, did ministers feel they could start talking about the fact that women in police custody are not being given adequate sanitary protection. These women find themselves bleeding through their clothes onto the seats of prison vans, having been handed the sort of wafer-thin sanitary towel given to pubescent teens, or expected to wear a tampon for more than eight hours (which also carries a health risk). Most women have grown up with the fear of their period appearing on the outside of their clothes, and have a visceral reaction to anyone, whether innocent until proven guilty or convicted and on their way to prison, having to stuff their underwear with toilet roll so that they might avoid that indignity. Men are largely unaware – and largely wish to remain so – of the general inconvenience of having a monthly period, of the expense of the sanitary products, and of the fact that most women need more than just that thin sanitary towel to get them through even a couple of hours of bleeding.

Katie Kempen, a custody campaigner who led a national campaign on this issue, told me: 'It took a women-led campaign to make the change. It wasn't enough to tell the men, as they didn't think it was that big a deal.' She was joined in her campaigning by female MPs including Jess Phillips, who has managed to build a high profile in the media that she uses to raise awareness of women's issues. She told the Chamber shortly after joining that 'every man sitting in this House is now here because, at some point, his mother had a period'.[6] Most of the men sitting there looked as though they hadn't wanted to think in those terms. But failing to think in those terms has meant that an out-of-sight problem has existed for years.

Domestic violence has also moved up the political agenda in recent years, and again it cannot be a coincidence that this happened as the number of women in Parliament was rising and a female Home Secretary (Theresa May) was calling the shots. As women are disproportionately the victims of domestic abuse and domestic homicide, this issue would simply not have figured for many of the men sitting in the Chamber. Perhaps this is why there has been so little outcry over regular and continuing closures of safe and specialist refuges for women fleeing abuse. But perhaps it is also because domestic violence is a crime that takes place behind closed doors. It can be out of sight for all politicians, even those whose own family members and friends are victims of abuse. Yet those victims tend to have somewhere to flee to. Women who need refuges will have been isolated from their friends and families, their money stolen and their access to work blocked. They have nowhere else to go – something that is difficult for politicians, who operate daily within an intense social network, to imagine.

The culture of sexism that I described in Chapter 6 has a lot to answer for when it comes to Parliament's ability to forget about women. If their complaints are belittled as a bit fussy and over the top, and their views are taken less seriously by even a small section of the Westminster population, then it is no wonder that it takes so long to introduce policies protecting their basic dignity. Women are still treated as a niche section of the population, rather than a majority group with the same diversity of views and interests as men. David Cameron was frequently advised to ask his wife Samantha for advice on what female voters wanted, as though she might be able to tap into an invisible 'lady network' and produce the Women's

View on Palestine. Yet campaigners struggle to get a hearing for their pleas about what women actually need.

Out of mind

The Grenfell Tower disaster of 14 June 2017 is by far the worst example of a problem seeming out of sight and staying out of mind. The residents of the London block had been in touch with their MP, Victoria Borwick, for years about their battles with their landlord over whether their homes were safe. She took up their fight and helped them communicate with the Tenant Management Organisation (TMO) and the council. Their complaints turned out to be part of a national scandal over fire safety standards that threatened many people in low-income housing across the UK. And yet we only found out about this scandal once families had burned to death that terrible June night.

To understand how much the failure of the political system lies behind the Grenfell disaster, we need to travel back. A fire breaks out at a tower block in London. Residents burn to death in their own homes, having been told by firefighters to stay inside and wait for help. The physical scars of the burnt-out building are there every day as the community mourns and grows steadily angrier with those in power whose mistakes may have led to the blaze spreading. This wasn't Grenfell, but the fatal fire at Lakanal House, which took place on 3 July 2009. At the time, it was the worst tower block fire in history, with six people, including three young children, losing their lives. The fire brigade had assumed the fire safety measures in Lakanal House would mean it was less risky for them not to move through the building. But those measures were inadequate: the landlord, Southwark Council, pleaded guilty to four counts of breaking fire safety regulations.

'Never again,' declared trade magazine *Inside Housing* as it launched its safety campaign for social housing in 2009.[7] Except it did happen again, and not without warning. The charred Grenfell Tower stood like a terrible black punctuation mark to what turned out to be years of complaints from its occupants.

Grenfell residents had been agitated for years about the absence of sprinklers in the 24-storey block, but their landlord, Kensington and Chelsea Council, hadn't fitted them. Even though the coroner at the Lakanal inquest had recommended them, and even though a coroner at the inquest of two firefighters killed in another tower block fire in Southampton had also made a rule 43 report – an alert issued in an attempt to make something examined at an inquest a 'never again' event – there was still no requirement from the government to comply.

Eric Pickles, then the Communities and Local Government Secretary, had replied to the Lakanal coroner in 2013, saying his department was giving councils funding to develop guidance on fire safety. 'I consider that it addresses sufficiently those issues that have been highlighted in your rule 43 reports,' he wrote.[8] The following year, housing minister Brandon Lewis told MPs that 'it is the responsibility of the fire industry, rather than the government, to market fire sprinkler systems effectively and to encourage their wider installation' and that 'the cost of fitting a fire sprinkler system may affect house building – something we want to encourage – so we must wait to see what impact that regulation [requiring sprinklers to be fitted] has'.[9] The BBC's *Panorama* found that the All-Party Parliamentary Group [APPG] on Fire Safety had written to communities minister Stephen Williams in 2014 and asked for the guidance to be updated sooner than planned, but he replied saying, 'I have neither seen nor heard anything that would suggest that consideration of these specific potential changes is urgent and I am not willing to disrupt the work of this department by asking that these matters are brought forward.'[10] Williams would later claim that the letter was written by a civil servant rather than himself.[11] By 2017, the review of fire regulations still hadn't been implemented, and a meeting between the APPG on Fire Safety and housing minister Gavin Barwell was postponed due to the snap election.

Fire experts argued in the aftermath of the Grenfell disaster that sprinklers could have saved lives, and maybe even stopped the fire in the room where it had broken out.[12] But they couldn't have stopped the fire spreading, because it spread on the outside of the building at an alarming pace. Grenfell had been refurbished at a cost of £8.7 million just a year before, and that work included smart new cladding being fitted to the exterior of the building, partly to make it more energy efficient and partly to spruce it up. Yet that smart new cladding went up like a tinder box.

The government ordered urgent testing of the cladding on other tower blocks. Hundreds failed, terrifying residents across the UK who feared they might be stuck in the next Grenfell.

How had a council managed to fit combustible cladding on a tower block? Why had residents' warnings about sprinklers and general fire safety measures in the tower not been acted upon? The public inquiry and police investigations into what happened at Grenfell will last beyond the publication of this book. But there are clearly lessons that politicians can learn now.

The first is that the residents were either ignored or powerless. Their blog, Grenfell Action Group, set up in 2012, throbbed with frustration and a sense that the powers-that-be were either ignoring them or seeking to do them over. In the hours after the fire, one campaigner wrote: 'We also share the sense of anger and injustice that has troubled this community for years. That is why we started this blog and that is why we will continue as we started, speaking truth to power whether or not they choose to listen.' They added: 'ALL OUR WARNINGS FELL ON DEAF EARS and we predicted that a catastrophe like this was inevitable and just a matter of time.'[13]

Even though the residents' MP in the run-up to the fire, Victoria Borwick, was sympathetic and accompanied them to meetings with the tenant management organisation, it seemed there was little she could do. Cast your mind back to Chapter 3, when her neighbouring MP Karen Buck met a woman living in unsuitable social housing. Buck was sympathetic but honest, telling the woman that while she would do everything she could to help, not much was likely to change. In their Westminster roles, MPs have less power than visitors to their surgery might hope. Unless an issue has political potency, it is very difficult to get ministers to listen. And because this was an issue that affected people so different to the political class, who didn't struggle with councils and tenant management organisations over basic fire safety measures, few in Westminster felt the same sense of panicked urgency that the Grenfell residents did.

What's more, MPs had little power to scrutinise or to try to change the guidance that led to the cladding being fitted to the tower in the first place. Government regulations state that materials used in high-rise buildings must be of 'limited combustibility', but since buildings are inspected by organisations in the building sector rather than officials to check they meet these requirements, developers can use substandard materials and still be signed off as safe. The BBC's Chris Cook looked into the regime shortly after the Grenfell fire and found that 'The net effect of the sector bodies' guidance is to set weaker standards than the government's rulebook.'

This included deeming cladding to be of 'limited combustibility' using 'desktop tests' based on previous tests of cladding in different scenarios. Cook explained: 'There are problems with all of this: it has allowed substandard material through. It is a deeply opaque process. We do not know when desktop studies get used. We do not know who writes these desktop studies. They are not lodged anywhere so that people living in these buildings can go and check on them.'[14]

The vetting process for building regulations makes the legislative process appear comparatively transparent and smooth. And yet it is about fire safety, not the colour of the cladding or the interior decor. Residents couldn't get to the bottom of it, and MPs didn't know what was going on because external organisations such as the Building Control Alliance and the National House Building Council, who were running the show, were not required to lay anything before Parliament, not even so much as the oblique sentence on the Order Paper that a statutory instrument gets.

Naturally, the grieving relatives of those killed or missing in the Grenfell disaster, and those who escaped the blaze, grew steadily more furious with the response of the local council and the government in the days after the catastrophe. It was partly the botched response of Kensington and Chelsea Council, and partly the refusal to update the death toll, when so many people on the ground claimed it was much higher. But there was also a growing feeling – expressed on the posters that appeared all over the borough alongside flyers pleading for news of those missing – that politicians hadn't really cared enough about them to begin with. Broadcasters spoke knowingly of a 'tale of two cities', for Grenfell was situated in one of the most expensive boroughs in the UK. Celebrities rushed to help their neighbours in the aftermath of the attack, but some commentators claimed that before then, the local communities were barely aware of one another.

Londoners are notoriously bad at noticing each other, even when sharing millimetres of space on the Underground. But politicians are supposed to notice problems. Would ministers really have been so complacent about updating building regulations and inspection regimes if they themselves had lived in properties like the Grenfell Tower? Did even the MPs helping those angry residents in the years before the fire see the people who came to their surgeries as people apart, people in crisis who weren't quite the same as the rest of the world? Perhaps they raised these points with ministers, but the civil servants advising them on the detail also couldn't quite see the problem, or at least they could see the problem but felt they had more important things to deal with. The reality of the residents' lives felt out of sight from Westminster.

The Grenfell residents had been banging their head against the wall of officialdom for years. Would their long blog posts and complaints to the council have been ignored for so long, all the way to a disaster, had they been more like the people they were complaining to in terms of background – or, more powerfully, had the people they were complaining to been more like them? This book started by observing the social backgrounds of MPs. Few spent their childhoods in council tower blocks. Fewer still would have been living in them in the years before joining the Commons. Many of them, however, have been or still are small-scale landlords, very aware of the burdens of regulation on small businesses. The response of Coalition ministers to requests for tougher fire regulations was that they could jeopardise house building. Too much 'red tape' does indeed unnecessarily stifle new development, but the operative word in that clause is 'unnecessarily'. This wasn't unnecessary stuff about how far you could expect residents to drag their own wheelie bins, but about saving lives if a fire broke out. Of course developers need an incentive to build, but that cannot come at the cost of basic safety.

And this is why the culture and make-up of Parliament matters. The following two chapters will show that even a properly representative Parliament will still make colossal mistakes, but the stories above are some of the most desperate in this book. And we will continue to read desperate stories if we continue to think it acceptable that someone should spend tens of thousands of pounds to be able to have a shot at being an MP. We will continue to read desperate stories if all those who even think about becoming MPs are drawn from a narrow social group and tend to be men. A representative parliament isn't just something to boast about. It could also save lives.

CHAPTER 10

ALL THINGS TO ALL MEN

MPs are so desperate to counter accusations that they are out of touch that they can end up creating another problem for themselves and the policies they work on. Most politicians want to do the right thing. But so do most of us, and we can all end up stumbling. Politicians would like to answer the big problems facing our society, but they can find that the painful uproar associated with building a new runway or telling people just how much they'll need to spend if they're unlucky enough to suffer from dementia makes realising that aspiration very difficult indeed. Better to try to get someone else to do it, whether an unelected boffin who doesn't have to face the furious voters at some point, or even better, the next generation of politicians, who will have to deal with an even more acute problem.

MPs have to try to be both policy fixers and political winners. The two don't always mix very well. On top of that, they're busy people. Increasingly so. They are strung out between many competing demands, particularly between the cases flooding their constituency surgeries and the need to read legislation before voting on it. They need to be all things to all aspects of their job, and as the old saying goes, one man cannot serve two masters. They end up being too frightened of the political consequences to make policy decisions, and too frightened of the personal consequences to turn away work generated in their constituency in favour of being scrutineers.

When MPs try to be all things to all men, they can end up letting down the most important people – those affected by the government's policies. They avoid making decisions that, while necessary and urgent, will upset voters. They take decisions that they don't need to in order to appear to be doing something about a problem that might not even exist. And they will do anything they can to get someone else who doesn't have to face those pesky elections to make a decision on their behalf.

Taking the politics out

How do you, as a politician, show that you're really much, much better than all the venal, backstabbing MPs around you? It is difficult to appear different when so many of your colleagues have the same background as you. It's even more difficult when you realise how all-consuming parliamentary life is, to the point where you lose touch with your non-political friends and find yourself with no one to go on holiday with, as happened to the ex-MP in Chapter 8.

Some politicians make breaking the political mould their speciality. Boris Johnson built his profile in the media as someone who could laugh at themselves, who could end up stuck on a zip wire without it being totally humiliating, and who appeared comfortable in his own skin as a rather posh buffoon. Nigel Farage made being a non-politician part of the UKIP brand, insisting on conducting interviews in a pub, and scoffing at MPs in the Westminster Bubble. Similarly, Jeremy Corbyn used his rather rough-around-the-edges appearance as an allotmenteering, manhole-cover-inspecting, jam-making backbencher to his advantage when standing for Labour leader. He didn't look like the other candidates, though in reality he hadn't come from a working-class background, and had been involved in politics for as long as all the identikit politicians his supporters derided. Even Ed Miliband had a crack at appearing to be different, claiming in his 2011 conference speech that he had the 'heritage of the outsider, the vantage point of the insider'.

This sort of political positioning is pretty obvious. Far more insidious is the way politicians try to seem different to their colleagues by disparaging politics itself. If you want to look really honourable and measured, you can promise to 'take the politics out' of a particularly thorny issue, suggesting that you're a serious, policy-focused character who sails far above the pettiness of Parliament. What this phrase actually means, however, is far less impressive.

What politicians might rightly want to remove from a serious debate is the pettiness, partisanship or dogma. These things can very easily stop governments taking the right decisions. Ministers can even be so petty as to refuse corrections to spelling in a bill if those corrections come from the opposition party. But what 'taking the politics out' really means is that in their desire to be all things to all men, politicians try to avoid doing something that might upset voters. They try to wash their hands of the responsibility for a controversial policy area by landing it with an external 'expert' of one sort or another who sets up a Royal Commission or some other lengthy process to make the uncomfortable decision on their behalf. Let's remember that politicians are elected and paid by the people to make decisions, and to be accountable for those decisions. 'Taking the politics out' means politicians washing their hands of the responsibility given them by voters.

Take aviation policy. Apparently, it was so important that Britain had sufficient airport capacity that the building of a new runway at a UK airport needed the politics taking out of it, and one of those 'experts' – in this case Sir Howard Davies – was appointed to make the decision on politicians' behalf. Conveniently, the decision to take the politics out of aviation capacity, which David Cameron magnanimously made in 2012, also allowed the prime minister to avoid contradicting his own 'no ifs, no buts' pledge about no third runway to voters living under the Heathrow flight path. The Airports Commission also had three years to produce its final report, thus delaying the evil moment when anyone would have to even start thinking about making a decision. And because it was a non-binding report, politicians didn't need to stick by its recommendations anyway.

Oddly, the commission didn't report until after the 2015 election, which was presumably another important element of taking the politics out of aviation capacity, in that voters living under flight paths wouldn't have the opportunity to base their vote on whether they were bothered about more planes whizzing over their roofs. When it did report, it unanimously recommended a new runway at Heathrow. Eventually, the government responded, though David Cameron was no longer its chief. Theresa May, who had taken over, was forced to partially suspend cabinet collective responsibility in order to let leading opponents of Heathrow expansion Boris Johnson and Justine Greening express their own views. Her statement to the House of Commons on the matter also triggered a by-election in Richmond Park, a constituency under the flight path, after its MP Zac Goldsmith carried out his threat to resign in protest at the government's decision (he lost to a Lib Dem in an election that was far more about Brexit than planes, and then returned to Parliament a year later in the snap general election of 2017).

The new runway could be built by 2025, by which time the UK will need to have another lengthy debate about aviation capacity that involves politicians running as far away as possible from confronting voters with a difficult decision. Taking the politics out of a debate is not something we should welcome. It is a sign that politicians are trying to be all things to all men, juggling their desire to stay in office with their commitment to do something while in office.

It also doesn't work. No matter what sort of Royal Commission or quango politicians set up, they still get blamed for the outcomes of a policy decision, and they are still tempted to meddle. The Health and Social Care Act, which we will examine in detail in the next chapter, was supposed to take the politics out of the NHS, yet no Health Secretary will ever really be able to avoid being accountable for a winter crisis in Accident and Emergency, for instance, and neither should they. The Fixed Terms Parliament Act was rather ludicrously supposed to take the politics out of elections, as it meant political parties couldn't call an election at a time they thought was advantageous to them. In reality, what it meant was that the Coalition government stopped doing anything interesting in 2014 so that the parties had a long run-in to the 2015 campaign without any controversial rows, and Theresa May then used the mechanisms within that Act to call a snap election at a time of her choosing anyway.

There is nothing wrong with politicians wanting to behave like adults, and perhaps even reaching a consensus on a reform to ensure it is implemented. But when they start suggesting that politics itself is a force for bad, rather than just the forum in which decisions are made, then they are doing themselves down, and in the process appearing more out of touch with voters.

Avoiding the dirty work

Everyone wants to be popular, politicians probably a little more than the general population because so much of their entry into the job is about persuading people to like them enough to select them as a candidate or vote for them. But being a good politician also means saying and doing things that will prevent groups of people from liking you. Your electorate chooses you and then pays you to be as informed as possible in order to make decisions on their behalf. Decisions involve choosing between things. People who wanted you to choose the other thing will be upset. They'll also be upset if you tell them that whatever decision you take will involve you asking them to pay more money in taxes.

This is why MPs have been so squeamish about restoring their own workplace. Parliament is a UNESCO World Heritage Site, yet it is crumbling. Every time the prospect of carrying out the urgent renovation work is raised, ministers find a way to delay it a little longer, fearing a public outcry about the cost. Of course, the longer Parliament is left crumbling, the higher the cost of repairing it will be. But politicians are so frightened of their own shadows that they daren't make the right decision and get on with the project. As with the decisions on their own pay outlined in Chapter 2, they don't seem to realise that the public already despise the political class. Deciding against restoring one of the most famous buildings in the world is hardly going to make them love MPs all of a sudden. It would also be a huge dereliction of duty.

This fear of upsetting voters with a necessary decision is also why politicians haven't yet resolved the issue of social care. It involves making a decision that will inevitably entail massive levels of public spending and a huge input from taxpayers in one way or another.

Being honest with the electorate about what it will take to reform and properly fund social care has been a political nightmare for years. After the 2017 election, in which the Conservatives were punished by the electorate for, among other things, proposing a 'dementia tax' in order to fund the system, it has become even more difficult to solve.

One of the biggest political problems with the reform of social care is that people don't know what the current system is like until they or their aged parents end up in it. For those mystified by what social care actually is, it is the support needed to help a person live as independent a life as possible. It ranges from visits at home from carers to day centres and residential homes. It is currently a means-tested system, and because of the rising demand that results from people living much longer, most people have to arrange for their help privately. Many believe that social care is part of the NHS and therefore free at the point of access. It isn't. Because many voters do not realise this, proposals from politicians to fund the system properly using one sort of tax or another come as a shock and seem like an excessive demand from the government when infirmity is already massively expensive.

This means that politicians are very good at wringing their hands over the many case studies of elderly people dying from hospital-acquired infections when they have been medically fit for discharge but have had no suitable care at home. But it is also why they are very bad at making a decision on what needs to change so that everyone is able to access social care.

England is one of the few major developed countries that hasn't made any reforms to its approach to long-term care, even though like most other countries it has an ageing population. Instead, politicians have spent a decade taking the politics out of the decision on social care funding, in order to 'work together' to find a solution, before promptly dumping all over any party in government that might decide to do something.

The Blair government set up a Royal Commission on social care in 1997. When it didn't like the commission's recommendations that all long-term personal care should be free, it rejected the proposals. In 2009, it looked as though social care might actually be about to be reformed. The then Health Secretary Andy Burnham launched a Green Paper proposing a National Care Service, funded by a compulsory levy on a person's assets once they passed away. The Tories had initially promised their support for a better-funded social care system, but with an election looming, they turned on Labour, calling the funding plan a 'death tax'.

Years of warm words followed. MPs became increasingly worried about the precarious situations in their constituencies, with families coming to them to complain about poor-quality yet hideously expensive care. The Coalition government set up the Dilnot Commission, an independent body that was supposed to take the politics out of social care funding, and which would examine how to fund care and support in England. It reported in July 2011, recommending a cap of around £35,000 on the amount that people should have to pay for long-term social care over their lifetime. The government responded in 2013, setting the cap much higher, at £72,000. The reforms were supposed to start from April 2016, but shortly after the 2015 general election, ministers slipped out a statement in which they said they would be delaying implementation until 2020, citing the £6 billion cost of the scheme. The response from councils and charities involved in social care was mixed, as some had feared they wouldn't be able to implement the cap anyway, but most pointed out that the funding situation remained so dire that they would rather there was a delay in the cap and additional money now for care services.

Despite the cancellation of the Dilnot plan, George Osborne did pay heed to the growing political clamour for more money for social care. His own backbenchers were starting to come to him to pass on complaints from Conservative-led local authorities. Now that the row had reached Parliament, it was time to act. The Chancellor announced that local authorities would add 2 per cent to council tax bills and use the extra money to fund social care provision. They could also hold local votes on raising their council tax much higher, if they wished.

The Tory-led Local Government Association gave a rather cool welcome to this announcement, and then staged a series of revolts against the Westminster Conservatives for repeatedly cutting council budgets while expecting them to continue providing social care. In 2016, the Care Quality Commission warned that the 'sustainability of the adult social care market is approaching a tipping point'.[1] Under the new prime minister, Theresa May, ministers interested in this area hoped to be able to push for a proper settlement. They were soon frustrated, repeatedly suggesting that social care was in crisis and that something needed to be done now, and repeatedly being fobbed off. In desperation, Surrey Council announced in 2017 that it would be holding a referendum on raising its council tax by a whopping 15 per cent to fill its funding black hole for social care. The council leader, David Hodge, was so horrified by his own idea that he did everything he could to try to prevent the referendum from happening, including sending a series of messages to special advisers begging them for a way out. Unfortunately the messages ended up in the wrong hands and were read out by a jubilant Jeremy Corbyn at Prime Minister's Questions, with the

Labour leader alleging a 'sweetheart deal' for the Tory-led council.

Ministers had secretly been quite keen on this referendum idea. They felt that if Surrey won the case for a council tax hike, they could say that local democracy was alive and well, and that other councils who complained about their funding situation should be brave and honest with their voters. If the taxpayers of Surrey decided they didn't fancy giving more money to their local authority (as everyone expected they would), then ministers could argue that there was no public appetite for raising taxes to fund the system.

Eventually, the Conservatives decided that they themselves would be brave and honest with their voters, making a rather bleak pledge on social care a central part of their manifesto in the snap election of 2017. So confident were they (and most people in Westminster) that the Labour Party would be decimated by the surprise poll that Theresa May and her advisers decided they could afford to avoid silly election gimmicks like the 'tax lock' promised by the Conservatives in their 2015 manifesto, and instead tell voters what they planned to do without fear of a strong opposition undermining their difficult decision.

In many ways, using an election campaign to tell voters that you want them to pay for their own care using the value of their home until the last £100,000 worth of assets is a rather honourable thing to do. You're certainly not deceiving the electorate about what life will be like if they put you back in government. There are few incentives to be honest with voters about how much of their money your plans will take up. So if you're going to be so bold, you'd probably want to make sure that the policy you're upsetting them with is properly worked out.

Unfortunately, the Tories hadn't done this. Having gone from worrying about upsetting people to being honest about costs, they became careless about the design of a policy that they were going to throw at the public without any warning. It wasn't until they unveiled it that they realised people weren't going to warm to a proposal that meant they would have to pay a great deal more for social care, and that didn't include any sort of cap on that spending either.

While the poll tax was cooked up by a homogenous group of politicians and civil servants who didn't quite realise its political implications, the 'dementia tax', as it quickly became known, was cooked up by the tiniest group of advisers possible. Not even the Health Secretary, Jeremy Hunt, or the Communities and Local Government Secretary, Sajid Javid, had been told about the plans that the team around Theresa May had drawn up for the manifesto – until the night before it was launched. Perhaps they might have pointed out some of the political and intellectual problems with the policy, which outsiders then quickly broadcast as soon as the manifesto saw the light of day.

The Tories may have forgotten their political instincts at just the wrong time, but Labour MPs hadn't. They were expecting to lose dozens of seats, and were therefore on the lookout for anything they could use to attack the Conservatives. The all-things-to-all-men instinct kicked in even for Labourites who privately told me that they thought the plan was probably as fair as any other, and they jumped all over the dementia tax.

When the Tories lost their majority, the social care fiasco was quickly pinpointed as one of the reasons for their humiliation in an election they had chosen to hold. Nick Timothy, one of the aides who drew up the policy, confessed in *The Spectator*: 'I accept that the manifesto might have been too ambitious.' But he also fretted that 'the implication of this argument is that politicians should not be straight with the electorate', adding: 'You can criticise the policy, but we need to be honest with ourselves. Since we have an ageing population, we need to spend more on health and care, and we need to decide how to pay for it. We can ask older people to meet the costs, subject to certain protections, from the wealth they have accrued through life, or we can tax younger generations even more. Somehow we have reached a point where older people with assets expect younger, poorer people to pay for their care. With Britain's demographics, that is not sustainable; neither is it socially just.'[2]

Timothy was right on every point, save that he didn't acknowledge that the best way to be honest with the electorate is to make sure your policy actually works before you start announcing it, rather than chaotically changing it in full view of the voters. As a very experienced political operator, he would have known that the opposition's support for social care reforms couldn't be guaranteed, given the way his own party branded Burnham's 2009 plans a 'death tax' for partisan purposes. The Conservatives' clumsiness over this policy has made it harder for politicians to be honest with the electorate about social care in the future.

Whoever does finally decide to plough ahead with reforms to the incredibly frail system will have to accept that people will be in uproar at the sums of money involved – as they are individually now when confronted with the current situation. Social care is a classic example of politicians' failure and unwillingness to deal with long-term problems because they fear the short-term consequences. Commissions make them sound serious while allowing them to delay telling voters something unpleasant. Elections make important ideas a partisan football even for those who claim a desperate desire to take the politics out of the matter in the mid-term. Politicians do not want to see politics as being the dirty, difficult work that the electorate would rather someone else do. They are very good at saying that something must be done, and even better at hoping that someone else will end up having to do it.

Something must be done

A very important word in the English language is 'they'. The way it is used colloquially gives an amusing insight into the British psyche. 'They' can refer to the weather presenter who told you it would rain later, the council closing a road, the people in charge of taxation, or a less easily identifiable person who nevertheless should be responsible for doing something. They've closed the road again. They were wrong about the weather and now I'm carrying around this stupid umbrella. They should sort out that derelict building. They shouldn't let people walk through that field when it's got a rare wild flower in it. It's not always clear who 'they' are, but they should be doing something about it.

Politicians can end up being rather self-centred and assume that 'they' refers almost exclusively to the people in Westminster, rather than wider society: they must do something about this bad thing that everyone is talking about. It's a dangerous instinct, the desire to show that something is being done. In the rush to do something, politicians often don't stop and check that what they're doing will actually solve the problem.

Worse, any opponents of the 'something' policy will be criticised for not caring enough about the victims of the tragedy politicians are trying to stop, even if their opposition comes from a fear that actually this policy either won't have any effect, or it may even make things worse.

Every government is guilty of feeling it should do something. In 2011, riots in cities and towns across the country had led to commentators suggesting that something must be done to stop certain sections of society feeling as though they were above the law. In a speech in December of that year, David Cameron said: 'As I said after the riots, I have a duty to speak clearly, frankly and truthfully about the problems in our society and an equal duty to do whatever it takes to fix them.' The programme he then announced would focus on the 'relatively small number of families [who] are the source of a large proportion of the problems in society'. That meant a Troubled Families Programme run by the Communities and Local Government department, which would spend £448 million 'turning around the lives' of 120,000 families who cost the taxpayer £9 billion a year.[3] It sounded good. It sounded like the prime minister was doing 'whatever it takes'.

Three years later, the government's own evaluation, carried out by analysts at Ecorys, suggested that Cameron had in fact just been doing 'whatever' to respond to the riots. The report pointed to a 'lack of evidence that [the programme] has had an impact on the outcomes that it seeks to effect for families'. It couldn't confirm that the programme had improved school attendance, safeguarding, child welfare, employment or benefit claims for these families.[4] Previously, ministers had claimed a 99 per cent success rate, which sounded pretty astonishing, and led to questions about what sort of metric the government could possibly be using.

When the evaluation was completed, it stayed mysteriously unpublished for months until the BBC's *Newsnight* got hold of a leaked copy. It turned out that the children might still largely be absent from school, the parents might still be out of work, and the families might continue to be what David Cameron described as 'the neighbours from hell', but if there had been progress on one measure, according to the government's definition, their lives had been 'turned around'. Which is a bit like a smoker who 'turns around' their life by just smoking 39 cigarettes each day, rather than the full 40.

This programme hadn't required much in the way of primary or secondary legislation to get going, and had received a reasonable level of support from the Labour benches in Commons debates, though MPs often asked how progress was going to be measured. Everyone had agreed that something should be done: it was just that they were a bit hazy on how that thing would actually work.

The Coalition government's response to the grotesque practice of phone hacking by some newspapers was another example of doing something new and expensive when the existing laws just hadn't been enforced properly. Phone hacking was already a criminal offence, but the response was to usher in state regulation of the media through a series of last-minute votes in Parliament. The press, naturally, wasn't too happy about this, but many parliamentarians dismissed it as turkeys suggesting that December was their least favourite month. When the legislation enabling a new press regulator came before Parliament, just hours after it had been agreed in late-night talks between the parties and press regulation campaigners, MPs had barely had any time to read it – and most had already decided that because something needed to be done, this something that was being tabled for debate was the right thing. Not necessarily.

Some MPs had thought about the consequences of the amendments to the Crime and Courts Bill, and spoke out against them in the Commons. Those amendments created a system of 'exemplary costs and damages' for newspapers that refused to join the new press regulator. David Cameron insisted to the Commons that this wasn't state regulation of the press, while confirming, in the manner of a René Magritte painting, that there would need to be legislation. Ed Miliband supported the changes, telling MPs: 'Today represents a huge moment for the House. We are doing the right thing. Politics has failed to grasp this issue for decades, but today politicians have come together to put the victims first.'[5]

Most journalists were appalled at the treatment not just of the phone hacking victims but also of those people, often not powerful or rich, who were harassed or had stories made up about them in the press. But they were also appalled at the idea of politicians, who are after all not exactly strangers to a bit of rough treatment (mostly justified) from the press, deciding how to tame the media. It doesn't serve the public well either. Indeed, in the run-up to the introduction of this legislation, *The Spectator* received a threat from a leading politician, who cited press regulation when complaining about a comment piece he didn't like. Worse, Maria Miller, at the time the minister overseeing this policy, then found herself in hot water when it emerged that her adviser had threatened the *Telegraph* using the discussions following the conclusion of the Leveson inquiry into the culture, ethics and practices of the press, saying, 'Maria has obviously been having quite a lot of editors' meetings around Leveson at the moment. So I am just going to flag up that connection for you to think about.'[6] Whether she was aware of her adviser's threat or not, this is a handy connection to have if you don't want a newspaper investigating whether you've wrongly claimed taxpayers' money in expenses for your London home.

Fortunately, one of the heroes of this book, Charles Walker, wasn't in the mood for doing just anything to stop the press behaving badly. An hour into the debate, he piped up: 'This House is at its best when there is an element of tension in the debate, and I am concerned that there is not that tension today. We have a pretty revolting press in this country; I realised that from about the age of 18 onwards. It is pretty unpleasant, to be perfectly honest; there is not much merit in much of its coverage. However, I am concerned that so many speakers are saying that we must have a free press, must respect that free press, and must enshrine the freedom of the press in some form or in some law, because I thought that a free press was simply part of the deal of living in this democracy. I also worry when we say that we are not enshrining these new laws in statute. We have amendments on the Order Paper and we talk about having to pass this into law both in this House and in the House of Lords. To me, that feels very much like statutory regulation and legislation.'

Walker and 12 other Conservative MPs voted against the amendments, which passed 530 votes to 13.

Did the legislation work? Yes, if you believe that having two regulators, one independent and the other underpinned by legislation, is a good result. Half the press is signed up to the Independent Press Standards Organisation (IPSO), which editors set up themselves, and the other half is regulated by Impress, which was the first such organisation officially recognised according to the government's terms, and which claims to be the only one fully compliant with the recommendations set out by Leveson. The government initially planned to bully the press into joining Impress by setting up an exemplary damages system. However, they later backtracked, realising that it would cripple an industry already in its death throes. The idea had been that politicians who had a grievance against a publication not in Impress could take out a legal action against that newspaper, which would be forced to pay the legal costs of the politician even if the paper won the case. This wouldn't so much be regulation of the press as prematurely killing it off.

Doing something for the victims of a terrible incident is an admirable human instinct, but that doesn't mean that doing just anything to help them will work. Another example of a law that politicians agreed should be passed to stop bad things happening is the Dangerous Dogs Act 1991.

A string of attacks in which infants either died or were seriously injured led to parliamentary pressure for something to be done, and the government acted quickly, introducing emergency legislation that would ban the breeding and ownership of pit bull terriers and other dogs kept especially for fighting. Philip Johnston, in his book *Bad Laws*, points out the rather obvious problem with this, which was that 'most dog attacks were not carried out by the breeds identified by Home Secretary Kenneth Baker but by Alsatians, Rottweilers, terriers and collies'.[7] Consequently, the courts found themselves having to decide what a pit bull terrier actually was, which sucked in a number of other types of dog deemed to be covered by the Act and therefore eligible for destruction.

The Act has since been watered down so that it doesn't focus so much on the breed as the owner. Dangerous dogs are made dangerous through bad training and management: Staffordshire bull terriers, for instance, are very sociable, soppy dogs if well trained, while supposedly 'family' dogs – including those used historically for picking up prey at shoots, such as retrievers – can maul children if they think the child is stealing their food, or if their owner hasn't bothered to train them properly. The legislation is still active at the time of writing, as are dangerous dogs.

In another, rather more ludicrous example of unnecessary action, John Major's government introduced the Cones Hotline in 1992 in response to heavy traffic caused by loitering cones that appeared to have no purpose. Members of the public could phone the hotline to ask whether the cones they'd seen were doing anything important, or whether they were blocking the road unnecessarily. It's a shame a similar hotline hasn't been set up so that the public can ask whether ministers are doing something important, or whether they're just spewing out unnecessary legislation.

Backbenchers regularly fall prey to the 'something must be done' instinct too, leading to the ridiculous rigmarole of private members' bills outlined in Chapter 4. It is almost fortunate that this instinct is so easily quashed on a Friday when other MPs can talk their colleagues' badly designed bills out; it is far less easy when the government is driving the change.

Being all things to all men creates a tension in politicians' lives where they are at once keen to do 'something' and reluctant to venture near another important part of their job. They want to seem popular and on the pulse, but don't want to do what their constituents have sent them to Westminster to do, which is to make difficult decisions. They have so little confidence in themselves that they struggle to have the courage of their convictions, or indeed to accept that though this difficult decision may make them unpopular, it still needs to be taken.

CHAPTER 11

YES-MEN

The most pernicious and inexcusable culture in the House of Commons is that of the yes-man. MPs may not notice their own unconscious biases and blind spots. They might even be forgiven for worrying about the response of voters at an election to difficult decisions on social care and aviation. But they know that they are taking part in a culture of subservience on legislation, and they do little about it.

Yes, the rewards in applying oneself to proper scrutiny are few. But this is a poor excuse for those who are supposed to be public servants. The rewards for being a lower gastrointestinal surgeon are also few, according to the measures that MPs use: spending a lot of time with the lower digestive tract is not glamorous given the sort of things you can encounter when that tract has gone wrong. People don't really want to talk about bowel movements at a dinner party, and so avoid discussing your job with you. You are rarely interviewed on the radio about the laparoscopic rectopexy you performed that week. Being an MP involves dealing with a different sort of shit, but parliamentarians have ostensibly signed up to dealing with it in the same way as lower GI surgeons have signed up to the realities of their job.

Good parliamentarians know that scrutiny isn't just about

rebelling. In fact, rebellions are a last resort after months of raising an issue in questions, engaging with the detail of a policy in bill committees, and holding private meetings with ministers to try to persuade them that there really is a problem with this piece of legislation. People often claim that Parliament would be much better if it had more rebels, but rebels can be as intractable and unable to listen to arguments as those who meekly file through the lobbies at their whips' bidding. As we saw in Chapter 4, MPs who want to get things done know that making a noise in the Commons Chamber is often the least effective way of doing it.

That said, if a policy is bad and needs changing, and ministers are getting rather uppity about the idea of changing it now that the proposed legislation is public, then voting against it or in favour of an amendment should be regarded as doing one's job, not being a naughty boy. Currently even causing a bit of friction in a bill committee is considered really not on. The whips will of course try to encourage this culture of turning up, keeping your head down, and voting as you're told. But MPs are adults. They don't need to accept it.

Often, parliamentarians only realise that a policy is a total mess once it's on the statute book and a desperate soul is sitting opposite them in a constituency surgery clutching one of those bags stuffed full of papers. One example of MPs only finding out what a policy meant when they were confronted with a real-life case came in 2014, when a man accused of rape and sexual assault endured a lengthy trial during which he considered suicide. He was acquitted of all charges, but found as he left the courtroom that he wasn't so free after all. He had a £130,000 legal bill to pay, and even though he had done nothing wrong in the eyes of the law, he would still have to cough up for at least part of that because of cuts to legal aid introduced by the Coalition government.

Legal aid is a complex issue that confuses even the politicians charged with changing the laws around who is eligible for it. Which is perhaps why this man, Nigel Evans, the Conservative MP for Ribble Valley, was shocked to discover that he couldn't claim back all his costs after his trial. He was even more shocked to discover that this was as a result of cuts introduced by his own party, and though he hadn't voted on the specific legislation because he was Deputy Speaker at that point (the Speaker and Deputy Speakers do not vote in divisions), he confessed that 'I might well have gone with whatever the government was promoting at the time. It's only when you actually go through these sorts of trauma that you see the first-hand consequences of that.'[1]

Evans was annoyed about what he described as the 'unintended consequences' of the legislation. But while none of his colleagues who were able to vote on the legislation would have wanted one of their friends to find themselves saddled with a huge legal bill after such a trauma, they had been warned. When the public bill committee scrutinising the Legal Aid, Sentencing and Punishment of Offenders (LASPO) Bill met in 2011, they started by taking evidence from leading figures and campaign groups in the criminal and civil justice sectors. Some were positive about the proposals for sentencing and probation. Others were rather nervous about the implications of cutting the £2.2 billion legal aid bill by £350 million, warning that it could restrict access to justice for the most vulnerable.

How did the Conservative members of the committee ensure that their government was getting these cuts right so that people were not wrongly denied access to justice? They were a sharp bunch of MPs who all went on to government jobs, including cabinet posts. Along with their Labour and Liberal Democrat counterparts, most of them had legal backgrounds, to the extent that when they stood up to declare their interests before the debate began, the committee's chair, Jim Sheridan, remarked, 'It is a bit like an Alcoholics Anonymous meeting.'[2] So a whole nest of legal eagles.

Bright and expert these MPs might have been, but they behaved according to the principles of a bill committee that we learned about earlier in this book. Ben Gummer, then the Tory MP for Ipswich, grilled one witness on 'how many barristers travel first class on the railway' before trying to work out if he agreed with a witness from another organisation about alternative cuts. The Tory MP Liz Truss made the very important point that the British legal aid bill was much higher than other countries with similar legal aid systems, asking: 'Is the British system not pretty generous in terms of the eligibility for legal aid and the scope that is being proposed under this Bill?'[3] This was later followed up by her colleague Damian Hinds.

The questions weren't bad in and of themselves; it was just that the stance of all the Tory MPs on the committee was adversarial. They saw their role as trying to trip up the witnesses over the principle of cutting legal aid costs, rather than asking whether the bill was actually drafted correctly. There is nothing wrong with ensuring that a witness is offering useful evidence – indeed, this is why cross-examination in the courts is important, especially when done by a barrister rather than a victim who does not have access to legal aid, for instance – but surely once that had been ascertained, the Conservative MPs also wanted to make sure they weren't going to be approving a messy bill. The tenor of their questions throughout the four days of evidence was that of members of the government defending what had already been decided, not probing whether it should go through unamended.

Yes-men are intelligent, articulate types, often hugely successful in their previous careers. They can show loyalty with more panache than some of their more plodding colleagues who spend months asking dozily faithful questions in the Chamber. But they're still committing the same offence, of disregarding their responsibilities as members of the legislature in favour of a bright and hopefully effective career in the executive.

The bill passed its Commons committee stage as all bills do, with only government-backed amendments being agreed, and went through its remaining stages with all non-government amendments failing. It then suffered 14 defeats in the House of Lords on matters such as eligibility for legal aid for domestic abuse victims and those who had developed asbestos-related cancers. Ministers were forced to make concessions on the latter. All the other changes made in the Lords were overturned by MPs at the final Commons stage, and the bill gained Royal Assent on 1 May 2012. The legal aid bill dropped from £2.4 billion to £1.6 billion by the end of the 2010 parliament, so at least ministers were successful in their aims to reduce it. But the government had also promised that this wouldn't undermine access to justice.

In March 2015, the Commons Justice Select Committee published a damning report on the cuts to civil legal aid. It concluded that 'while it made significant savings in the cost of the scheme, the ministry had harmed access to justice for some litigants and had not achieved the other three out of four of its stated objectives for the reforms'. These objectives were to 'discourage unnecessary and adversarial litigation at public expense', to 'target legal aid to those who need it most', to 'make significant savings in the cost of the scheme' and to 'deliver better overall value for money for the taxpayer'. The MPs reported that there had been a substantial increase in people with no choice other than to represent themselves in court, 'who may therefore have some difficulty in effectively presenting their cases'. This meant the courts were having to spend more money on helping these litigants, and there were various other knock-on costs to the public purse in cases such as repossession.[4]

In the three years after the cuts, 11 law centres closed. There was a 25 per cent decline in the number of solicitors undertaking civil legal aid work. The Law Society found that a number of areas of the UK had become 'legal aid deserts', where there was no legal aid advice available, and that the hardest hit were lone children adopted from overseas who had been trafficked but hadn't been recognised as such, and children with immigration issues following the death of a parent or a family break-up.[5]

It wasn't just Nigel Evans who became wise after the event when it came to legal aid. His Conservative colleague Bob Neill took over as chair of the Commons Justice Select Committee in July 2015, whereupon he became a vocal critic of the cuts, saying the government had gone 'too far' and needed 'to look at some areas again', also writing in *The Times* that 'there are serious questions around access to justice' as a result of the legal aid cuts, on which his 'personal view is that we have now removed more than the system can take and should rectify the anomalies as soon as possible'.[6]

Even David Cameron latterly realised that some of the proposals his government was seeking to implement wouldn't work. In January 2016, Justice Secretary Michael Gove announced he was cancelling plans introduced by his predecessor Chris Grayling for a 'dual contracting' system for criminal solicitors that would restrict the number of firms able to do duty work in courts and police stations. He also dropped a planned 8.75 per cent cut to the fees for solicitors doing this duty work.

What prompted this change of heart? In Chapter 3, I revealed how a criminal solicitor came to Cameron's surgery and explained the problems with the proposed arrangements. Once again, a problem was turning up not in Parliament but in the constituency surgery – and fortunately for the justice system, it was the prime minister's surgery in which it was raised. Solicitors are far better able to represent themselves in these contexts than many of the people normally directly affected by government policies. It was lucky that Cameron heard the problems articulated to him directly, as it was unlikely that any of his ministers would have passed the concerns on voluntarily.

Perhaps it doesn't matter that the cuts have created a two-tier justice system in which some people cannot access the advice they are entitled to. Perhaps it doesn't matter that costs have been offloaded onto other areas of the public purse. LASPO 2012 is still a bad law, however, because it is doing what ministers promised it wouldn't. And their own party colleagues weren't prepared to check that those promises had a chance of being kept as the bill was passing through Parliament. They agreed with the principle of cutting the legal aid budget. But their job was to make sure that this principle was being carried out in the best way. They didn't.

We told you so

As far as scary policies go, the 'size criteria in the social rented sector' regulations don't sound all that threatening. But this cut to housing benefit for council and housing association tenants who had more bedrooms in their homes than they needed has caused endless misery for tenants since it was announced in 2010 – and made the government look stupid and arrogant. Most people know it as the 'bedroom tax', a name that one of its critics cooked up before the Conservatives, who introduced it, could think of a snappier one that would appeal to the electorate. Many years after it was first announced, it is still difficult to find a Tory MP who really thinks it is a decent, well-designed policy that works as it is intended. Yet the bedroom tax (not a tax, but a benefit cut) has remained in place.

Initially, few people noticed this cut amid the wider debate about the housing benefit bill. But in 2013, housing associations started to receive letters from Tory MPs angry that their constituents were being asked to pay more rent for homes they'd lived in for years. The landlords politely pointed out that these demands for higher rent were in fact a result of the reduction in housing benefit enabled by the Welfare Reform Act that they had passed into law just a year before. How had MPs failed to notice the consequences of this benefit change until it pitched up in their surgeries? The cut was in fact announced in the Emergency Budget following the 2010 election, and had been the subject of repeated rows in Parliament. Yet it was only when cases started appearing in constituency surgeries that Conservative MPs started to understand the design and effect of a policy that they had approved.

The underoccupancy penalty – the most neutral name for this highly controversial policy – sounds like the sort of idea that only a churlish character could disagree with. Social housing in the United Kingdom is horrendously oversubscribed: at the time the policy was announced, 250,000 social homes were overcrowded, with serious impacts on mental and physical health and on children's education. At the same time, 400,000 social tenants were living in homes that had more bedrooms than they needed, and the new Coalition government was seeking to cut £11 billion from welfare spending over five years.

But like so many policies that sound like no-brainers, this turned out to be a nightmare. Firstly, until 2010, all social tenants in England had lifetime tenancies for their homes, which meant that there was no legal reason why they should move out, regardless of whether they still needed the three-bedroom house they had moved into many decades previously. The Coalition quickly abolished the automatic right to a council house for life, but existing tenants were unaffected because ministers felt it was unfair – and possibly unlawful – to change the terms on which those homes had been given to them. But the underoccupancy penalty took no account of that, and so someone who had a right to their home for life now didn't have the right to the housing benefit to help them pay for that home for life. Worse: the penalty applied whether or not you were able to move into a smaller home – and there weren't enough one-bedroom homes for social tenants to move into. So even those tenants who had done everything they could to find a new home were still being penalised while they were trapped in their existing one.

Hence this policy, sold as fair, was in fact anything but. Few would disagree with the principle of only paying housing benefit to new tenants for the rooms they actually needed. But that wasn't how the penalty had been designed. It hadn't been cooked up because of a hunger for fairness in the two departments responsible for housing and housing benefit – the Work and Pensions department (DWP) and the Communities and Local Government department (DCLG) – but because of a hunger for savings in the Treasury.

Even though ministers were talking tough on spending cuts, some who understood the housing sector baulked at the plan. Grant

Shapps, the housing minister at the time, took it upon himself to block the policy when it was proposed in the ministerial 'write-round'. He dug his heels in for months, trying to persuade DWP and Treasury ministers responsible for administering the penalty that it didn't work for existing tenants and that there at least needed to be a much bigger discretionary fund to cover cases where tenants either couldn't move or needed extra rooms – for dialysis machines, children who lived with an estranged parent for part of the week, or as 'safe rooms' to protect domestic abuse victims from their violent ex-partners. The stalemate continued 'for months', according to Shapps. 'Eventually Eric Pickles [then Communities and Local Government Secretary] came to me and said, "I know you disagree with this but I'm having to let it go." What had happened was that DWP started routinely blocking DCLG write-rounds. It was a really, really bad policy but it went through.'

So keen were DWP and Treasury ministers to get this policy approved by all the departments responsible and into legislation for the Commons to sign off that they were effectively holding DCLG to ransom until it yielded. And yield it did, allowing the underoccupancy penalty to start its journey through Parliament.

At the time, most political debate was concerned with the other cuts to housing benefit, one of which was dropped as a generous concession to campaigners. Sources who were in the DWP at the time insist that this particular cut, which was a 10 per cent reduction in housing benefit for those who had been on Jobseeker's Allowance for over a year, had always been included in the list of welfare reforms as a policy that would be easy to abandon so that other cuts could go through. The opposition also found itself in a sticky place on welfare, having lost the 2010 election partly because voters felt the Labour Party was 'soft' on benefits. At the second reading of the Welfare Reform Bill, which bundled in the benefit cuts (which Labour thought were bad but difficult to oppose) with the introduction of a massive overhaul of the entire benefits system called Universal Credit (which Labour knew it absolutely couldn't oppose), the party tabled an amendment arguing that the bill should have first been scrutinised in draft form, and that the legislation 'provides no safeguards for those losing housing benefit or appropriate checks on the secretary of state's powers'.

The party's shadow housing minister, Karen Buck, then tried to alter the bill in public bill committee in May 2011, so that the underoccupancy penalty would not apply to those who had not received a 'reasonable alternative offer' of accommodation. But this being a public bill committee, the proposal failed, with 15 Coalition MPs voting against the nine Labour MPs on the committee. It then sailed through report stage with no votes on the penalty, and proceeded to the Lords, where housing experts including cross-bench peer Lord Best did their damnedest to try to water down the measure. At first, the peers succeeded in amending the bill along the lines of the change that Buck had proposed. But the government invoked what is called 'financial privilege', which is the right of the House of Commons to approve matters of public spending when there is a dispute with the Lords. So the measure went to 'ping pong', where Lord Best kept pushing at the issue, and the Commons, with Coalition MPs on a strict three-line whip not to allow any Lords amendments, kept pushing back. The peer first tried to exempt certain tenants such as war widows and carers from the penalty, and eventually settled on forcing the government to review the impact of the penalty on those affected. The Commons approved this, as it meant very little. Even a critical review didn't tie ministers' hands.

All the bill actually did was to allow the secretary of state to introduce regulations on the underoccupancy penalty. And so in 2012, MPs got another chance to scrutinise the actual detail of the policy when those regulations were laid, examining it in a delegated legislation committee on 16 October of that year. The MPs met for an hour and a half, but in that time, only two backbenchers from the government parties actually said anything. Those two Conservative MPs – Andrew Bridgen and Richard Fuller – interrupted questions from the Labour MPs merely to make the case for the regulations, rather than probe the minister on the design of the policy they had been asked to scrutinise. They were doing their job as they saw it, which was to do as the whips had told them, turn up to the committee and get the measure passed. Bridgen in particular is a notorious troublemaker on issues he disagrees with, so is no government patsy. But in this committee meeting, they weren't checking that the underoccupancy penalty was well designed. They were just ensuring that it passed, which it did, nine Conservative and Lib Dem votes in favour to four Labour votes against.[7]

Conservative and Lib Dem MPs were also presumably just doing their job when the regulations came before the whole Commons as a deferred division on 24 October 2012 – though the chances are that most of those voting didn't have a clue that they were marching through the 'aye' lobby to approve a cut to housing benefit. It passed by 260 votes to 206. And that was that.

Not only was there scant opportunity to scrutinise the actual design of the policy in detail, what little opportunity there was was not seized upon by government backbenchers, who saw it as their job to get the measure through, rather than ensuring that it would actually be effective. The yes-men were hard at work, and not for the good of legislation. Did they know that the policy took no account of whether a social tenant could actually move out of their home? None of them gave that impression. They argued according to principle, not design.

Does the bedroom tax work? Not politically, at least. Labour took up the scary-sounding name, and the Tories belatedly tried to regain lost political capital by calling it 'the removal of the spare room subsidy', a name invented by someone who had clearly never read a tabloid newspaper. It also, according to the latest DWP figures, does not seem to be saving the £500m a year it was supposed to: based on the 2017 caseload, it is only saving £300m.[8] Central government gave £150m to local authorities in Discretionary Housing Payment to help tenants who didn't 'deserve' the penalty.

In the year after the cut came into effect, over 57,000 families – around 60 per cent of those affected – fell into arrears on their rent as a result of the reduction in their housing benefit. Some political campaigners have claimed that a number of suicides were linked to the tax. It is certainly true that it has caused a great deal of mental distress, but it is irresponsible to suggest that suicide has one clear cause, not least because it suggests to others affected by benefit cuts that ending one's own life is the only solution. And just because people haven't killed themselves doesn't mean a policy is working fine. There are much clearer ways of telling that ministers have made a mistake.

In this instance, ministers did make a mistake. But even when it became clear that this was the case, government ego prevented anyone owning up to it. It would be more admirable to admit that the penalty needed tweaking. But though the Tories secretly considered offering to scrap the cut as part of any negotiations with the Liberal Democrats for a second coalition after 2015, they never accepted that it might just be a good idea to get rid of it anyway when it turned out they had won a majority. Ministers feared that admitting they were wrong on one benefit cut might bring the whole edifice tumbling down around them, with other groups then homing in on other controversial deficit reduction measures. And so it stayed, even though its flaws had been obvious from the very moment it left a desk in the Treasury in 2010.

How were we supposed to know?

Backing the principle without noting the details is a classic feature of yes-men politicians, and probably the commonest cause of government blunders. Many of these examples are found in the welfare system. This is because welfare is a potent combination of fiendishly complicated and politically salient, which means the incentives to get policies right are often outweighed by the incentives to sound as though you're saying the right thing. This, it turns out, can have disastrous consequences.

On the surface, the idea of ensuring that everyone receiving sickness benefit is actually in need of that benefit sounds uncontroversial. Stopping people from claiming incapacity benefit when they could in fact be helped back into work means that those who genuinely need it aren't losing out. It also means that the taxpayer isn't losing out. And finally, it means that those who are in need of proper support to return to the workplace after time off – or the small number of people who just aren't ill at all – make the most of themselves in the workplace.

Governments have frequently used incapacity benefit claimants as a means of making the unemployment figures a little less awful. The bill for sickness benefit rose sharply during the late 1980s and early 1990s under the Conservative government as those left unemployed by the collapse of the mining industry moved from out-of-work benefits to being 'on the sick'. Moving them back was inconvenient, and difficult, given that it would swell unemployment figures – and many had indeed developed mental health conditions. The reluctance over many years to go near these claimants could have featured in the previous chapter, as it was just too politically difficult for many to contemplate.

But towards the end of its time in government, Labour tried to toughen up the tests for sickness benefits. In 2006, the party announced that it would rename Incapacity Benefit 'Employment and Support Allowance' and would introduce stronger tests in order to move people back into work. Work and Pensions Secretary John Hutton told the Commons that the changes would lead to a million fewer claimants. In 2008, the then Work and Pensions Secretary James Purnell set up a series of stringent work capability assessments. The Conservatives said they would support the broad thrust of these reforms, which were introduced in the Welfare Reform Act 2007 – and in secondary legislation attached to that Act called the Employment and Support Allowance Regulations 2008. The tests were designed by and contracted out to private sector companies Unum and Atos Healthcare. The Coalition government extended these pilot tests introduced by Labour into a nationwide system.

Pretty uncontroversial stuff. But then again, assessing whether someone is ill enough to receive benefits is pretty tricky. Some conditions, like multiple sclerosis and depression, can relapse and improve so that a claimant can appear fit to work on the day they are assessed, but struggle to hold down a full-time job over a number of months. Other conditions can sound horrendous but are actually not a barrier to working, provided an employer makes reasonable adjustments.

When the regulations first came to the Commons in 2008, they were the subject of an unusual amount of debate in the delegated legislation committee considering them. Unusual in the sense that it wasn't just the opposition – at that time the Conservatives – who asked questions about their efficacy. A Labour MP, Neil Gerrard, raised concerns about a number of technical issues regarding the payment of the benefit, but he, like his other Labour colleagues, ended up voting for the regulations while the opposition parties voted against. And so the tests began.

Those regulations have been revised repeatedly over the years as ministers realised that they didn't take account of cancer sufferers who were between chemotherapy courses, for instance, or provide sufficient support for those with mental illnesses. The original legislation provided for annual reviews of the assessment, which the DWP uses to modify the test further. So ministers could argue that they are allowing adequate scrutiny of the tests, which were always going to be difficult to get right first time.

But are they right all these years later? And could they have been better when they were first introduced? John Hutton's promised reduction of one million claimants never materialised: when the Welfare Reform Act was in its final stages in 2007/08, there were 2.6 million claimants 'on the sick'. In 2016, there were 2.5 million. The tests themselves were always going to be controversial, as not everyone who is found fit to work will believe that they are, and not every decision will be entirely right. But the scale of successful appeals against decisions by Atos – in 2013, 42 per cent of appeals against fitness-to-work decisions were successful (and 40 per cent of decisions went to appeal, at no small cost to the state) – suggested that something wasn't working. Worse, in 2015, the DWP was forced to publish an assessment that found 2,380 people had died after being declared fit for work and losing their benefits. Some may have killed themselves (though, as we know, suicide is incredibly complex), but others died after being told they should return to the workplace, which seems an odd definition of 'fit for work'.

Some groups have always been implacably opposed to testing, but it wasn't just the obvious critics who found flaws. The National Audit Office identified weaknesses in the £100 million contract with Atos Healthcare in October 2012, followed by a similar verdict from the Public Accounts Committee in 2013. MPs on the PAC said the DWP was 'getting far too many decisions wrong' and at a 'considerable cost to the taxpayer'. Atos left the contract early, after years of angry protests, and was replaced by another contractor, Maximus.

The organisation running the tests may have changed, but they are still dogged by problems. The DWP's figures published in March 2017 found that 59 per cent of the 4,000 appeals on fitness-for-work decisions were successful.[9]

Now, while sickness and disability benefit tests were always going to be difficult, this is an insufficient excuse for ten years of problems. Even less excusable when you consider that the people caught up in this system are some of the most vulnerable in our society: sick, frightened, dependent on the state for help because of bad luck, not choice. The tests themselves have now become a fearful part of being sick, as claimants do not trust that they will be treated fairly and fear losing all their benefits for months on end, even if eventually they are vindicated at appeal.

When I mentioned the tests to an MP, he remarked, 'How on earth were any of us supposed to understand what those tests meant and distil that into a short debate in committee on the regulations?' MPs are too busy with all sorts of other things to become experts on everything, which is presumably why ministers engaged independent experts to assess the efficacy of the tests. But they end up being busier as a result of the genuinely disturbing cases that turn up in their constituency surgeries, including people with degenerative diseases who are not only unable to work but are clearly never going to get better and yet have somehow been found fit for work and therefore ineligible for benefits. Perhaps things would have been different if only those far-reaching regulations had been subject to at least a debate on the full floor of the Commons. Or maybe that would have made no difference, given that they would probably have been passed by a Parliament with a yes-men culture and precious little time for detail.

Visible from space

The really clever yes-men are the ones that sound like scrutineers but are actually as compliant as their colleagues. Take the Health and Social Care Act 2012. This was famously 'paused' when the Liberal Democrats (rather belatedly, given that it had already passed its second reading in the Commons) expressed concerns about its implications. Was this a sign of the Commons halting the progress of bad legislation so that ministers could come up with better policies? Maybe not.

This Act is in fact a prime example of how easy it is to look the other way and not notice something that, in the words of the man in charge of the National Health Service at the time, was so big 'you could probably see it from space'. The legislation was the brainchild of the incredibly clever Andrew Lansley, who had worked on it in opposition, believing he had the trust of David Cameron to draw up truly radical reforms. Indeed, David Cameron trusted Lansley so much that he didn't appear to have looked at the reforms at all until they were hurtling towards the statute book like an asteroid so big it could have had a disaster film featuring Liv Tyler written about it.

Unfortunately, this disaster film featured someone with far less impressive communication skills than Liv Tyler. Lansley was convinced that his reforms, which would radically change the way NHS hospitals worked, would improve the service. But he wasn't quite able to explain what they would actually do – and it seems that no one managed to work that out until far too late. Indeed, it is now difficult to find a Conservative MP who thinks that the legislation their own party introduced was firstly a good idea, and secondly worked in practice. This book is less about which policies are morally right – of course, different parties will disagree over the extent to which the state should be involved, and so on – and more about whether policies that governments introduce actually work. But the Health and Social Care Act fails both those tests.

The reforms made NHS England, rather than the Health Secretary, responsible for people's health, abolished primary care trusts and strategic health authorities, and set up clinical commissioning groups of local doctors, nurses and lay members, which would be responsible for around two thirds of the NHS budget. Everyone had plenty of warning about the bill. The Conservative manifesto referred to it vaguely as 'a reform plan to make the changes the NHS needs' and 'decentralise power', followed by a commitment in the Coalition agreement to 'strengthen the power of GPs as patients' expert guides through the health system by enabling them to commission care on their behalf' (though, confusingly, the agreement also promised to 'stop the top-down reorganisations of the NHS that have got in the way of patient care'. This was most certainly a top-down reorganisation). Then there was a White Paper called 'Equity and Excellence: Liberating the NHS', followed by another publication called 'Liberating the NHS: legislative framework and next steps'. And then came the bill itself, which was published in mid January 2011 amid a rumpus in the health policy world, but which passed its second reading in the Commons at the end of that month.

In that second reading debate, Labour opposed the plans, focusing mainly on fears that the 'ideological' legislation would further open up the NHS to profit-making companies, who would compete on the basis of price, not quality; and the fact that doctors weren't too sweet on the reforms. Margaret Hodge warned Lansley against making things worse through 'the unnecessary institution of reform'. Hodge had spent enough time in government herself to recognise the weakness of all ministers for making their mark on a sector just for the sake of it. Some Conservative backbenchers asked for reassurance about their local NHS services, as did some Lib Dems, though they were as likely to attack Labour during the debate for its previous reforms as they were to talk about their local services. The bill passed by 321 votes to 235. All Conservative and Lib Dem MPs supported the legislation.

So into committee it went. Aware of the growing opposition in the medical world, Lansley tabled a series of amendments to rule out some of the more controversial aspects, such as price competition. The MPs spent days taking evidence from organisations ranging from NHS England itself to patient groups and doctors' bodies, before moving on to line-by-line scrutiny of the legislation. There was just one Liberal Democrat backbench member of the committee, John Pugh, and one Liberal Democrat health minister,

Paul Burstow. Outside the committee room, members of Pugh and Burstow's own party – and the medical profession – were going into rather noisy revolt. While Nick Clegg didn't appear particularly well versed in the finer details of the reforms when he was grilled about them in interviews, his party's grass roots were becoming increasingly agitated.

In March, the British Medical Association voted to reject the reforms. Then the Liberal Democrat spring conference voted in favour of rewriting the legislation to remove what it considered to be an undue emphasis on competition and to give councillors a greater role in the commissioning process. Conservative MPs including Dr Sarah Wollaston, who had tried and failed to get a place on the bill committee, signed a cross-party motion calling on ministers to listen to concerns about the bill. Nick Clegg held talks with David Cameron over the legislation, and on 6 April 2011, the government announced a 'pause' to the bill's progress in order to carry out a two-month 'listening exercise'.

Cameron was privately furious with Andrew Lansley for dropping such a big political bomb. He should also have been furious with himself, given the size of the bomb and the amount of warning that he too had been given about it. *Times* columnist Rachel Sylvester quoted one frustrated Downing Street figure saying the Health Secretary should be 'taken out and shot'.[10] But while Lansley was indeed hopeless at communication, surely it would have been easier for those Downing Street figures to engage with the legislation when it was still in the bowels of Whitehall, rather than exploding messily in the public eye? *The Times* later reported that neither Cameron nor George Osborne had realised how explosive Lansley's plans were because they were 'unintelligible gobbledegook', according to one insider.[11] Of course, legislation will generally appear like gobbledegook to the layperson. But that's why MPs enter Parliament, isn't it, to check on the implications of gobbledegook? So presumably the prime minister and his chancellor would be in the habit of doing so. Perhaps not, if, like Cameron and Osborne, you were rather more interested in moving from the legislature to the executive, where both had previously worked as special advisers.

Clegg, meanwhile, was still in the early phase of Coalition, in which the most important thing was unity of purpose so that the deal between the two parties might last and the government could get on with deficit reduction without distracting rows. He too had clearly failed to pay sufficient attention to Lansley's gobbledegook. But other Lib Dems hadn't. Nicholas Timmins's comprehensive account of this legislative disaster quotes Baroness Shirley Williams saying she spent the February recess reading 'the bill, I read the impact statements, the quality statements, all these huge documents'.[12] Williams had much more time on her hands than those in government, naturally. But she didn't have ranks of special advisers who could do this on her behalf, as those in government did. It was only when she approached Clegg and told him that she was going to lead a rebellion at the Lib Dem spring conference that her party's leader read the bill. And at that point, he realised that he needed to make it stop.

Did the 'listening exercise' result in gobbledegook that might actually work in practice? When the government's amendments to the bill were published in June, everyone from every side claimed victory. But it quickly became clear that many of the fundamental objections to the legislation remained. Worse, Conservative cabinet ministers were privately expressing concern – though this seemed to be far more about the politics of reforming the health service than whether they had a clue that the reforms in question were actually going to help.

By now, though, the government ego that we mentioned in Chapter 4 had kicked back in. It had been an extraordinary suspension of ego for ministers to admit during the passage of the bill that it needed substantial amendments. To have to concede even more would appear dreadfully weak. Worse than the bruised egos of Whitehall was the fact that many of the changes connected to the legislation had already started happening. Staff were being made redundant at primary care trusts. To kill the bill at this stage would have caused even more upheaval for the NHS.

Naturally it was in the Lords where the battles on substance raged. While the Lib Dem leadership had tried to claim that the thousands of amendments tabled represented a significant change to the bill, their own peers and many medical and legal specialists sitting as cross-bench peers disagreed. And at the end of the bill's tumultuous passage through both Houses of Parliament, Lansley was able to claim that its 'fundamental principles' remained intact.[13]

So all that sound and fury, and thousands of technical amendments that only a handful of parliamentarians really truly understood, and still the bill was the same? Well, perhaps that's the prerogative of a party in government. But is it the government's prerogative to pass bad legislation that doesn't turn out to work so well?

From the outset, the implications of the Act were messy. Timmins writes that 'Monitor [the regulator] now has a wide range of apparently conflicting duties which may not be irreconcilable but which will take some reconciling: not just the twin duties to prevent anti-competitive behaviour and promote integration, but also to tackle health inequalities, promote research and much else. Its senior executives are unclear whether this welter of duties in practice gives it much freedom of action, or whether it lays it open to endless legal challenge.'[14]

There were a number of factors that made it more difficult than usual for Parliament to scrutinise this bill. The first was that there was a lot of legislation going through the Commons at the time. Cameron had learned from the Blair government that serious public sector reform should take place as early in a parliament as possible, and so alongside the health bill were big, controversial reforms on legal aid, welfare and education. MPs had plenty to be looking at, and the Health and Social Care Act wasn't exactly light reading, in terms of either length or clarity.

With a lot of new MPs keen to do their leadership's bidding in the hope of getting a job in the executive, and a coalition trying to find its feet, there were added incentives not to read the bill at all. So while the storm that blew up outside Parliament among the doctors' bodies was policy-focused, it remained largely political in nature inside Westminster because the majority of MPs didn't know the substance of the bill, and therefore didn't know what the changes to that bill entailed. Mind you, they got more opportunity than was strictly necessary to look at it. Indeed, Lansley remarked rather sourly during its pause that he could have carried out his reforms without primary legislation, shunting the majority of the changes into secondary legislation, which would have gone before committees with a government majority and a group of pliable backbenchers. So the Commons should have counted itself lucky that it got the chance to have such a glorious row at all.

Just two years after the bill passed into law, Conservatives privately accepted it was a disaster. One senior cabinet minister told *The Times*, 'We've made three mistakes that I regret, the first being restructuring the NHS. The rest are minor.'[15] Stephen Dorrell, who had served as Health Secretary under John Major and as chairman of the Health Select Committee under the Coalition government, supported the bill in Parliament, but told the *Observer* in 2015 that the reforms were his party's biggest mistake in government, largely because they created a huge amount of upheaval over management structures.

The reforms cost £3 billion and a great deal of political capital. They didn't solve the question of the NHS's long-term financial sustainability, nor that of social care (see Chapter 10), nor the problem of how a service set up to treat largely acute illnesses could deal with so many people living longer with chronic conditions. They were supposed to remove the secretary of state's political oversight of the health service, yet Jeremy Hunt's focus when he took over from the beleaguered Lansley as Health Secretary was on standards and mistakes in individual hospitals, to the extent that he had a whiteboard in his ministerial office with a list of the most recent 'never again events' – such as doctors amputating the wrong limb. Simon Stevens, who was appointed chief executive of NHS England in 2013, has since taken on the task of reform – as perhaps he might be expected to, given the responsibilities outlined in the Act – undertaking to repair the 'fractured' health and social care system.

Of course ministers can be mistaken in their judgement about what will help the health service. The problem is that if they pursue that judgement onto the statute books, it then causes another big mess, and years of disruption to the fragile NHS if anyone tries to unpick the policies that have been implemented. So big you can see it from space, and so complicated that not even an astrophysicist would relish fixing it.

CHAPTER 12

—

TRAPPED!

Governments who manage to whisk a complicated bill past bewildered MPs initially count themselves lucky to have got away with it. They then repent at leisure as the realities of the policies, which no one cared or dared to point out, wreak havoc in voters' lives. In many cases, this is the fault of the yes-men of the previous chapter: MPs who have chosen to suck up to the executive because they want a job, or those who are so busy with other non-legislative business that they simply don't have time to look at the laws.

Even though the cultural pressure to behave in this way is strong, it is still a choice. But governments can force even conscientious parliaments into yes-men moulds by denying them the powers and opportunities to probe big, serious policies. Even very earnest scrutineers can end up being trapped by the system of legislating. Chapter 4 didn't just show us that the legislative process is complicated; it also showed how little power MPs really have, even when they want to make decent changes or introduce thoughtful laws. Secondary legislation is a classic way by which governments trap MPs into approving laws without proper scrutiny. But it goes much further than that – and has deadly consequences.

The war trap

Ask anyone whether we get the wrong politicians and it won't be long before the word 'Iraq' crops up. Whether or not removing Saddam Hussein, a brutal dictator who unashamedly killed his own people, was the best thing for Iraq in the long run is a question far beyond the scope of this book. But the run-up to war, and Parliament's involvement in scrutinising the conflict as it unfolded, and its aftermath, is another example of how the executive is able to trap legislators into being yes-men.

This is despite the fact that the decision to invade Iraq was hotly debated in Parliament. Indeed, it is despite Tony Blair's own awareness of the conditions that he would need to satisfy in order to secure parliamentary approval for the conflict. It is also despite the fact that members of his own cabinet dissented publicly, with Clare Short and Robin Cook both criticising the decision and resigning from the government in protest.

But while MPs poured considerable effort into examining the arguments that the prime minister put before them over several months, what they were unable to do was force ministers to reveal certain details that would have helped Parliament reach a more informed decision. In this case, it wasn't that there was a lack of willing MPs to scrutinise the government. It was that the structures of Westminster made it impossible for them to do their jobs. They were forced into the yes-men mould even though, for once, few of them wanted to be. And so we get the wrong politics not just because of a culture, but because of a design that is in the interests of the executive to perpetuate.

There was no formal requirement for Blair to seek the approval of Parliament: going to war is the preserve of the executive. Yet

Parliament was recalled from recess in September 2002 for the publication of the dossier of evidence of Saddam Hussein's weapons of mass destruction. MPs endorsed seeking a solution through the UN. Then, in March 2003, the cabinet agreed that they should be asked to endorse military action in Iraq. There were two votes on the matter in the Commons on 18 March, with a quarter of Labour MPs rebelling against the motion. Blair himself told MPs as he opened the debate that 'at the outset, I say that it is right that the House debate this issue and pass judgement'.

It is not Parliament's fault that the evidence presented to it was not of the highest standard. *The Spectator*, which supported the Iraq war, judged in 2016 after the publication of the Chilcot report that 'there is a huge difference between campaigning and governing. When it comes to Parliament making grave decisions such as whether or not to go to war, the information put before it should be unimpeachable. Tony Blair treated winning Parliament over to his military adventure in Iraq like just another election to be won. It was an error of judgement for which he and many others have suffered ever since.'[1]

Blair had told George W. Bush, 'I will be with you, whatever' long before turning to Parliament for approval. He was in campaigning mode, and wanted Parliament to approve what he had already decided.

Former Conservative MP and committed Commons scrutineer Andrew Tyrie was scathing about the relationship between Parliament and the government. In a 2004 pamphlet entitled *Mr Blair's Poodle Goes to War*, he wrote: 'The executive has succeeded in frustrating Parliament . . . Congress has fared only a little better. Ultimately, the losers are not just our legislatures, nor even our electorates. Executive obstructionism and parliamentary weakness threaten to erode trust in politics and politicians, leaving our system of government the biggest casualty.'[2]

Tyrie was particularly unimpressed with the information Parliament was able to extract about the post-conflict planning for Iraq. What Blair and his ministers had considered for the country after the invasion was inadequate, something even those who supported the principle of removing Saddam agree about in hindsight. Blair told the Chilcot inquiry that 'with hindsight, we now see that the military campaign to defeat Saddam was relatively easy; it was the aftermath that was hard. At the time, of course, we could not know that and a prime focus throughout was the military campaign itself.' The next line of the report's executive summary is dry and scathing: 'The conclusions reached by Mr Blair after the invasion did not require the benefit of hindsight.'[3]

Blair was well aware of the importance of long-term planning after an invasion. But perhaps his mind would have been more acutely focused on this had Parliament been able to force ministers to articulate what exactly they were going to do afterwards. As Tyrie pointed out, 'Parliament's cross-examination of the executive failed, for the most part, even to establish whether or not the executive had done much forward planning.'

Blair's opening speech on 18 March did state that 'What happens after any conflict in Iraq is of such critical significance.' He set out his plans, which covered a UN resolution for humanitarian help, the administration and governance of Iraq, and protection for the country's territorial integrity. This was as much to answer the accusation flying around at the time that it was 'all about the oil': he then added, 'This point is also important: that the oil revenues, which people falsely claim that we want to seize, should be put in a trust fund for the Iraqi people administered through the UN.'

Iain Duncan Smith, then the leader of the Conservative Party, complained in the Chamber about 'the lack of preparedness' of the government. Plaid Cymru MP Elfyn Llwyd, who vehemently opposed the war, shot back, 'If those preparations are so ill-advanced, why is the Right Honourable Gentleman so keen on going to war?' Other opponents of action, such as Tam Dalyell, asked how an aftermath might be measured a 'success', pointing to the circumstances in Afghanistan. MPs also raised concerns about how well equipped the troops being sent into combat would be, but the focus of the debate was squarely on the case for war and the legality of it. This is understandable, given that the House was voting that night on whether to go to war, but it did mean that the prime minister was able to sidestep the question of how much planning really had been done.

Perhaps the job of examining post-conflict planning, both before and after the decision to go to war, was better done by select committees anyway. They have the time and space to go into details in a forum that lacks the theatre of the Commons. But they too were frustrated by their lack of powers, and the executive's refusal to cooperate. Andrew Tyrie believes the committees – of which he was not a member – were 'unable to provide the whole House leadership on the issue', and that they were also unable to obtain much more information than the Commons at large or the media could. This was the case before and after the war: neither the Defence nor the Foreign Affairs Select Committee was allowed to access the relevant papers and records that they needed to see as part of their inquiries. Their reports made statements to the effect that they were 'entitled to a greater degree of cooperation from the government on access to witnesses and to intelligence material' and that the relevant ministries had 'demonstrated on occasion less cooperation and openness than we have the right to expect as a Select Committee of the House of Commons'.

So who did get to the bottom of whether the government had made adequate plans for Iraq after the invasion, and indeed whether the intelligence on which it based the invasion was sufficient? It was never MPs. There were three separate inquiries into the conflict: the Hutton inquiry, which examined the circumstances of the death of weapons expert Dr David Kelly, whose off-the-record chat with BBC journalist Andrew Gilligan had sparked the row about whether the government had 'sexed up' its dossier on Saddam Hussein's weapons of mass destruction; the Butler Review of Intelligence on Weapons of Mass Destruction; and the Chilcot inquiry, which only concluded in 2016, having been set up in 2009 by Gordon Brown. So it was only when the executive deemed it appropriate that a properly powerful examination of the events was carried out, and that wasn't done by Parliament but by an independent body.

The consequences of this were enormous and are well known. By July 2009, at least 150,000 Iraqis had died as a result of the invasion and subsequent instability. A vacuum was created into which Islamic State came charging, which led to further military action in the country. In September 2014, Parliament approved Britain joining air strikes against Islamic State in Iraq, but Prime Minister David Cameron was so scarred by his failure a year earlier to secure approval for strikes against President Assad's regime in Syria that he did not feel confident enough to ask for approval of strikes against IS in Syria too.

Of course, everyone makes mistakes: it's just that in government these can be colossal ones that lead to the deaths of troops and innocent civilians. At least governments can learn from those colossal mistakes and not repeat them, right?

Wrong. The Iraq war certainly taught everyone many lessons about how to do politics, but it doesn't seem to have helped all that much in the way of post-conflict planning, if the conflict is even approved in the first place. Now, whenever the question of military intervention arises in the House of Commons, MPs fall into a frenzy of apologising for their sins or those of their forebears, even accidentally referring to the latest brutal dictator as 'Saddam', as a number of members did when debating military action against Assad in 2013.

Iraq has enshrined a convention of prime ministers consulting the House of Commons on military action, but this has not been put into law, partly because of the difficulties involved in deciding when a leader must consult the House and when it would be more effective not to highlight that action is about to be taken. David Cameron was anxious to avoid the accusations that Blair faced of 'sofa government' over matters of foreign policy, and so set up the National Security Council when he became prime minister.

But it did not lead to greater caution about post-conflict planning in Libya, for instance. In March 2011, NATO forces took action against Muammar Gaddafi, who it was feared was about to launch a genocide in the city of Benghazi as the civil war in his country intensified. MPs approved the action after it had begun, though many expressed concerns about 'mission creep' from the original objective, which was to prevent the genocide, to regime change in the country. Leader of the opposition Ed Miliband urged the prime minister to prepare for every eventuality, as did others, but once again the House of Commons was unable to extract much further detail from the government on what that would involve.

The same month, Cameron held a conference in London that focused on the importance of planning for a post-Gaddafi Libya. But in June of that year, Foreign Secretary William Hague described the Libyan rebels' plan for democracy after Gaddafi as 'embryonic'. The *Financial Times* then revealed that just 12 officials in the International Development department were planning the reconstruction of the country, with no one in either the Foreign Office or the Ministry of Defence working solely on the matter. In an interview with Cameron's biographer Sir Anthony Seldon, the former chief of the Defence Staff Sir David Richards criticised the absence of long-term planning: 'There is a lack of strategy and statesmanship. The problem is the inability to think things through. Too often it seems to be more about the Notting Hill liberal agenda rather than statecraft.'[4]

Barack Obama agreed with this in March 2016, claiming in an interview with *The Atlantic* that Libya was a 'mess' (he is reported to have described it as a 'shit show' in private). He argued that he had 'more faith in the Europeans, given Libya's proximity, being invested in the follow-up', but pointed out that President Sarkozy had lost his job in 2012 and David Cameron was 'distracted by a range of other things'.[5]

The Europeans couldn't be distracted from Libya forever, though. That 'shit show' included the collapse of the country's democracy and its economy, a humanitarian crisis that led to a migration crisis, with Libyans joining Syrians risking their lives in totally unseaworthy boats to cross the Mediterranean and start a new life in Europe. It also saw Gaddafi-regime weapons making their way into the hands of Islamic State. In late 2011, Cameron and Sarkozy made an emotional visit to Benghazi, where they were cheered by crowds. But this was followed by the collapse of the country in the long term.

In the aftermath, the Commons picked over what had gone wrong. By this time, select committees had been given more teeth. Their chairs were elected rather than being chosen by the whips, and so were their members. In September 2016, the Foreign Affairs Select Committee produced a damning report of the conflict, which was described by some as Parliament's equivalent of Chilcot for Libya. The MPs on the committee said, 'We have seen no evidence that the UK government carried out a proper analysis of the nature of the rebellion in Libya.'[6] They criticised the 'international community's inability to secure weapons abandoned by the Gaddafi regime', which 'fuelled instability in Libya and enabled and increased terrorism across north and west Africa and the Middle East'. And, specifically on the question of post-conflict planning, they suggested that the government had perhaps learned the wrong lesson of the Iraq war: 'We recognise that the damaging experience of post-war intervention in Iraq engendered an understandable reluctance to impose solutions in Libya. However, because the UK along with France led the military intervention, it had a particular responsibility to support Libyan economic and political reconstruction, which became an impossible task because of the failure to establish security on the ground.'

The committee placed the blame squarely on Cameron, saying: 'Through his decision-making in the National Security Council, former prime minister David Cameron was ultimately responsible for the failure to develop a coherent Libya strategy.' But his failure to do so was inadequately tested by Parliament at the time. Once again, MPs spent so much time debating the principle of intervention that they failed to pressure the government for more detail on plans for the aftermath.

David Cameron, like Blair before him, still insists intervention was the right thing. He refused to give evidence to the committee's inquiry, and left the Commons at the same time as the report was published, so has never really had to answer for his decisions. This is another weakness in the parliamentary system. You can be questioned ad nauseam on your plans for a shit show. But once that shit show is on the road and its consequences are plain to see, if you're out of the Commons (or even if you are in it and no longer in the government), you don't have to help MPs with their inquiries – inquiries that may at least stop someone making the same mistake all over again.

Brexit

Could Brexit be the next big complicated disaster, so big you can see it from space, and yet also too big for MPs to understand or scrutinise properly? Since the 2016 EU referendum, MPs and ministers have been engaged in a tug of war over who really gets to 'take back control' of making laws. Yet the position they will eventually arrive at still won't guarantee that the British people won't feel as though their lives are being messed about by a higher political power.

It's not just the new relationship between Britain and its closest trading partner that is in the balance, but also the way Parliament will scrutinise the laws for which it may now have responsibility. To begin with, there was a threat that Parliament wouldn't even get a chance to look at much of the new Brexit legislation, with the government's original plan for the Repeal Bill being that tens of thousands of EU regulations would be replaced without scrutiny. Eventually Parliament won that fight, with a new 'sifting committee' being set up to decide how much debate each change deserved. If it was merely removing the letters 'EU' from a regulation, it could pass without a fuss. If the piece of legislation actually represented a dramatic shift in policy, then the committee would send it to MPs for proper consideration.

Except, of course, we know what 'proper consideration' of secondary legislation really looks like in Parliament. Whatever your view of Brexit, it is hard to argue – as both Remainers and Leavers have – that Parliament has really 'taken back control'. This book has shown that MPs are scarcely in control of the issues they've been responsible for over the past few decades, let alone anything new. And the shortcomings don't just concern the structure of the Commons, but the culture too.

Ministers' desire to dodge scrutiny as much as possible was laid bare by former Brexit Secretary David Davis, who seemed to regard his role as part negotiator and part obfuscator, sending up clouds of confusion about the government's policy on leaving the EU at every turn. He had a habit of blustering in the Commons about how well things were going, and managed to dig himself into a bit of a hole when he told the Foreign Affairs Committee in September 2016 that the government was working on a number of detailed reports on the impact of Brexit on different sectors. MPs wanted to see these reports, funnily enough, and held an Opposition Day debate in the Commons calling for them. The government was terrified of showing its vulnerability by fighting anything, even non-binding Opposition Day votes, that it would be defeated on, so it ordered Conservative MPs to abstain. The motion passed.

Commons Leader Andrea Leadsom then said the government was happy to release the papers, but that there might be some delays while ministers worked out how to avoid damaging the ongoing Brexit negotiations. Eventually they were passed to the Brexit Select Committee, which was so unimpressed with the quantity of information contained in them that it summoned Davis to explain himself. In an extraordinary hearing on 6 December 2017, the Brexit Secretary admitted that in fact there was 'no systematic impact assessment', no 'formal quantitative assessment' of the impact of leaving the customs union, and that it didn't necessarily follow that 'because you use the word impact, you have written an impact assessment'.

The MPs were furious, and published the documents themselves. Some threatened to have Davis held in contempt of Parliament, which could have led to him being suspended, expelled, or locked in the clock tower (while this last has not been done for centuries, Theresa May must have considered reviving it for her Brexit Secretary, given the number of blunders he made).

Not long after this, MPs voted to hold the entire government in contempt of Parliament, albeit with a different Brexit Secretary at the helm (Davis had long since resigned, and had been replaced by Dominic Raab, who also resigned, to be replaced by Stephen Barclay). This was because ministers had refused to publish legal advice on Brexit – even though the Labourites who were demanding this publication admitted that they wouldn't want to set a precedent that meant they would have to do the same for every big decision a future Labour government might end up taking.

Some argued that this was Parliament taking back control. Still more made this case when, in January 2019, MPs started to formulate their own plans for what Brexit should actually look like. When Conservative MP Nick Boles proposed that the Liaison Committee, which is made up of the heads of all the other select committees in the Commons, should take over the design of the Brexit plan after Theresa May's first attempt had failed, the members of that committee refused, pointing out that that they did not have the necessary resources or experience to write legislation. This was a fair response: select committees may well be one of the bits of Parliament that work relatively well, but the Boles plan would have represented a significant change to the way in which those committees operate. It would have been unreasonable to expect even the most proactive legislators to take on the biggest project politicians have faced in their lifetime, having had no experience at all on smaller matters.

Beyond that structural barrier, though, was a cultural one. Parliament was unused to taking big decisions; even less so than those politicians in the executive who had managed to dodge tricky issues before. Theresa May had procrastinated wildly on many of the toughest matters, such as the Northern Irish border, presumably because she had cut her teeth in a political culture that generally either rewarded or at least tolerated putting things off for as long as possible.

Given that the government has 2,000 lawyers, Parliament has 20, and the Opposition has limited resources at the best of times, the chaos before the Brexit deadline of 29 March 2019 is just the start of a crisis that does not bode well for one of the greatest political changes in modern British history.

———

CAN WE GET THE RIGHT POLITICIANS?

Here's a confession. I've led you on rather in this book, suggesting with its title about the 'wrong politicians' that we do indeed have a bunch of self-serving toffs in the House of Commons. Of course, you will have realised by now that I think of them rather more charitably, and perhaps you are sorely disappointed, because this isn't what you expected.

What we hope for from our politicians will inevitably lead to disappointment. We want them to tend to our every parking problem, but also spend all their time in the House of Commons Chamber, where we can see them. We want them to have their family home in the constituency, but also to have a perfect life when in Westminster. We want them to earn less than us but make crucial decisions on our behalf. We want them to keep the prime minister up to speed on the issues we care about, but also to be 'in touch' with ordinary people. We also expect them not to mess up our lives further by churning out bad laws. In addition, we want to punish them for the expenses scandal, regardless of whether they were even in Parliament at the time, and to stop them from getting too big for their boots by abusing them on social media. And then we wonder why 'ordinary' people don't want to go into politics.

Time to separate?

Ah, you say, so it's my fault that we get the wrong politicians. All I did was place a cross on a piece of paper a few years ago on my way home from work. Not my fault that the Bubble is the way it is.

This is true, and it would be both trite and rather odd if a book that had detailed quite how frustrating, powerless and personally miserable the life of an MP can be then ended by telling people that it's their own fault for not standing for Parliament themselves. There are much bigger problems than a grumpy public, and they lie well within Westminster itself. The first is the structure of the place, which is obvious and the sort of thing that constitutionalists can have exciting debates about that then fall flat when presented to the public in a referendum about how the country should vote, or about House of Lords reform – though this book has shown that the House of Lords is one of the few places where scrutiny does actually happen. But the second problem is more pernicious, and that is the culture.

Let's first look at the structure, and what we might do to change that. We do not have a full separation of powers in this country. Thus, when an MP is elected, he or she might be joining Parliament not just for the love of backbench life, but because they want to work in government and achieve things for the country that way. A noble aim, but it's not strictly the job named on the ballot paper. MPs who are ministers do not scrutinise bills, because they are busy working on them in their own departments. So at any one time, over a hundred MPs aren't actually doing their job as members of the legislature because they are in fact members of the executive.

To solve this, we would have to separate the government from Parliament, so that MPs and ministers were entirely different jobs.

This is the system in America, where ministers are appointed to the government, and members of Congress are elected to the Senate or the House of Representatives. The president is elected in his own right, and then appoints his government. Of course, many Congressmen aspire to be in the executive. But the leap between the two is bigger. Indeed, it is an actual leap, rather than a situation where an MP has their parliamentary office and their constituency office and their ministerial office – and to vote against the government would be to lose the ministerial office.

Appointing ministers also gives the president a much bigger pool to choose from than just his parliamentary party. That pool will include experts in the field, rather than simply people who are quick learners and have been loyal as backbenchers. It means a minister isn't required to mug up on housing for 18 months before suddenly needing to hold their own in front of the Chief of the Defence Staff. Of course ministers would still want to make their mark by spewing out legislation. But at least they might have a chance of understanding what that legislation actually entailed.

There are a number of MPs who are advocates of separation of powers. They tend to be those who admire American politics, and who also enjoy working on legislation rather than aspiring to be ministers. Graham Brady, the powerful chair of the Conservative 1922 Committee, is one such. He believes that taking the executive out of Parliament would remove patronage as a corrosive force in the culture of the place, as well as preventing the government from having control of the legislative agenda in the way it does currently.

Ministers would actually have to make the case to their party colleagues in Parliament in order to get support, rather than knowing that, bar an unusual rebellion, they're pretty certain to get at least the bulk of a bill through because of their inbuilt Commons majority.

But then again, Congress is hardly a bastion of political virtue. A study of American voters in 2017 by Pew Research Center found that just 6 per cent expressed a 'great deal of confidence' in their legislature. It is beset by the same partisan bickering as Westminster. And the dream of ministers having to make their case to elected party colleagues can all too often become a nightmare involving 'pork barrel politics', in which those party colleagues are promised funding, infrastructure and other incentives for their constituencies in return for support, or in which a Republican-dominated Congress repeatedly frustrates the government's desire to pass legislation promised by the president, who was elected by the American people. Both wings of government are elected, but they end up at loggerheads over what the voters really want them to do. In Britain, voters back a party with a programme for government, and it is therefore reasonable to expect that the government should be able to deliver what it has promised without the 'losers' – the opposition – being able to intervene. In the US, if both houses of Congress are dominated by the president's opponents, then he becomes a 'lame duck', unable to deliver anything particularly radical.

There are other problems besides the legislative deadlock that critics of the American system cite. Speaker John Bercow is fervently in favour of strengthening Parliament, but very cool on the idea of a full separation of powers. When I asked him about this, he explained: 'I think that the case would have to be made quite strongly as to why it is or how it would be that we would be better served if ministers were not directly and immediately accountable to the House . . . It is a risky enterprise to move away from a situation where, however powerful they might be, they are members of our Parliament and we've got them.'[1]

Bercow's delight in granting troublesome urgent questions to backbenchers and members of the opposition is an example of this, though the minister responsible for a crisis can quite easily send someone to answer on his behalf. David Gauke, for instance, became the go-to minister first for George Osborne and then for Philip Hammond whenever those chancellors were in trouble. He would calmly spend an hour at the dispatch box, insulated from MPs' anger by the knowledge that the crisis wasn't his fault, and able to calm the Chamber with his cool sense of humour and general likeability. An impressive skill, but not particularly good for accountability.

Committees in Britain also have far less power than in other countries, including the US. They can summon a minister, but no MP can be forced to attend. Of course, the parliamentary and media pressure to turn up is a powerful incentive against hiding from an angry select committee. Other democratic systems give committees the legal right to summon ministers, even though many do not exercise this right very often. Members of the executive do not appear on the floor of Congress, but once again the committees have powers to subpoena departmental secretaries if necessary.

One final objection to a full separation of powers in the UK is merely practical. It isn't going to happen. The British public tend to be disgusted by the political system but bored by attempts to change it, as the 2011 Alternative Vote referendum showed (that is one reason why the process by which MPs are elected isn't covered by this book: there is a case for electoral reform, but it was made and voters didn't like it). Constitutional change interests only a niche group of people in Westminster. Even when voters are angry, they aren't excited by the prospect of further upheaval of their institutions. Brexit, which represents the biggest change to our institutions since the Second World War, is another case in point.

But that's not to say that full separation of powers is the only game in town. Indeed, the changes made to select committees in recent years show the value of incremental reform, which beefs up Parliament structurally and also encourages a culture of seriousness about being a parliamentarian rather than a minister. Speakers like Bercow, who believe that their job is to make Parliament appear to be serving the voters, whether it be through granting urgent questions, extending PMQs far beyond the half an hour it is supposed to last, or scolding MPs for behaving like children during certain debates, can make the Bubble a better place without the bother of referenda about changing the way the whole system operates.

Turbocharging Parliament

How could you turbocharge the existing parliamentary system? Firstly by shrinking the executive. The Public Administration Select Committee suggested in 2010 that the payroll vote (that is, ministers and their parliamentary private secretaries [PPSs]) shouldn't exceed 15 per cent of the overall size of the Commons.[2] It is not just the plethora of ministers who are removed from the day-to-day role of scrutiny and guaranteed to support the government on every vote, but the myriad unpaid government roles such as PPSs, backbench policy boards, trade envoys to this, special ambassadors to that and so on. All of these promotions are offered on the understanding that the MP in question stays loyal to the government, so they too become passive members of the legislature.

After the expenses scandal, a committee of MPs proposed a series of reforms to improve public confidence in Parliament. Their suggestions, known informally as the Wright report after their chair Tony Wright, included ending the system by which select committee chairs and members were chosen by the whips. The Coalition government implemented almost everything, except a proposal to give MPs control over the amount of time allowed for debating each bill. Currently the government decides this, though technically MPs approve it through a 'programme motion' at the second reading of each bill. This motion, though, is as heavily whipped as the rest of the legislation, and it is only in exceptional circumstances, when rebels in the governing party want to kill off a bill – such as the Coalition's attempt in 2012 to reform the House of Lords – that the government loses a vote. MPs have control of non-government time through a backbench business committee, which was also recommended by Wright and which decides topics for debates that MPs are interested in. But the House Business Committee, which would take away power from the government to decide how much time MPs need to spend debating a bill, remains a pipe dream, and one that Labour hasn't been too keen on either. Critics argue that such a committee would either be a rubber-stamping exercise for what the government wants, if it has an inbuilt majority, or a means by which oppositions could prevent the democratically elected government from getting its way.

Even if we stick to the same system of the executive deigning to give the legislature a certain amount of time to debate laws, there are still ways to make those debates better. Bill committees and statutory instruments are currently the obvious weak structural link. They are so pointless that the only people who would miss them would be the whips, who often use delegated legislation committees as a punishment for MPs who have recently rebelled. Abolishing the whole stage would just mean that the government would need to table more amendments at report stage, and members of the opposition wouldn't have to draft such long speeches about the problems with the bill that no one really listens to.

This would be rather defeatist, though, and committees do in theory have a hugely important function in scrutinising the detail – it's just that they're currently not doing their job. Other parliaments, including the Scottish Parliament and the German Bundestag, have linked their select committees with public bill committees, which means that the members charged with looking at the detail will at least have a chance of understanding what that detail actually entails, as a result of their time taking evidence on the select committee. Anthony King and Ivor Crewe have suggested that this increased level of expertise would lead to fewer messes making it onto the statute book, arguing that 'perhaps it is no accident that governments in Germany since the Federal Republic's inception in 1949 have almost certainly committed fewer egregious blunders than governments in the UK'.[3] It would also mean that another key weakness of public bill committees that those authors identify – their lack of professional staff – would be solved, as select committees have a small staff attached to them.

Stronger bill committees made up of MPs with an interest in the policy area would at least mean a possibility that someone might spot a potential mistake before it went any further. But the incentive not to pipe up about that mistake would still be strong. Most MPs have concluded that, to be effective, you have to be a member of the executive. Complaining about the drafting of a bill means wrecking your chances of joining the executive. Not complaining about it means a mess, but MPs are rarely held accountable for the mistakes they make, whether as ministers or as the people whose votes enabled ministers to get their way on a bad policy.

This means that the incentives involved in being an MP need to change. The Wright report and countless other examinations of Parliament's problems all make a powerful case for better post-legislative scrutiny. There is currently little reason for a minister to fear being hauled over the coals because their policy turns out to have been a dud. Some policies take years before their utter folly manifests itself, by which time Parliament has not, in Bercow's words, 'got the minister', because the minister left the government, resigned as an MP and is now enjoying a quieter and more lucrative life elsewhere. Prime ministers are in charge of the government and therefore tend to have to take the blame for mistakes made by their juniors. But even former prime ministers don't spend much time answering detailed questions about what they got wrong years ago. Tony Blair is unusual in that he regularly ruminates in public about why he went to war, and why he still sincerely believes that he made the right decision. He is hardly the only leader who has made a mistake.

It's not just ministers, though, who don't need to fear the long-term consequences of bad legislation. Even when a reform is widely accepted to be a mess and those who approved it are still in Parliament, they are rarely asked to account for what they did. Liz Truss, for instance, did a good job on the public bill committee for the legal aid reforms, and even served as Conservative Justice Secretary. But she hasn't had to answer for her actions in approving some of those cuts, partly because she was performing her role in the way that every other member of a governing party who is put on a bill committee does. But what if every MP who served on a committee scrutinising legislation had to answer to their colleagues and the public when that legislation turned out to be a terrible mistake?

An important new stage of post-legislative scrutiny could be public payback, whereby a panel of people who were either experts in the field or members of the public directly affected by a government policy could ask the members of the committee that approved it why they voted the way they did. Some of those experts would be able to point out that they had warned the MPs when giving evidence at committee stage in the first place, but that the MPs had been more interested in undermining them as witnesses. The people whose lives had been wrecked by a clumsy benefit cut could explain to the backbencher what losing their home meant to them, and ask them why they had thought that this or that cut was OK when they voted on it. Yes, these panels would be angry, bruising affairs for MPs who would have to admit to those asking the questions that they had only voted a certain way because they had been ordered to do so by their whips. But MPs already encounter the heartbreaking consequences of bad legislation in their constituency surgeries: public payback panels would merely make a direct link to the members who approved that bad legislation. It would mean that attending a legislative committee would not be either an opportunity to suck up to the whips or a punishment, but something that MPs were anxious to get right, because they would know that getting it wrong could result in having to face someone whose life had been ruined. They would then not be merely advocates of their party's policy in the committee room, but people who wanted to ensure that everything was being done to get that policy absolutely spot on.

Public payback would also answer the desire among voters to break open the Bubble. Jeremy Corbyn made admirable attempts to do this in his early Prime Minister's Questions to David Cameron by crowd-sourcing his questions. His execution of this 'phone-in' format left a great deal to be desired, but he was right to try to make PMQs more about the people affected by the government's decisions. Public payback would do that in a targeted way, outside of the partisan hurly-burly of PMQs. It could be organised in a similar manner to the petitions that MPs already debate in Parliament, with a petitions committee deciding how to deal with causes that have reached a certain threshold of signatures. The sessions could be chaired by an MP to ensure a relative level of civility and structure, and the questioners could be approved by the payback committee. Some MPs might fear that these panels would be too chaotic and angry, but that suggests a rather low view of the public that may have developed as a result of too much time in the Bubble. They might also risk becoming overtly partisan, though the culture of select committees, where partisanship is frowned upon, would be a good blueprint to prevent this.

Changing how MPs view their time on committees, both by linking them to the expertise of the select committee and adding an incentive to get it right or face the music, would help shift the culture of the Commons. This book has repeatedly shown how being a legislator is rarely celebrated in our political culture. The changes to select committees have helped develop an alternative career path to being a minister, and there are more developments that could help. The right-of-centre think tank Reform recommends paying members of select committees an attendance-based supplementary salary, which would again add an incentive for taking the whole thing more seriously.[4] If there was a shrinking of the gap between senior legislators' salaries and those paid to ministers, the legislative powerhouse would become even more powerful, as very few people don't want to get on and earn a higher wage.

But it cannot be the case that the Commons is strongest outside the Chamber. Currently few MPs see the physical House of

Commons as the best forum for getting things done, even though their constituents tend to believe it is. The way their performance is assessed by the public and the media does not help with this. We are obsessed with how many questions or speeches MPs contribute in the Commons, but not the quality of those contributions. As I was writing this book, I started a blog called the Burn Book[5] (based on a book of 'dirt' compiled by characters in the film *Mean Girls*), which lists the utterly pointless questions that MPs ask at PMQs. Some got rather shirty about this, arguing for instance that their pointless question that drew attention to the fact that Jeremy Corbyn supported the Venezuelan government despite rampant injustices in that country was in fact an important way of scrutinising Labour. (This rather ignored the fact that Labour hadn't won the election, didn't have any real power, and therefore didn't require much time to be given to scrutiny.) But it did force them to answer for their questions. If MPs were anxious about the quality, rather than quantity, of their contributions, perhaps they wouldn't feel quite so comfortable about helping out their party leader by producing parliamentary candy floss whenever they stood up to speak.

It is more important to change the culture rather than the overarching structures of our political system. MPs should want to be MPs, not to become ministers. There should be more rewards for being serious about what Parliament does. Currently the majority of people standing for Parliament want to be either a minister or a glorified social worker, devoting themselves to constituency work. There are few who want to devote themselves to the Commons by being a legislator. Instead, being an MP is a rung on the ladder to something else. There isn't even any training in how to scrutinise bills. MPs just work it out as they go along. Surely Parliament could offer something a little better.

The biggest culture change involves select committees once again. If they became legislative powerhouses, possibly even able to draft decent backbench legislation that was debated properly rather than tossed about on the floor of the Commons on an idle Friday to those who enjoy devoting themselves to filibustering about wine cellars, then joining a committee could become a sincere aspiration of equal merit to joining the executive. You would get a pay rise. You would get more attention. You could change things. You could feel intellectually satisfied as you developed expertise in a subject. You would have a higher place in the hierarchy of the Commons, being called earlier in debates by the Speaker as someone more senior than other backbenchers, and someone whose contribution was likely to be meaty, rather than pointless partisan waffle. You would even be as busy as a minister, given the number of inquiries and legislative committees you would be involved with.

Some of these things sound like rather petty reasons for MPs wanting to be better legislators. But remember that all humans respond to small rewards, and currently most of the rewards, big and small, lie in the executive. Media attention and praise, a sense of power and the belief that you might actually be able to change things aren't insignificant considerations when it comes to an MP deciding what sort of politician they want to be.

One of the reasons why we sometimes get the wrong politicians is that they don't really see any reason to be the sort of politician who scrutinises legislation. But this book has made clear that we have the wrong kind of people going into Parliament too. Yes, our MPs tend to be hard-working and sincere in their desire to make the world a better place. But they are drawn from too narrow a pool to ensure that we get the best politicians with the best breadth of experience.

There is a great deal of incentive to sound concerned about this if you are a politician, but little incentive to really do anything once you're actually in Westminster. Countless MPs brag about how they are different to all the others, often with comic consequences. Take Andy Burnham's claim in a Mumsnet Q&A during the 2015 Labour leadership contest that he didn't really like biscuits, but 'give me a beer and chips and gravy any day'.[6] Burnham was attempting to appear a northern man of the people rather than an Oxbridge graduate who had worked as a special adviser before becoming an MP. But even if your backstory does involves being northern and going to a comprehensive (still not the norm in Parliament), you are probably going to have a more recent story involving either working in Westminster or earning lots of money outside it. This doesn't make you a 'wrong politician' individually. It's just that those types of occupation are not the only source of wise and decent potential parliamentarians.

Changing this would be more difficult than changing Parliament. It would involve more outreach into communities where people are active in helping one another but detached from party politics because those already in the Bubble look different and inaccessible. It couldn't be done by the political parties alone, but would need involvement from organisations with a non-partisan interest in improving the make-up of Parliament. The Speaker's Parliamentary Placement Scheme and the Social Mobility Foundation are two opportunities for students from disadvantaged backgrounds to get into Parliament and see that they have as much of a right to be an MP as those who by accident of birth have had a more comfortable upbringing. We need to encourage people from all walks of life to realise that they have a right to stand for election, so that the Commons bursts at the seams with experience from across the board. This would mean both parties and non-partisan campaign groups approaching people outside their existing social and political networks. And it would require money from somewhere, as parties tend to want to spend what funding they do have on winning elections in the short term, not improving the overall supply of candidates in the long term.

All parties have made admirable attempts to increase the proportion of female MPs, but still too few women are even applying to be candidates. As well as Parliament appearing to be a place that welcomes rather than belittles women, more women need to be asked that important question: 'Have you considered standing as an MP?' And though society may be moving slowly towards encouraging mothers and fathers to share the burden of childcare, it is still the case that in the vast majority of families, women are the primary caregiver. This makes it more difficult for them to juggle Parliament and family, though the presence of a nursery on site has improved this. Some MPs such as Caroline Lucas have proposed job shares so that MPs could work part-time. But it really isn't clear how this could work in practice. Unless the co-candidates for each constituency have totally identical political and moral views, they would disagree on important issues such as going to war or abortion, as well as the intricate detail of policies.

But there will be little point in anyone doing any parliamentary headhunting if the cost of standing remains so high, in terms of both personal finances and time. This is a major and rarely acknowledged barrier to a better Parliament. In a strange way, the 2017 snap election helped, as it meant there was no lengthy run-in in which candidates were selected early and became embedded in their target seats. But the strangeness of that election result could make such short-notice polls less likely, as prime ministers will be afraid of suffering the same fate as Theresa May, who set out to win big and ended up losing seats and her political authority.

Parties need to reform their selection process for candidates so that those who cannot take six weeks off work to campaign are not as disadvantaged as they are now. But they also need to pay their candidates so that leaving your job to stand as an MP isn't the ridiculously risky decision that it currently is. If we expect our politicians to go through lengthy and expensive job interviews with no guarantee that they'll win at the end, we will continue to get a self-selecting bunch of people who think that this sounds like a sensible and financially viable thing to do.

There is little incentive for the parties to pay candidates a salary, even just at living wage level, since it isn't going to make any difference to whether they actually win their seat. However, both Labour and the Tories have toyed with the idea of bursaries for low-income candidates. The Tories have even set one up, though it doesn't come close to the average cost of standing. But it's a start, a recognition of the current ludicrous situation. External non-partisan organisations could make a huge difference here in offering bursaries. Some might have certain political criteria for supporting a candidate. Others might want to offer financial support to people from particular backgrounds. But it would be a much more effective way than setting up a new party that doesn't get anyone elected, as the well-funded Women's Equality Party has done.

It's true that none of these changes are particularly glamorous. They're not the populist revolution that some politicians, comedians and writers would like. They're not even an overhaul of the major structures of British politics, though the fuss that would be made about some of them might suggest otherwise. But revolutions and constitutional upheaval disappoint as much as they promise, because while the new system might look shiny and exciting, it still involves humans, who are all flawed, sometimes selfish and sometimes stupid. Better, surely, to make use of those humans by breathing life into the existing parliamentary system and giving the best, not merely the best-placed, the chance to be the most effective politicians we could possibly hope for.

NOTES

Introduction: A Mistrusted Class

1. P. Kellner, 'Democracy on Trial: What Voters Really Think of Parliament and Our Politicians' (YouGov, 2012).

2. http://www.independent. co.uk/news/uk/home-news/ teachers-banned-classroom-sexual-misconduct-record-numbers-statistics-investigation-a7828891.html.

3. http://www.gmc-uk.org/ Analysis_of_cases_resulting_in_doctors_being_suspended_or_erased_from_the_medical_register_FINAL_REPORT_Oct_2015.pdf_63534317.pdf.

4. BBC *Question Time*, 11 December 2014.

5. https://www.suttontrust.com/ wp-content/uploads/2017/06/ Parliamentary-privilege-2017_FINAL_V2.pdf.

6. I. Robertson, *The Winner Effect: How Power Affects Your Brain* (Bloomsbury Publishing, 2012).

7. Speech to Commons Press Gallery Lunch, 18 December 2012.

8. https://www.suttontrust.com/ wp-content/uploads/2017/06/ Parliamentary-privilege-2017_FINAL.pdf.

9. http://researchbriefings. parliament.uk/ResearchBriefing/ Summary/SN05125.

10. https://www.local.gov.uk/ sites/default/files/documents/ national-census-local-aut-1b1. pdf.

11. C. Durose et al., *Pathways to Politics* (Equality and Human Rights Commission, 2011), p. 88.

Chapter 1: Getting In

1. *Mail on Sunday*, 21 March 2015.
2. http://www.bbc.co.uk/news/uk-32011321.
3. http://www.fabians.org.uk/wp-content/uploads/2015/12/Practising-what-we-preach-14.12.pdf.
4. A. King, *Who Governs Britain?* (Pelican, 2015).
5. http://www.fabians.org.uk/wp-content/uploads/2015/12/Practising-what-we-preach-14.12.pdf.
6. http://conservativehome.blogs.com/goldlist/2006/08/the_costs_of_be.html.
7. Response to candidate survey.
8. Response to candidate survey.
9. Response to candidate survey.
10. Response to candidate survey.
11. Response to candidate survey.

Chapter 2: Starting Out

1. R. Prince, *Standing Down* (Biteback Publishing, 2015).
2. Speaker's Conference on Parliamentary Representation, 2010.
3. https://www.hansardsociety.org.uk/projects/a-year-in-the-life-from-member-of-public-to-member-of-parliament.
4. http://parliamentarystandards.org.uk/transparency/Our%20consultations/Pay%20and%20Pensions/MPs%27%20Pay%20Consultation%202015/MPs%27%20Pay%20Consultation%202015.pdf.
5. Quoted in 'MPs' pay in the 2015 Parliament: Final Report' (IPSA, July 2015).
6. Ibid.
7. Ibid.
8. https://www.facebook.com/TobiasEllwood?fref=ts.
9. 'A Year in the Life: From Member of Public to Member of Parliament' (Hansard Society, 2011).
10. https://eprints.soton.ac.uk/394835/1/__userfiles.soton.ac.uk_Users_nl2_mydesktop_Deposits_One%2520off_The%2520rise%2520of%2520anti-politics%2520in%2520Britain.pdf.
11. M. Jack et al., *Erskine May: Parliamentary Practice* (Butterworths Law, 2011).
12. https://d25d2506sfb94s.cloudfront.net/cumulus_uploads/document/pkc8kmvyqs/HansardSociety_Results_150918_PMQS.pdf.
13. http://www.standard.co.uk/news/politics/chuka-umunna-turn-parliament-into-a-museum-10363578.html.

14. Hansard, 28 October 1943.

15. Reported to the author by MPs who were present.

Chapter 3: Getting Out There

1. http://www.younglegalaidlawyers. org/sites/default/files/YLAL_ Nowhere_else_to_turn.pdf.
2. N. Vivyan and M. Wagner, 'What do Voters Want from Their Local MP?', *The Political Quarterly*, Vol. 86, Issue 1 (2015), pp. 33–40.
3. P. Norton and D. M. Wood, *Back from Westminster: British Members of Parliament and Their Constituents* (University Press of Kentucky, 1993).
4. O. Gay, 'MPs Go Back to Their Constituencies', *Political*

Quarterly, Vol. 76, Issue 1 (2005).
5. Hansard, 3 June 2015: https: //publications.parliament. uk/pa/cm201516/cmhansrd/ cm150603/debtext/150603- 0003.htm.
6. Quoted in *Observer*, 23 January 2016.
7. https://twitter.com/jessphillips/ status/758670826732412929?.
8. https://www.politicshome.com/ news/uk/social-affairs/politics/ house/60356/james-gray-what- mp.

Chapter 4: Getting Things Done

1. R. Prince, *Standing Down* (Biteback Publishing, 2015).
2. http://www.theguardian.com/ politics/2011/feb/13/new-tory- politics-claim-sham.
3. http://www.telegraph.co.uk/ news/newstopics/mps-expenses/ 5381509/MPs-expenses-Why- I-want-to-open-up-Tory- candidate-selection.html.
4. A. Tyrie, *Mr Blair's Poodle: An Agenda for Reviving the House of Commons* (Centre for Policy Studies, 2000), p. 11: https:// www.cps.org.uk/files/reports/

original/111220125131- Mrblairspoodle2000 AndrewTyrie.pdf.
5. http://www.publications. parliament.uk/pa/cm201314/ cmselect/cmproced/writev/216/ p21.htm.
6. Evidence to the House of Commons Procedure Committee, 19 June 2013.
7. A. King and I. Crewe, *The Blunders of Our Governments* (Oneworld Publications, 2013).

8. L. Thompson, *Making British Law: Committees in Action* (AIAA, 2015), p. 64.
9. http://parliamentlive.tv/Event/Index/b5f17295-ec67-41ba-a5df-1e67da5b2e9a.
10. Interview on BBC's *Daily Politics*, 27 September 2016.
11. https://www.hansardsociety.org.uk/resources/the-devil-is-in-the-detail-parliament-and-delegated-legislation.
12. House of Commons committee, 14 July 2016.
13. http://www.parliament.uk/business/publications/hansard/commons/this-weeks-public-bill-general-committee-debates/read/?date=2012-09-10&itemId=126.
14. Hansard, 28 January 2014: https://hansard.parliament.uk/Commons/2014-01-28/debates/14012854000023/TopicalQuestions.
15. Hansard, 4 July 2016: https://hansard.parliament.uk/commons/2016-07-04/debates/1A2C4E40-ACAD-4E55-B521-374C3A8B5BF6/TopicalQuestions.
16. Hansard, 7 June 2016 (Treasury Questions).
17. *Guardian*, 3 August 2011.
18. Based on a calculation of how much MPs spend on staff on average, assuming that one researcher spends half their time working on petitions and subscribes to a pooled research unit service.
19. https://petition.parliament.uk/archived/petitions/106477.
20. https://petition.parliament.uk/archived/petitions/171928. The petition seems to have attracted more signatures after the debate – a total of 1,863,708.

Chapter 5: Getting On

1. R. Prince, *Standing Down* (Biteback Publishing, 2015).
2. https://www.conservativehome.com/thetorydiary/2015/01/interview-grayling-as-lord-chancellor-its-an-advantage-not-being-a-lawyer.html.
3. https://twitter.com/priskmark/status/387191608325992448.
4. Evidence to the House of Commons Select Committee, 16 January 2013.
5. Quoted in *The Times*, 3 December 2016.

Chapter 6: Getting Caught

1. https://twitter.com/GregHands/status/529730515830833152.
2. Quoted in the *Daily Mirror*, 2 July 2011.

3. *Daily Mail*, 17 May 2016.
4. http://www.thetimes.co.uk/article/family-man-who-stood-for-pm-sent-sex-messages-cddmxmvgb.
5. https://www.buzzfeed.com/hannahalothman/former-labour-cabinet-minister-ivan-lewis-has-apologised?utm_term=.flv39BwJ2#.xyBrjqWEX.
6. B. Sones, *Women in Parliament: The New Suffragettes* (Politico's Publishing Ltd, 2005).
7. Ibid., p. 94.

Chapter 7: Getting Ill

1. House of Commons, 24 April 2013.
2. Interview with BBC Radio Kent, 11 July 2010.
3. https://www.totalpolitics.com/articles/interview/boozing-parliament.
4. *Sunday Times* magazine, 20 May 2007.
5. B. Wright, *Order, Order! The Rise and Fall of Political Drinking* (Gerald Duckworth & Co., 2016).
6. House of Commons, 14 June 2012.

Chapter 8: Getting Out

1. K. Theakston et al., *Life After Losing or Leaving: The Experience of Former Members of Parliament* (The Association of Former Members of Parliament, 2007).
2. C. Byrne and K. Theakston, 'Leaving the House: The Experience of Former Members of Parliament Who Left the House of Commons in 2010', *Parliamentary Affairs*, 2016.
3. https://www.thesun.co.uk/news/1338757/why-should-i-do-the-hard-st-teary-pm-admitted-he-didnt-want-brexit-grief-moments-before-he-quit/.
4. Quoted in the *Evening Standard*, 19 April 2017.
5. K. Theakston et al., op. cit.
6. Ibid.
7. R. Prince, *Standing Down* (Biteback Publishing, 2015).
8. K. Theakston et al., op. cit.

Chapter 9: They Just Don't Get It

1. Hansard, 21 March 2012: https://publications.parliament.uk/pa/cm201212/cmhansrd/cm120321/debtext/120321-0001.htm.
2. Ibid.

3. Quoted in *Guardian*, 21 March 2012.
4. *Sun*, 29 May 2012.
5. A. King and I. Crewe, *The Blunders of Our Governments* (Oneworld Publications, 2013).
6. Hansard, 26 October 2015: https://hansard.parliament.uk/Commons/2015-10-26/debates/15102612000001/FinanceBill?highlight=period#contribution-15102633000102.
7. *Inside Housing*, 25 September 2009.
8. https://www.gov.uk/government/uploads/system/uploads/attachment_data/file/205567/

Annex_B_-_SoS_DCLG_Rule_43_response.pdf.
9. House of Commons, 6 February 2014.
10. BBC, *Panorama*, first broadcast 19 June 2017.
11. https://www.bristolpost.co.uk/news/bristol-news/bristol-mp-stephen-williams-warned-124266.
12. *Guardian*, 15 June 2017.
13. https://grenfellactiongroup.wordpress.com/2017/06/14/grenfell-tower-fire/.
14. http://www.bbc.co.uk/news/uk-40418266.

Chapter 10: All Things to All Men

1. http://www.cqc.org.uk/sites/default/files/20161019_stateofcare1516_web.pdf.
2. *The Spectator*, 17 June 2017.
3. https://www.gov.uk/government/speeches/troubled-families-speech.
4. https://www.gov.uk/government/uploads/system/uploads/attachment_data/file/335261/

National_Evaluation_of_report_web_copy-ecorys.pdf.
5. House of Commons, 18 March 2013.
6. *Daily Telegraph*, 4 April 2014.
7. P. Johnston, *Bad Laws: An Explosive Analysis of Britain's Petty Rules, Health and Safety Lunacies, Madcap Laws and Nit-Picking Regulations* (Constable, 2010).

Chapter 11: Yes-Men

1. Interview with *ITV News*, 13 April 2014.
2. https://publications.parliament.uk/pa/cm201011/cmpublic/legalaid/110719/am/110719s01.htm.
3. Ibid.

4. House of Commons Justice Committee, *Impact of Changes to Civil Legal Aid under Part 1 of the Legal Aid, Sentencing and Punishment of Offenders Act 2012* (Stationery Office, 2015).

5. Law Society of England and Wales, *Access Denied? LASPO Four Years On: a Law Society Review* (June 2017).

6. https://www.thetimes.co.uk/article/bob-neill-we-have-urgent-work-to-do-on-prisons-probation-legal-aid-and-brexit-86rp5qpk7.

7. https://www.publications.parliament.uk/pa/cm201213/cmgeneral/deleg1/121016/121016s01.htm.

8. https://www.gov.uk/government/uploads/system/uploads/attachment_data/file/614096/

housing-benefit-caseload-data-to-feb-2017.ods.

9. https://www.gov.uk/government/uploads/system/uploads/attachment_data/file/601874/esa-wca-summary-march-2017.pdf.

10. *The Times*, 7 February 2012.

11. *The Times*, 13 October 2014.

12. N. Timmins, *Never Again? The Story of the Health and Social Care Act 2012* (The Kings Fund and the Institute for Government, 2012).

13. Ibid.

14. Ibid.

15. Ibid.

Chapter 12: Trapped!

1. *The Spectator*, 9 July 2016.

2. A. Tyrie, *Mr Blair's Poodle Goes to War: The House of Commons, Congress and Iraq* (Centre for Policy Studies, 2004).

3. http://www.iraqinquiry.org.uk/media/247921/the-report-of-the-iraq-inquiry_executive-summary.pdf.

4. A. Seldon, *Cameron at 10: The Inside Story 2010–2015* (William Collins, 2015).

5. Quoted in *The Atlantic*, March 2016.

6. Foreign Affairs Select Committee, *Libya: Examination of Intervention and Collapse and the UK's Future Policy Options* (Stationery Office, 2016).

7. https://www.gov.uk/government/publications/the-repeal-bill-white-paper/legislating-for-the-united-kingdoms-withdrawal-from-the-european-union.

8. Evidence to Select Committee, 6 December 2017.

Conclusion: Can We Get the Right Politicians?

1. Response to a question at a Policy Exchange event, 21 September 2015.
2. Public Administration Select Committee, *Too Many Ministers?* (Stationery Office, 2010).
3. A. King and I. Crewe, *The Blunders of Our Governments* (Oneworld Publications, 2013).
4. C. Hagelund and J. Goddard, *How to Run a Country: A Parliament of Lawmakers* (Reform, 2015).
5. https://medium.com/@ IsabelHardman/hardmans-parliamentary-burn-book-da5cf37e4c22.
6. https://www.mumsnet.com/ politics/politicians-best-answers-mumsnet-biscuit-question.

ACKNOWLEDGEMENTS

Every author needs a small army in order to get to the end of the first draft, let alone the moment when the first physical copy of their book appears. My own army didn't just ensure the development of this book and its ideas but also kept me going through the rather difficult personal backdrop to writing it.

I am tremendously grateful to my researcher Tiffany Trenner-Lyle, who has an extraordinary ability to discover and analyse nuggets of information. She is also very patient when it comes to dealing with sudden deluges of bizarre requests for said nuggets of information.

My agent, Andrew Gordon, managed to tell me just with a certain facial expression that my first book idea was rubbish, and then got the proposal for *Why We Get the Wrong Politicians* into shape so quickly and precisely. My editor, Mike Harpley, has been so encouraging but also perfectly blunt when something just hasn't worked. Working with Mike meant I loved writing this book so much that I immediately went into writing another.

My boss at *The Spectator*, Fraser Nelson, has always been a kind mentor and gave me both ideas and the time to write the book itself. He also supported me through my period of depression in a manner that I will always be grateful for and never able to repay.

Philip Cowley of Queen Mary University of London has been very generous with his time and advice, even humouring my requests for his favourite private members' bills and failed backbench rebellions. Though I suspect he was also just delighted someone had finally asked.

Before I gush about my partner, I should also explain his role in this book. I fell in love while writing it. John is, though, an MP, and before we started a relationship he was a case study in the constituency chapter. I have deleted this from the text, but I think losing 300 words about the 'It's all happening on Walney' event is a fair exchange for finally finding happiness. As I wrote much of this book in 2017, I had presumed that I would be thanking the 'former Labour MP for Barrow and Furness', given his chances of holding his seat in the snap election of that year, but even *I* had reckoned without John's tenacity. He is both absent and present in this book: I cannot write about him or the town I now call home with any objectivity, but I could not have written this book without his wisdom and practical support. He is the kindest and bravest man I know.

Finally, I have four Ms to thank. Marion and Michael, my parents, who are both ridiculously loving and just quite wonderfully ridiculous, and Maisie and Molly, John's children, whose existence I had no role in but who have become stitched into my heart. I am grateful for the girls' timely distractions in the final month of writing, especially for summoning me away from a particularly difficult passage with the announcement that 'Molly's got a fish finger in her hair'. Without them, I would have gone quite mad.

INDEX